Ritual and Knowledge
among the Baktaman of
New Guinea

FREDRIK BARTH

Ritual and Knowledge among the Baktaman of New Guinea

1975
Universitetsforlaget   Yale University Press
Oslo   New Haven

ISBN 82-00-04847-0 (Universitetsforlaget)
ISBN 0-300-01816-9 (Yale University Press)

Library of Congress catalog number: 74-19572

Published simultaneously in the United States of America
by Yale University Press, New Haven, and in Norway by
Universitetsforlaget, Oslo.

Printed in Norway by
A.s John Griegs Boktrykkeri

Preface

I went to New Guinea to experience a world entirely different from anything I had known before — different both in its overt features and in the reality that its residents construct. In this task I was profoundly dependent on the help of others. My debt is greatest to Nulapeng, who provided the major bridge for me to cross into the world of the Baktaman. Nulapeng was born in the village of Abologobip, but spent some years of his childhood in fosterage among the Baktaman and speaks their dialect as well as his own. Some time after his return home for initiations, Abologobip experienced its first contact with Australian patrols. Nulapeng swiftly acquired a full command of Pidgin, and gained some experience of school and work in Kiunga, Daru, and Olsobip. He served me as interpreter and assistant; and his intelligence and social skills made our cooperation highly productive.

I do not know in what way the Baktaman (or Nulapeng) understood my purposes. But unwittingly or not they have all aided me, and I hope this text will repay them by salvaging some of what they now value from the oblivion of imposed change and induced disintegration which looms ahead. Some of them helped me greatly with clear intent and persistent sensitivity and patience. Outstanding among these were Kaineng, the village headman, who used his rhetoric in my support at the first meeting where the tribe decided whether to accept me as a resident or not, and later was my friend and ally in most matters; Kimebnok, the cult leader, who after a period of doubt accepted me as a pupil and colleague and bent rules to make me a participant in his religion; Kayimkayak, a Seltamin cult leader who lived in Feisabip during the first half of my fieldwork and cooperated in my instruction; Ngaromnok, who shared something of my curiosity and need for understanding and made his insights as

5

available to me as he could; and Amireng, who, though we probably understood each other less, gave me the closest I came to a personal friendship.

Other persons also gave generously of their time and thought in support of my work. John J. McGregor, at that time patrol officer at Olsobip, provided me with every assistance possible, and also with good companionship on two patrols on which I was allowed to join him. Alan Healey gave me immensely valuable help in 1967 before my fieldwork, collecting and writing out a brief vocabulary of (west-central) Faiwol and a sketch of its grammar, both of which were essential to all subsequent progress I made with the language. John Barnes, Ralph Bulmer, and Ronald Crocombe all gave me professional support as well as private hospitality as needed.

Despite all this, I found my fieldwork among the Baktaman extraordinarily demanding. To reduce my impact on the community in the small ways possible I lived a very frugal life in physical discomfort, giving small gifts of salt in return for irregular provision of taro from women in my hamlet, hunting (largely unsuccessfully) with bow and arrow with the men and receiving shares (as my initiation rank entailed) of wild pig, cassowary, and certain marsupials. This diet I supplemented with a small store of tinned meat. More discouraging was my failure to develop language fluency: though I was able to understand and participate in everyday conversation in the latter half of my fieldwork, I never reached the point where new topics or complex explanations were available to me without the assistance of Nulapeng. Finally, most exhausting of all were the continued efforts and frustrations of trying to cross into a world so different from my own, and make human contact with persons entirely unacquainted with Man in any other form than themselves.

The work of analysing this material has also been a sustained and demanding effort. I have tried to let intuitions and concrete understandings emerge as they could, as untrammelled as possible by anthropological schemata and pre-established premises and habits of thought. In this work I have been stimulated by the intellectual companionship of Unni Wikan, my wife, who has participated in every step. Sidney Mintz, Knut Erik Tranøy, and Edmund Leach have read the manuscript and made valuable comments; I have also benefited from discussions with numerous other colleagues in many places.

An initial survey visit in spring 1967 to New Guinea and Melanesia was supported by the Wenner-Gren Foundation. The fieldwork

6

during January–November 1968 was jointly financed by the Wenner-Gren Foundation and the Norwegian Research Council for Science and the Humanities. Finally, the typing and classifying of my notes were assisted by a grant from the Wenner-Gren Foundation. I gratefully acknowledge this support.

Publishing this monograph raises a vexing question, since much of its data are part of a secret cult. As a participant I was told these secrets in trust and naturally never failed this trust while I was part of the world of the Baktaman. I made it clear that in my distant homeland I would share their knowledge with others who had passed through all *our* initiations; and that was acceptable. But I did not explain that this would include women as well as men. I also asked whether, in the absence of Baktaman type cult I should need to persist in observing all the Baktaman taboos — and they decided it might be best for me, but it made no difference to them once I was not among them.

My reasons for wishing to publish are twofold: to make use of the data in trying to further our understanding of ritual, within the general purpose of the discipline of anthropology, and to document one of the many rapidly disappearing cultural constructions man has created. Making the information thus available can only hurt the Baktaman if it is used irresponsibly (with or without evil intent) among them by external agents. I appeal to those few who may come into a position where this might happen to show the necessary care and humanity. It is my hope that the picture I give is one that will inspire the admiration and respect for what this small and vulnerable population has created which should motivate such care. If so, the present monograph will not constitute a threat to them today, but only a resource for them tomorrow.

Contents

Introduction

The following monograph gives a close description and analysis of the ritual corpus of the Baktaman community in New Guinea, and through this exercise attempts to contribute to a general theory of ritual. Though the monograph thus presents a considerable substantive body of ethnography, its major purpose is theoretical: to develop ways of analysing ritual as a mode of communication and, behind that, a mode of thought. These theoretical aspects are mainly explicated in Part IV and, especially, Part V. Throughout the text I seek to discover just what is being communicated in the rituals of this community; what are the features or aspects of ritual acts and objects which make them capable of serving as vehicles for concepts, understandings, and emotions; and finally how do the topics and ideas so communicated reflect the potentialities and constraints of the ritual codes in which communication is cast and the social organization in which it is embedded.

The structure which I seek to expose is thus semantic rather than grammatical: I understand Baktaman ritual to embody a tradition of knowledge, and I wish to know what vision of Man and Cosmos it sustains, and what one needs to know and understand to participate in the communication of this knowledge. It follows from this that I must look at the elements of ritual in the context of the *messages* in which they occur, interpreted with reference to the social *personae* of the participants and their previous knowledge. Since Baktaman religion has the character of a secret mystery cult, this entails considerable complexity. Nor is one aided by any native tradition of exegesis or by more than a meagre corpus of myth. As our interest is in what is being said in Baktaman ritual rather than what such a presumed code might be capable of expressing, the soundest methodology is to focus on what a novice learns from seeing and doing the rites.

This question is approached initially in a highly concrete and descriptive way. Part I summarizes the context of experience which a participant must take for granted and on which he may draw for associations and connotations of signs and symbols in rites. Part II presents the rites of initiation through which men progressively pass. Part III presents other idiom clusters, and the social praxis, different from formal initiations, in which they are embedded. Through these descriptions and analyses, a series of focal sacred symbols emerge. Part IV analyses the more important of these, and tries to establish sub-sets of them and to investigate the nature and extent of their interconnectedness and interdependence. Through this analysis it becomes apparent — not as an artefact of its stepwise synthesis, but as an empirical feature of the corpus — that the sacred symbols that are joined in Baktaman rites show a considerable diversity and independence in their sources of meaning. Briefly, I argue that the meanings of these symbols do not arise from their interconnection in pattern and contrast. Rather, each of the sacred acts and objects has its separate fan of connotations and associations, in part inherent in its appearance and occurrence and in part contrived through ritual manipulation. The codes of ritual are thus not based on digital structures but on metaphor and analogy — a mode of codification which has very different properties as a communicative device, and entails very different procedures for analysis, from those of a digital code. Some of the implications of this view are elaborated in the various chapters of Part V.

Finally, a note of warning. This text does not seek to construct or present precise verbal definitions of central concepts such as ritual, symbol, idiom, etc. I hope that the senses in which these words are used will become sufficiently clear through the concrete descriptive statements in which they occur through the first parts of the book. In this way the detailed necessary ethnography I present should also serve the useful purpose of absolving me from having to enter a number of tedious and very rarely fruitful debates.

PART I

Cultural and organizational setting

CHAPTER 1

The cultural conventions
of communication

Every culture is an ongoing system of communication and contains
a corpus of replicated messages. In this book I seek to describe and analyse Baktaman culture from this point of view; its focus is thus on the
forms and contents of symbolic activity. Confronted with a rich and
active ritual life, I am particularly concerned to understand the structure and content of non-verbal communication in this culture.

The Baktaman are a nation of 183 persons occupying a tract of
mountain rain-forest near the centre of New Guinea. They compose a
highly self-contained face-to-face community in only intermittent contact with their immediate neighbours, quite recently contacted by the
Australian administration and very little touched by the outside world
(see Appendix I). In all essentials they sustain, through their own
activities, a whole culture and world of their own; and it is the processes of perpetuation and transmission of this culture that interest
me. Obviously, neither field data nor analysis can embrace a description of all the knowledge and skills of the Baktaman population. What
I have sought is to capture the basic premises of Baktaman knowledge in terms of the explanations of self, man, and environment
which they transmit to each other through discourse and ritual,
much of which is organized in an instituted system of male initiations.
The study will present what appear to me to be the main substantive
features of the Baktaman world view; it will explore the structure of
the codes in which this world view is transmitted, and it will analyse the
sociology of the Baktaman tradition of knowledge.

In the literature of social anthropology we are accustomed to treat
such topics subsequent to, or as derivatives of, major features of social
organization. Yet, to reveal the 'social construction of reality' I should
rather prefer to proceed from the other side of the circle and order
my data on encounters and cases of interaction primarily in a frame-

15

work of categories based on the kind of occasion and activity, the medium of communication, and the kind of knowledge contained in the messages. This way, I am also freer to discover and explore the features of social organization that effect the release of a message (whether a conventional item of knowledge or a creative excursion) and thus the social processes that sustain and modify the cultural tradition. By way of introduction I therefore choose to give only a brief orientation on (i) the codes and idioms through which knowledge is expressed and communicated (ii) the basic conceptualizations of space and occasion in terms of which the experiences of an actor seem to be ordered, and (iii) a few features of the organization of persons and audiences. This may also serve as an inventory of the major kinds of data on which the study is based. More conventional features of social organization should become clear as the description of initiations and other ritual behaviour unfolds in the major part of the text. Readers who feel the need for a more detailed and exact documentation of such data are referred to the census materials and diagrams of Appendix II.

(i) *Codes and idioms.* Communication between the Baktaman takes place by means of speech and the manipulation of a number of other symbols. My preliminary classification of the major media of communication was as follows:

Language. All Baktaman speech takes place in the Seltaman dialect of the Faiwol language or dialect chain; no Baktaman knows any other language. By means of this dialect a person can communicate more or less fluently with perhaps 1,000 speakers of the same or closely similar dialects, residing in 6–8 territorially and politically distinct communities. There is no system for symbolizing any linguistic item by writing or any other form than sound; but language is used in a number of conventional styles, which are clearly distinguished. Apart from the predominant (1) normal conversation and argument, it is modified in characteristic ways such as (2) baby-talk, spoken by both sexes, and (3) tales and myths, distinguished in several categories appropriate to men, women, or both. These allow the speaker to engage in relatively uninterrupted monologue and are characterized by clear narrative structure, the simplest of which is sub-cycles of repetition. The corpus of such tales and myths is small, and the frequency of their telling low. (4) Descriptive monologue, signalled by special pitch and diction. This is used especially by men recounting a journey or giving a chronological account of a day's events away from the village. Such monologues provide a favoured form of pas-

Plate 1. Feisabip, the main Baktaman hamlet, looking west. Extreme left: Yolam temple; next, on stilts: Katiam temple; facing: two men's houses. Houses to the right are women's houses.

Plate 2. Women's houses in Kerabip at dawn, looking north-east. The main Murray valley is to the left. On the ridge outlined against the white cloud are several previously inhabited village sites. The most distant ridge is unknown territory to the Baktaman.

Plate 3. Woman of Kerabip hamlet. The string across her forehead is against headache. She is also wearing a cassowary amulet, and a set of mourning tassels. The nasal decoration is made of kangaroo-bone. Over her head is a bark rain-cape.

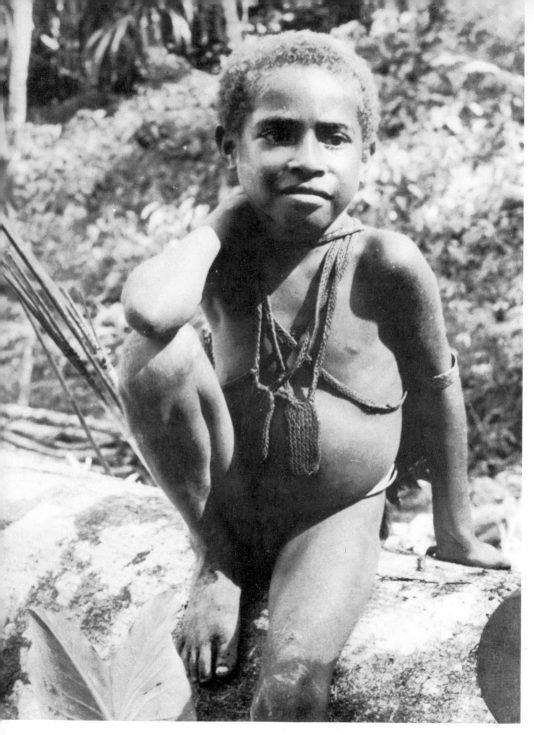

Plate 4. Young boy, 1st degree novice, visiting a garden planting area for lizard-hunting. Note the diagonal breast bands worn as insignia of 1st degree.

time during eventless periods in the men's house. (5) Speeches or harangues. Rhetoric is very poorly elaborated by New Guinea standards but is occasionally indulged in by senior males to collective audiences. It is mildly signalled by posture and diction. (6) Prayers. These are addressed to ancestral relics and contain much beseeching and flattery in an insistent, pep-talk style; they are brief and repetitive. Spells, directed towards ancestors and other spirits in connection with sacrifices and curing, seem to be basically of the same kind, but are mumbled and whispered since they are often uttered in the presence of ritually more inhomogeneous audiences. (7) Ritual formulae. These cryptic phrases or verses are recited by ritual officers and sometimes repeated in unison by the congregation. Compact and often incomplete in sentence structure, they are linguistically highly ambiguous and their meaning properly known only to initiates. In part, these formulae employ a secret vocabulary to refer to sacred objects. (8) Songs. These are known and sung by both men and women, and new songs are composed by identified authors. Often sung in an alternation between solo and chorus, they are linguistically cryptic in a way similar to ritual formulae, above; some of the words and expressions in them are not used in normal speech and are thought to be archaic by some informants. The corpus of such songs is large, and they diffuse readily between neighbouring communities.

Non-verbal idioms. These may be characterized as objects (public vs. secret) and acts (taboos vs. positive ritual acts) — a set of distinctions that also remain meaningful in terms of the emic categories that will emerge through the main body of description. Among public objects, i.e. objects not shielded from public view, the Baktaman attach meaning especially to buildings, gates, fences, and some tools; to the whole or part of a variety of animals and plants; and to feathers, clothing and other items of personal adornment. Other objects derive their major significance from the fact that they are secret and known only to persons of authorized ritual status; these are especially skulls and other ancestral relics, a few other categories of sacra, and a variety of ritual equipment. As for taboos, Baktaman religion is sustained or embedded in a very elaborate wealth of taboo places, objects, and actions. Some of these prohibitions are universal, but most of them are associated with particular social statuses and/or temporary ritual states. Finally, as will emerge from the descriptions, religious observances are composed of a wide variety of positive ritual acts, often in elaborate sequence stretching over weeks of continuous ceremonies; some of these meanings depend on individual acts, others on collective configurations.

Much of the more highly valued information is cast in codes known only to a few members of the community. While this is true only of a few songs among the verbal messages (since the sacred vocabulary must be kept secret and should not be spoken in the presence of non-initiates) it is generally true of the non-verbal symbols that their meanings are deepened and modified by progressive initiations, so their message content will differ from spectator to spectator. As a result, different kinds of knowledge will be obtained from a single ritual sequence by members of the same congregation, depending on their differing equipment for de-coding the message. The difficulties of harmonizing these different meanings and in general of operating such a complex and multivalent cognitive system, pose a major theme in the analysis of this material.

(ii) *Space, time, and occasion.* Baktaman are highly oriented towards *space* in ordering their experience. The vocabulary and grammar of their language impel a speaker constantly to specify relative location (distance, direction, and above/below on a slope) of observer and actor in describing events; and they have a variety of means to describe landscape features and shapes. There is also a wealth of place-names of differing order by which to designate area and specific location; in describing or inquiring about events much discussion focuses on the exact details of location. Places also serve to recall events in the past — stories and anecdotes that I was unable to elicit in conversation in the men's house would suddenly surface in the forest with the opening 'this is the spot where . . .'.

In more general terms, some categorical distinctions and allocations of space are of fundamental significance. Firstly, the Baktaman occupy a territory of their own, in which they monopolize the rights of exploitation and resist unauthorized trespass. This territory consists of c. 250 km² of mountain slope and valley ranging from 500 to 2,000 m in altitude (see map I); it adjoins the territory of several cognate political communities, the most important of which is the Seltaman, with whom they are most closely related and in most intensive contact — both friendly and violent. With these adjoining communities the Baktaman entertain some ceremonial trading relations; they occasionally hold joint feasts and initiations; and until pacification in 1964 they were intermittently at war with some or many of them (cf. Barth 1971 for inter-tribal relations). On rare occasions, peace and political alliance would reach a stability where

18

Map 1: New Guinea, with location of Baktaman territory.

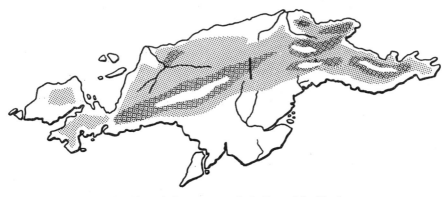

The line of the transept is indicated in black.

Baktaman territory in close stipple.

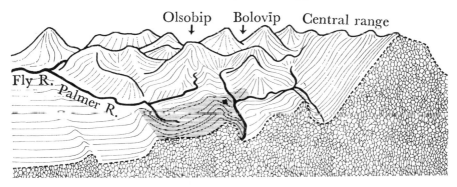

mutual trust would allow the reciprocal passage of groups of men through neighbouring territories to reach a further circle of second order neighbours; but these were so rare as to produce little knowledge of these more distant territories, and the known world of the Baktaman remained very small. Thus in an easterly direction one may sit on the men's house platform and see landscape, including smoke from garden fires, in unknown territory for which the Baktaman have no name for land or people, while to the north, west, and south the known world extends for approximately two days' journey. Detailed knowledge of the countryside is limited to their own and closely adjoining sectors of neighbouring territories; it is significantly wider for men than women and for adults than children.

19

The major subdivision of Baktaman territory as life space is a tripartite schema of village/garden/forest,[1] each associated with characteristic taboos and observances. The two former are limited to areas of present or recent use, so that known but long abandoned village sites, and gardens under forest fallow, are treated as forest. From this must be subtracted certain taboo areas: the haunts of malignant spirits, which should always be avoided (mostly around fearsome stone crevices and roaring waterfalls or areas of limestone sink-holes), and the Baktaman necropolis, where the bones of most of the dead are deposited and which cannot be visited without causing death pollution. There are also a few shrines, of men and dogs who have died and been buried in distant places. Caves occur, against which special precautions are needed. Further, some springs and streams are regarded as polluting and should be avoided. There is thus a fairly complex sacred geography of the whole Baktaman territory, which affects all behaviour.

Another equally pervasive dimension of spatial differentiation is the vertical one from below ground to sky. This coincides with a basic gradient of purity-pollution. Objects, and particularly animals, found below the ground are regarded as impure, those crawling on the ground likewise, while objects and animals standing on the ground's surface are generally of 'normal' profane status. Bushes and trees constitute a purifying, good habitat, and the highest degree of purity is generally associated with the sky, free air, and birds. The harmonization of this view of purity and pollution with the basic facts of root-crop agriculture poses an essential problem to Baktaman knowledge.

Within the village, finally, there are house types and areas of differing degrees of sacredness and purity. Menstrual huts are placed on the ground, outside the bounds of the village; menstruating women must not enter other houses, cross the central plaza of the village settlement, or use the main paths close to where they open on to this plaza. Women's huts, in which women, children, and pigs reside, are built low but with their floor off the ground; they are located in a circle or semicircle around the central plaza and are reluctantly entered by men, in the daytime only. Men's houses, forbidden to women and children, are generally larger and built on higher posts well off the ground at one or another end of the plaza circle or oval. Finally, several categories of temple are constructed, often straight

[1] *Abíp/Yoŋ/Sép.* For *Sep*, alt. *Kut. Yoŋ* in strict sense: new garden, contrast to *Binál* = garden being harvested, *Binarmún* abandoned garden going into fallow bush.

20

across the plaza from the men's house and somewhat withdrawn from the immediate neighbourhood of women's houses, surrounded by a sanctified area of ground. The temples are invarably raised on posts, their door opening is kept boarded up whenever they are empty, and they are forbidden to all who are not ritually authorized to enter them.

In contrast to this complex and precise attention to space, Baktaman orientation to *amount* and *time* is diffuse and vague, and their means for specifying them poor. The numerical scheme is a cumbersome system capable of quantifying up to 27. The complete set of numerals are:

1 *māγup*, 2 *arēp*, 3 *arēpmáno*, 4 *arēparēp*, 5 *aōk*, 6 *nowʒ/bgūp*, 7 *fēt*, 8 *dūan*, 9 *teip*, 10 *kiʒ*, 11 *kūm*, 12 *kēnu*, 13 *kīn*, 14 *mutūm*, 15 *kīnmári*, 16 *kēnumári*, 17 *kūm-mari*, 18 *kiʒmari/naʒar*, 19 *teip-pūn*, 20 *dūan*, 21 *bénkūn*, 22 *nowʒ/bgūp*, 23 *aōk*, 24 *iorōnim*, 25 *iorōnim-farep*, 26 *katkēt-arfēp*, 27 *katkēt*. Most of these numerals are also terms for body parts, and counting is invariably associated with a routine of indicating or touching appropriate body parts, starting with the right little finger. The numerals translate as 1-one, 2-two, 3-two-one, 4-two-two, 5- thumb (up to this point each finger is bent as you count, ending up with a clenched right fist at five. From this point on, the index finger of the free hand is used to point and touch at the appropriate body part): 6-wrist, 7-lower arm, 8-elbow, 9-upper arm, 10-shoulder, 11-neck, 12-ear, 13-eye, 14-nose, 15-other-eye, 16-other-ear, etc. Numerals beyond 3-4 are very rarely used in spontaneous speech; numerals up to 8 are used to specify rules about the duration of temporary taboos. By insisting on the specification of how many men participated in a raid, how many children a woman has, etc., I have elicited numerals up to 10 but then always as a listing of names that are counted as they are spoken. I have never heard figures higher than ten spoken except in the exercise of teaching me to count.

Unlike space, time is very difficult to specify without linear quantification, and the precision which Baktaman achieve is consequently low. The units of time recognized are day and moon; these are mutually unconnected and there is no calendrical system. Phases of the day and night are indicated by positions of the sun and characteristic animal sounds and activities associated with each phase; but measured in absolute duration these designated phases are highly unequal and imprecisely separated. Days are counted in both directions from the present (three days ago, in two days) but rarely in larger quantities and there is no way whereby one can keep a tally of the passage of days, so any longer-range planning on this basis would break down. For longer time spans, moon months are used and also on occasion moon phases; but Baktaman can only make rough guesses at the number of days contained in even short moon phases, such as from half to full moon. No Baktaman is aware of the number of days in a full moon cycle. As with days, longer time spans are measured in moons in both directions from the present (two moons ago, in one moon). With only slight and irregular seasonal changes, there is no awareness among Baktaman of the year and consequently no opportunity for an annual cycling of moons and the construction of a calendar. Beyond a time zone of approximately 3 months before or after the present there is no absolute time measure, only the entirely relative one of 'before' and 'after.' This seems to attract interest only in the context of 'senior' and 'junior' as between siblings, and initiations sets. The one exception to this is the historical division point between 'before contact' and 'after contact'; remembered events are sometimes referred to, and can usually be placed, in terms of this milestone.

Otherwise, the flow of activities is naturally ordered in phases; but there is little interest in correlating between several such phases and cross-locating events in time. The phases of relevance for various purposes are as follows: (a) *Garden maturation:* gardens are cleared, planted, harvested for the main crop (taro), harvested for secondary crops (sweet potato, banana), abandoned. Planting and harvesting are never allowed to overlap in one garden. Taro appears to mature c. 6–8 months after planting; the total period of use of a garden would seem to be about two years. (b) *Cultivation and fallow:* a longer gardening cycle is that of clearing, cultivation, abandoning, and regrowth. Judging by the maturity of persons remembered to have been born when certain gardens were in use, the Baktaman seem to regard old garden sites as ready for recultivation after periods of 15, or preferably 20 years. (c) *Village sites:* the location of settlements is changed in response to misfortunes of war and disease, and the sequence of occupancy of abandoned sites could provide a relative time scale. A reconstruction of the history of Baktaman village locations is given, facing p.; there is, however, much disagreement between informants about the sequence of occupation, and ignorance and lack of interest among younger people about older sites from before their personal recollection. The sequence is thus not used to provide anything like a collective reference system for the construction of a vision of Baktaman history.

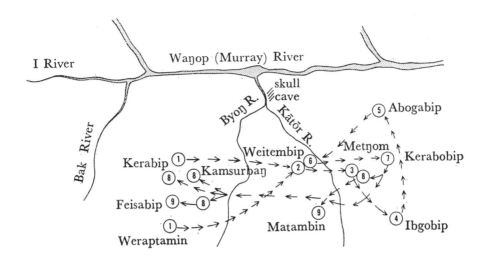

In the shorter run, life is punctuated and channelled by certain special *occasions*, triggered by the decisions of self or others, or by external events, and not controlled as to time of occurrence. These are most frequently births and deaths in the community, causing brief periods of taboo on gardening and hunting, and thus collective leisure for 2–3 days. Secular dance evenings are also improvised when desired, and irregular rituals are held, prepared for and followed by brief periods of communal taboos. Of larger events, there is the irregular recurrence of male initiations, involving the whole community in a major and elaborate sequence of activities. Finally, until pacification there was the recurring alternation between peace and war, affecting the whole of life (though peace was not coincident with security, since it was always associated with the possibility, and fear, of ambush and sudden attack). These phases, again, were not correlated with the phasing of garden work or ritual, but happened independent of, and as interruptions of, those other phase sequences.

(iii) *The organization of persons and audiences*. Communication always takes place in a predefined context of occasions and social relationships that affect the meanings of symbols and idioms. It is useful to note some of these basic preoccupations and premises which permeate Baktaman social life, and seem significantly different from our own.

(a) *Male-female, and domestic organization*. The Baktaman dichotomize very sharply between man and woman as two essentially different kinds of persons further separated by mutual distrust. Women

23

and men cannot fill the same statuses or enter the same sacred precincts (menstrual huts and temples respectively); women should remain ignorant of all important religious truths, and indeed religious cult has a persistent aspect of making the men independent of, and stronger than, women in all matters of public or collective concern. I should emphasize the character of Baktaman religion as a communal cult run by men, not a male cult; to the best of my knowledge there is no counterbalancing female cult, and the few ritual activities of women are mostly derivative from, or minor elements in, the male-run cult activities. From the male point of view, women are ignorant and/or sceptical of revealed knowledge and truth; careless and unreliable in their handling of both useful and dangerous cosmic forces and thus unhygienic, polluting, and destructive; powerful and evil in their sorcery; and weakening and debilitating in their everyday effect on men. Yet they inevitably remain a source of gratification and are associated with the provision of plenty, epitomized by cooked taro. Having had no privileged access to the corresponding judgements of women I can only guess that they have a similarly distant, but somewhat less damning view of men.

This dichotomy is not mediated by any marked jointness of the sexes in a domestic unit. Spouses are residentially separated both day and night; their joint garden is largely cultivated in distinct phases of male and female work. The connotations of some basic experiences, and thus the sources of some crucial idioms, are very directly affected by this. Thus, the prototype of commensality is not the holy family, but an aggregation of uniform-sex status equals. The pleasures of sexual intimacy are not associated with night, sleep, and body warmth and comfort but with daytime trysts in remote spots in the forest. The emotional assurance of love is expressed by the husband through a constant flow of gifts, especially of game and other strongly desired protein foods, by the woman through attentiveness in having good quantities of taro and other slow-cooking foods in readiness. In their activities and interactions, men and women move throughout in very distinct spheres, and consummate the majority of their limited cross-sex interactions in public.

(b) *Size and diversity of personnel.* The scale of the Baktaman society must be constantly kept in mind. One hundred and eighty-three people plus a scatter of known persons in neighbouring groups make a very diminutive social world where every person is known by all for his or her personality, failings, and predilections, and where there is no escape from social sanctions through anonymity. It is also,

24

characteristically, a society of peers, essentially limited to two living generations. Without native calendrical awareness demographic data are in many respects derivative (cf. Appendix II), but it is unquestionable that of the 82 persons below puberty in 1968 only 6 had a grandparent alive and nearly half (39) had lost one or both parents. The dead are thus in a literal sense very close and include a number of significant alters for all members of the society; the living are very prominently composed of one's age-mates and, progressively, one's juniors.

(c) *Corporate groups.* Appropriate to, but not entailed by, the small scale of society is an organization where collectivities are poorly constituted and conceptualized. There is an absence of definitive idioms and images for sodalities and basic prototypes for such groupings. Siblings are differentiated as to elder and younger, eldest brother and eldest sister are elevated to first ascending generation in kinship terms (cf. Barth, forthcoming, for kin terminology), collective rights (in sago palms, gathering areas, etc.) are vested in a steward who 'owns' the resource and allocates it to the others entitled to it. When flocks of people meet, each individual must greet each of the others; there are no collective signals and no recognition of group spokesmen. Patrilineal exogamous clans might be thought an archetype of corporation; but even these seem weakly conceptualized; they emerge more as a by-product of certain cult activities and their relevance in everyday life is suppressed because of this association with secret cult (cf. chapters 12 and 24). Notions of membership and solidarity are therefore obliquely and cumbrously fostered and expressed in ritual, and the search for their accompanying security and identity is continuous.

(d) Persons, on the other hand, are tightly integrated and unchanging. Since all alters have extensive information about all of a person's different circumstances and capacities, his performance tends continually to be judged in terms of them all, and not just with reference to particular statuses and facets of the person. Status changes are very explicitly and publicly signalled in rites-de-passages. They are also prominently expressed in taboos, which inevitably attach to whole individuals and cannot be assumed and shed at will. Social life among the Baktaman thus allows very little switching between situations in which persons activate different facets of themselves; all relationships tend to involve more of a whole *person* and to have more of the character of a 'total' relationship. Characteristically, unusual and fateful events in a person's life are often associated with a change of personal name.

(e) *Public, private, and secret scenes.* While the individual thus tends to present a whole and unchanging personality as he moves in social space, what constitutes appropriate behaviour is profoundly modified by the component of locality or setting. Occasions differ radically as to whether they are public, private, or secret, i.e. with respect to the nature of the audience present; and the management of information as one passes between these kinds of audiences is a major concern of the Baktaman.

Essentially, unless particular precautions are taken, all behaviour among the Baktaman is public behaviour. There are no recognized and respected ways in which the public gaze can be cut off, no way of separating oneself out from others present. Any conversation between two may be freely invaded, interrupted, or redirected by anyone present or arriving on the scene; sleep (e.g. in the communal men's house) may be interrupted by an alter for any purpose of his own choosing. Privacy can only be achieved by hiding from others; sexual gratification, peace to defecate,[1] and the opportunity to eat without sharing (except as protected by rules of taboo) can only be obtained that way.

By contrast, the village in all its constituent parts constitutes a demanding public arena. Thus, after exhausting hunting trips, Baktaman do not return directly to the village to collapse and rest in their houses, but halt a short distance from the village to relax and collect themselves. When struck by sickness or fearing sorcery, persons prefer to leave their houses and hide in shelters in the jungle, as do old people when they feel death coming. Likewise, when social pressures seem great and unbearable, people frequently move out and spend longer periods of time in garden houses — where the formalities of living are relaxed even to the extent of permitting coresidence of spouses.

The only other way in which audiences are controlled is by taboo and secrecy. The pervasive importance of secrecy to Baktaman society and culture will be discussed later; what I wish to point out here is simply the existence of certain sanctuaries in the form of temples, taboo to unauthorized persons. Rather than adjusting the contents of information to the personnel present the Baktaman appear

[1] Now, after contact, the Baktaman have very swiftly adopted latrines, acting on first encouragement from the patrol officer, as these relieve them of the fear of being surprised by others, especially of the opposite sex, while defecating and of the pigs eating fresh faeces to the detriment of the person and the ritual properties of the pork fat.

26

to regard secret information as forbidden except in the sacred localities, thereby obliquely achieving audience control. To some extent, this was manipulated in that persons could arrange to discuss more profane 'secrets' in these sanctuaries and thereby in privacy; the obverse of speaking about the sacred secrets when safely out of earshot of others was not equally acceptable. In this I recognize the same structural constraints on situational switching as those noted above as a characteristic feature of Baktaman social organization.

CHAPTER 2

Ecology and subsistence

As will be seen progressively from the description of initiation rites and other rituals, Baktaman religion is essentially a fertility cult and focuses on man's relation to nature, rather than to other men. Their world view is concerned with animal species, various wild and cultivated plants, agriculture, vegetative growth, and the strength and health of the community; ritual idioms are derived from such a world, while the explanations and understandings feed back on it. Thus tangible features of the specific environment and subsistence of the Baktaman constitute in large part the objects of knowledge and understanding towards which they strive in their ritual. It is therefore useful to sketch briefly some features of the environment and agricultural regime, and hunting and gathering.

Environment. An essentially seasonless high rainfall is one of the governing components of the environment. It rains most nights, often in the afternoon and sometimes continuously for days on end; heavy dew covers everything at night and in the early morning; and most days open with clouds and mists that rise and whirl and dissolve and reform, or descend in bursts of rain. A damp, dense rain forest covers the land except where it is kept clear by human activity. Swift and turbulent streams dissect the terrain. The main features of the land form are mountain ridges, prominently of limestone, running East-West and building up from the vast, low alluvial plain in the south towards the central cordillera to the north, forming the divide between the Fly and the Sepik drainage at about 3,000 m altitude. This creates a complex drainage pattern on the southern slope with rivers alternately running along the strike of the mountains, or breaking through them in narrow ravines and gorges. In some areas there are extensive sink holes, dams, and other karst formations. Sudden heavy precipitation immediately produces violent floods in the rivers, while erratic dry spells quickly reduce the flow, even in major streams. The high moisture together with the temperature result in deep oxidization of the land surface and produce the characteristic steep clay hills and sparse rock outcrops away from the sharpest limestone ridges.

The Baktaman divide this environment into six major zones of which all but the two extremes are found within their own territory (see Map I p. 19). The lowest zone of alluvial plains can be seen from the Dep range on the southern boundary of Baktaman territory, but has never been visited by a Baktaman. It is reported to be occupied by long-eared cannibals of various colours, and monsters with Janus faces. Residence in such areas is believed to cause fevers and red skin.

The lowest familiar areas are composed of the poorly drained flats of the Luap (Palmer River) and its smaller tributaries in the valley north of the Dep range, and also some spots along the Waŋop (Murray River). These areas are particularly valued for their sago swamps; the jungle is largely stunted and the fauna not particularly rich, and the area is not thought good for agriculture.

Above this is the 'warm' zone of 500–1000 m altitude, with stands of gallery forest including the red pandanus, breadfruit, giant fern, and black palm among a large range of other species. Present and former Baktaman village sites are all located in the upper part of this zone, in a slight rain shadow providing a fairly pleasant habitat; the bulk of the cultivated gardens are also found here.

Higher up is a 'cool' zone with lower temperatures and probably considerably higher precipitation, favoured for some cultigens and also suitable for taro cultivation. The forest in this zone rarely develops into true gallery forest, but includes a number of useful species such as the pandanus nut.

Above this again, at some points at as low as 2000 m altitude, lies the cloud forest — cool, damp, perpetually shrouded in mist, with a decaying forest grotesquely overgrown with moss and lichen. No cultivation takes place in this zone, but access to it is valued for the hunting of a considerable range of marsupials. Finally, to the north, outside Baktaman territory, is the high mountain zone, uninhabited except by fearsome spirits but known to be crossed by men on trading expeditions to the Feramin and the distant and fabulous Telefomin. I do not know of any Baktaman ever having made this journey.

Settlements are preferably constructed on ridges and high spurs for easier defence; they are surrounded by an area entirely cleared of forest for the same reason. The present Baktaman village consists of the three contiguous hamlets Feisabip (pop.:70), Kerabip (pop.: 56), and Kamsurbaŋ (pop.:31), each within shouting distance of the next and all in one continuous clearing in the forest. In addition, some few Baktaman live in the outlying hamlets of Metŋom (pop.:14) and Matambin (pop.:11). From the main village, two large and three smaller paths lead in various directions, as do another half dozen barely negotiable tracks used by pigs and persons on local foraging trips. The surrounding forest is also somewhat affected by the cutting of firewood and therefore in part more open and penetrable. It is also irregularly broken by areas of garden in present or recent use. Six to eight years after abandonment, however, such gardens become if anything even more impenetrable than regular jungle, whereas some stands of mature forest may provide a surprisingly open and penetrable forest floor.

Dominant subsistence attention is given to the cultivation of taro (the staple food), to the raising of pigs (the most favoured meat and the crucial provision for feasts and blood sacrifices), and to hunting, especially marsupials, wild pig, and cassowaries (which constitute the major source of protein and are used for sacramental meals and offerings to ancestors). The physical and technical requirements of these activities form constraints which Baktaman knowledge must accommodate and, to the extent they are questioned, explain. On the other hand, the organization of subsistence tasks also and simultaneously reflects Baktaman values and preconceptions; and the two are very difficult to separate. Provisionally, gross features of both will be seen together as 'facts of life' that present themselves as having the same inherent authority to Baktaman actors.

Agriculture. Taro is both ritually and economically the most important food, and is cultivated in most gardens, though occasionally an area may be opened up for the exclusive purpose of cultivating secondary crops of vegetables or sweet potatoes and bananas. The sequence of activities in taro gardening dominates Baktaman life and thinking.

All Baktaman cultivation is slash-and-burn, which implies continuous decisions about localization, allocation, lay-out, etc. For a number of reasons the Baktaman prefer to have their gardens together — it gives the security of numbers against ambush and spirit attacks, it is labour-saving in terms of fencing, and it is diffusely thought to be right, ritually good. But the collective decisions required

30

to assure this are not easy to achieve, and a number of features of taro subsistence exacerbate the difficulties. Thus, since the harvested root is spoiled within 6–7 days, production must be programmed for continuous harvesting, which means fairly continuous planting 6–8 months in advance of consumption. Once the cleared space available to a household is used up, it thus becomes essential to obtain new space for planting quite swiftly; and this need may not arise simultaneously for other households. Smaller ad hoc garden areas are consequently often prepared. There are also complex judgements of fertility, water requirements, labour demands, insect or blight risks, and convenience of transportation that enter into the comparison of alternative new sites for gardens, and thus provide much room for differences in judgement and preference. The Baktaman have no instituted leadership or decision-making procedure for these collective decisions. What happens is a great deal of conversation and fussing in dyads and small groups, whereby pressures to open a new garden build up. The final overt move must be made by senior men, but they are highly sensitive to the opinions of their wives and juniors and unwilling to clarify disagreements and impose a showdown — a reluctance springing from the weakness of their sources of authority, fear of sorcery retaliation, etc. The major case I observed had very much this character. Although there had been a protracted period of talk about the need for a new garden area the decision itself clearly came as a surprise to many and had a band-wagon effect of sudden release of excitement and instant rumour. In the course of less than an hour one morning, this led to the formation of a large, happy crowd of members of a majority of households, who trooped off collectively to one of the areas that had been broached during the preceding days' conversations. On the way, some major guidelines of allocation (from which side planting would start, how the eventual fence would run, what stretch of land would ultimately be cleared) spread in this crowd. Once in the area, spouses and friends went crashing through the bush trying to select a good spot for their particular garden and trying to find out where other people were locating themselves and what potential directions of progressive clearing they were envisaging; the criteria of choice, apart from the potentialities of soil and moisture, were previous use (the area had been cultivated by my estimate 16 years earlier and persons had sentimental and quasi-jural first rights to areas used by their parents or senior siblings at that time), while the direction of expansion was preferably up hill. Late arrivals who had not been present at the sudden departure from the village kept arriving and staking out their claims; trees came crashing down to mark the beginnings of gardens, women started clearing the ground, a few even planted the first, symbolic taro plants, boys climbed breadfruit trees to collect mature fruits for immediate cooking.

This diffuse pattern of decision-making stands in marked contrast to that which takes place when acts of cultivation are integrated in larger ritual cycles (cf. pp. 121 f.). In such cases, the leaders of cult activity coordinate and ensure that the required occasions and opportunities arise, and direct the activities of other men towards this purpose. The effects of an active ritual life thus include the incidental production of authoritative decisions to clear new forest areas and start new gardens, with implications which we shall return to later.

The main work of taro gardening is that of clearing the plot. This is men's work and involves the felling of dense stands of mixed forest, both hard- and softwoods (though casuarinas are often prominent in secondary growth, the Baktaman do not, like some New Guinea natives, plant them in fallow areas). A scattering of trees may be left standing — for convenience often mostly hardwoods. These are later killed by barking, and some of them are eventually cut down for firewood. The tool for this work was until 15–20 years ago exclusively a hafted polished stone adze; subsequently steel axes have filtered in through ceremonial trade so most men now own such an axe. Present hardships of disease, slow taro growth, loss of autonomy, and the death of parents and loved ones are blamed on the use of the steel axe; and a nostalgia for the previous golden age focuses on the stone adze as its symbol.

In the further work of the garden, branches and small trunks, as well as bushes and brambles, are burned or set aside as fencing materials; large tree trunks are allowed to remain where they fell. Fire is controlled by men; only senior initiates know the technique of making it. The procedure is simple, but demands a burst of energy: A transverse groove is made in a short hardwood stick; the stick is then split and a stone placed in the cleft to hold it open. In the groove across the cleft you pull a loop of dry rattan (such as men wear around their waist) while holding the stick under your foot, braced against the pull of the rattan. Dry tinder of shredded pandanus or similar material is placed directly under the point of friction. Pulling the cane back and forth forcefully, heat is quickly generated; as the first smoke starts rising you appeal for aid from a marsupial mouse, crying *Ubīr kir-kir-kir-kir*. (The place of this marsupial in ritual will be discussed later, pp. 186 f.) At this point the glow falls into the tinder, and by breath-

Plate 5. Group of women, married and unmarried, around entrance to a women's house. The scarification shown on the woman to the right is optional, and done at first menses. Necklaces are of pig's tusks, and Job's tears.

Plate 6. Taro-planting. Note the taro sticks in the foreground used for planting. In the background, an area planted some weeks earlier, with new leaves forming.

Plate 7. Weeding in a half-matured taro garden, husband and wife working together (she is bent over, below him to the right, with only her bark-cape showing). Note the pillar-like shade-trees. Compare Plate 13.

Plate 8. Boy (1st degree novice) shooting with bow-and-arrow.

ing and blowing carefully on it a flame is created. If women need fire in the gardens when their men cannot provide it, they must bring embers from the village.

Women enter the new gardens for clearing of shrubs and weeds (formerly with stone adzes and a chopping-board, now with axes and bush-knives) and in this phase of clearing both sexes may be simultaneously occupied in their joint garden. Smoke from the garden fires also signals the progress of work very widely; idle observers on the sitting platforms of men's houses enjoy watching for such columns of smoke during the day as indication of the activities both of other Baktaman and of distant communities, rarely or never visited.

Once a part of the graden is cleared, planting may start. For this one needs a store of taro sticks, i.e. the tops of harvested taro or their subsidiary off-shoots. These are carried to the garden from other gardens in the process of harvesting, but may be stored up to some weeks before replanting. Planting is done with a 6-foot digging stick; it is women's work, but may also be done by single and widowed men, whereas felling trees is only men's work and must be performed for single women by kinsmen or friends.

During its growth a taro garden needs to be weeded 3 or 4 times; this is done by women, or by both sexes together. At other times, men with adjacent plots in the garden area work in groups building sections of the encircling fence for protection against marauding wild pigs; but the mobilization of groups for this purpose is haphazard and difficult, and gardens have often come into maturity without the fence being completed. The alternation between male and female phases of work is coordinated by semi-public conversation between spouses in the village, often shouted at night between a husband inside the men's house and a wife in her women's house.

It is worth while dwelling on the visual characteristics of a taro garden, in contrast to jungle, since these features reappear in various ritual contexts. While the jungle is dark, damp, and chaotic, littered with debris, twigs, and rotting leaves, the gardens provide a very different image: still and ordered, they are bathed in a clear and uniform sunlight filtered through the few remaining shade trees. The trunks of these trees stand in an open scatter, like the columns of a hall or indeed an enlarged version of the fire-posts in a Baktaman house. The ground is tidy and weeded, free of twigs and debris, and covered only with a regular stand of heart-shaped taro leaves.

In essentially this condition the garden will stand for about six months. After a while, the leaves of the barked shade trees will fall — a process thought beneficial to the crop and regarded as an effect of the crop's beginning maturity. The weeds collected in the first couple of weedings are burned so that they will not reseed; but after some months grasses invade the gardens and these are mulched around the developing taro — to provide the roots with the smells on which they thrive.

Harvesting is done by women. The tops or sticks of the harvested taro are tied in bundles and carried to new gardens for planting; the taro roots are loaded into net bags and carried to the house. Short lines of women entering the village heavily laden with taro represent the fulfilment of the hopes and achievements of gardening.

Along the edges, or in suitable patches of the taro garden, other crops, particularly of banana, sugar cane, and pit-pit may be planted. These produce or will continue producing after the taro has been harvested. Likewise, sweet potatoes are planted alongside taro, or where taro has been harvested. In favourable spots it then runs riot over the harvested garden and produces an important subsidiary crop which is used as supplementary food and to feed the pigs.

Domestic animals. Pig raising is a second major preoccupation of the Baktaman; but their success is poor by New Guinea standards and is achieved in intimate dependence on the wild pig population. Firstly, a major fraction of the pigs kept are captured from the wild as piglets. Even more important, only female pigs are allowed to mature sexually, while male piglets are castrated and usually slaughtered before reaching full size. Female pigs are thus entirely dependent on wild boars for impregnation; they are encouraged to wander into the forest and find a mate, both in the expectation of the litter they will produce and in the hope, frequently realized, that on their return they will entice the wild boar close to the village, where he can be ambushed. Baktaman are aware that were all wild pigs to be exterminated, as they attempt for the sake of their gardens, then their domestic pigs would be in danger of dying out. In such a case, they claim they would allow a male piglet to grow to maturity uncastrated, to impregnate all the sows before being castrated (to make him edible by women and children) and slaughtered.

The sow gives birth unattended in the jungle, but then shortly brings her litter home. There is much conversation about the sow during her 'confinement' and rumour about the number of piglets born; and there is general public excitement and pleasure when the sow returns to the village, followed by her string of piglets.

The care of piglets and their training is quite elaborate. While

34

small they are constantly herded, or kept tied with a loop around their foot in the house. They are partly fed, partly helped during foraging; they are carefully taught to avoid snares and traps, and to stay away from garden fences; they are fondled and cuddled; most of them are given personal (pig) names. When a pig dies of disease or through an accident, the woman who has tended it may mourn it by painting her body with mud, as she would for a person. Fully trained pigs can be allowed to roam freely, despite pig traps and incompletely fenced gardens. Unless mating, giving birth, or on long foraging trips they will return home every evening to be fed a supplement of sweet potatoes and sleep in the women's houses, by the fire.

In addition to this care and supplementary feeding, pigs are also protected and encouraged by ritual means. Men who are eager to obtain good results will make a small shrine of sacra wrapped in a leaf so that women and children cannot see the contents and thus profane it, and place these in a container made of a pandanus leaf-base against the wall over the area where the pigs sleep. To enhance the pig's growth and the formation of fat all pig raisers must also obtain hallowed white earth (*Kwoŋ bayon*). This is collected by either men or women from special, secret places, or traded in from areas to the SW; it is dried, crushed, and wrapped in leaves, to be hung over the pig's sleeping area. In the evening when the pigs return to the house, some of this white powdered earth is taken and rubbed over the back and flanks of each pig.

Pigs are either owned by a man (when caught wild, or obtained by ceremonial trade from the SE) or by spouses jointly (when born to a sow fed from their garden). Ownership, however, does not necessarily imply tending; somewhat more than two of every three pigs are kept in fosterage by non-owners. The owner may choose to give a pig in fosterage for several reasons: (1) some women have a particularly lucky flair in looking after them, (2) you may wish to mark a particular relationship or do a person a favour, or (3) you may wish to be free to consume the flesh of the pig yourself. This latter point arises from an abhorrence, mandatory upon men, against eating a pig you have raised since 'it is like your own child'; some women observe the same rule of exophagy while others will take a share without regard to such sentiments. The person who fosters a pig must provide all its food and care. In return she (or accasionally he) receives at least one piglet from any litter produced by a sow, and the appropriate cuts (cf. below) of the pigs when slaughtered, to eat or use as gifts.

The decision to slaughter is made by the owner, and necessarily

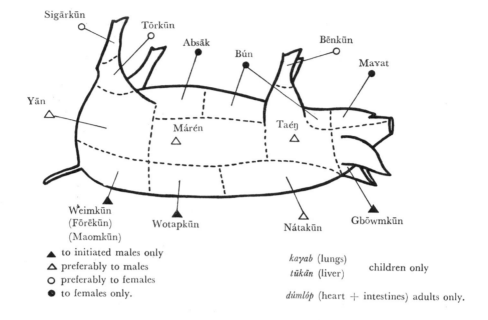

Sigārkūn

Tōrkūn

Absāk

Bún

Bēnkūn

Maуat

Yān

Márén

Taéη

Wĕimkūn
(Fōrēkūn)
(Maomkūn)

Wotapkūn

Nátakūn

Gbōwmkūn

▲ to initiated males only
△ preferably to males
○ preferably to females
● to females only.

kayab (lungs)
tūkān (liver)
children only

dúmlóp (heart + intestines) adults only.

entails a public distribution of meat. It may take the form of a simple slaughter for culinary purposes; a profane communal pig feast to impress a neighbouring group; a blood sacrifice as part of a private healing ceremony; or a sacrifice as part of a communal ritual. On communal occasions, whether profane or sacred, at least two pigs fostered by different persons must be slaughtered so that no one will be debarred by his relationship to the animal from participating in the feast. This may be taken as symptomatic of the great importance attached, and attention given, to the careful distribution of appropriate shares to all members of the community in every case of slaughtering.

Only fully initiated men are authorized to slaughter pigs, and only authorized slaughter renders the meat edible. The animal is tied by a front foot which is pulled forward to expose the flank between the elbow and the shoulder-blade; it is then shot in the heart or upper lung at close range with a bamboo-bladed arrow and allowed to bleed to death. Standardized cuts of meat are made and named as in the associated diagram; the slaughterering is done with axes and bamboo-sliver knives. The first piece to be cut runs from the lower jaw to the anus; much of the intestines come out with it. It is subdivided into three as indicated in the diagram and allocated strictly to women only. Obversely, the head, back, and most particularly the pelvis are male cuts, to be consumed only by senior men. These allocations concern domestic sows and piglets only; the rules governing the consumption of wild pigs will be described below.

As noted, the domestic pig population among the Baktaman is small; it also fluctuates rapidly. A census of the total stock of pigs in April 1968 gave 34 sows and piglets; by October 1968 this had changed by slaughter, capture, birth, and ceremonial trade to 63 sows and piglets. During the intervening six months, 13 pigs were slaughtered and about 20 newborn piglets died. A Table shows the relative importance of the alternative ways of obtaining pigs:

Census in:	April	October
Caught as wild piglet	9	15
Traded from partners in other villages	11	19
Born of a Baktaman sow . . .	14	29
Total	34	63

The only other domestic animal is the dog — indeed only the dog is fully domesticated in that it breeds in captivity and gives birth in the presence of its owner. Only men own dogs; they are used in hunting to locate game in dense forest. Dogs are small and very weak, and predominantly fed on taro though occasionally allowed to eat scraps of meat and intestine and to lick the spilled blood from sacrifices. They are generally carried by the hunter to a likely site for hunting so that they do not exhaust themselves on the way. None the less, they are associated with fierceness and virility, and used to symbolize or embody such qualities in several ritual contexts.

Dog meat is eaten, though not very highly valued for its taste. Sometimes their skulls are kept in secret storage for ritual purposes. Their bones, uniquely among animals but like the bones of unimportant people, are buried. Occasionally, when a dog dies far from a settlement, a shrine is built over the buried bones. As a token of respect and to avoid reprisals from the dog's spirit, persons passing the shrine will throw a twig or small branch on it, often accompanied by a prayer for taro and wealth objects.

Hunting and gathering. The Baktaman must not be thought of as cultivators who supplement their garden produce by hunting and gathering — they are people of the forest who utilize their whole environment for living, and whose attention is directed at all aspects of this environment. Thus the tripartite division into village/garden/ forest is not to separate out distinct worlds and concerns, but a way of ordering experience so as to understand their connectedness. Specifically, village cult, garden agriculture, and forest hunting are regarded as different refractions of the same reality and each is manipulated to achieve effects in the others. This preliminary description is concerned with sketching only the overt and technical features of subsistence, but even from this point of view the place of hunting and gathering is major; when we come to explore the conceptual and ritual role of these activities their importance and connections will become even more apparent.

Much time is spent in hunting, and much importance is attached to its rewards. Most hunting is a male prerogative, and a husband's concern and love for wife and children are judged by his reliability in providing them with game even more than by his gardening. Indeed, with the variety of status-specific eating taboos, and the prescriptions of sharing, such forest products are constantly being provided in a large network of relations and are a major source of social confirmation. The excitement and delight generated by the sudden appearance of an item of game — a snake, a bird, or some lizards — brought home by a hunter is surprising to an external observer. The importance of such food items is incidentally illustrated in a story told by an informant about fleeing from the dreaded Seltaman neighbours. Losing their dog in the flight, the couple in question stopped and the man returned to look for it. When he rejoined his wife to continue the flight, she had built a leaf shelter for the night. He scolded her for stupidly wanting to camp here where the enemy would find them — until she showed him a snake she had managed to kill. So they spent the night there, eating the snake, before proceeding with their escape.

Since much forest produce is consumed on the spot to circumvent rules of sharing, any estimate of its place in the total diet is difficult to make. However, special ritual rules affecting cassowary and wild pig, requiring the deposition of trophies from each kill in the *Katiam* temple, allow me to make an estimate of the number of such prey caught. In one *Katiam* temple, occupied by one man only for a period of approximately 10 years, I found 105 cassowary and 90 wild pig trophies, representing an average of one major item of such game every 2–3 weeks, or of the order of 1/2 kg of meat per day of cassowary and wild pig alone secured by one (slightly better than average) hunter.

The fauna which the Baktaman exploit is composed of the major categories of wild pig (*sāmin*), a large range of marsupials and rodents (*nuk*), bats (*yomnok* = flying fox, *siŋam* = smaller fruit bats, *sirōl* = insectivorous bats), cassowaries (*byā*), birds (*awon*), snakes (*dī*), lizards (*atim*), frogs and toads (*fagāp; faganiŋ* = 'frog-nephews', i.e. tadpoles), fish (*takám*), and a large variety of invertebrates. Techniques centre on the use of bow and a range of specialized arrows, falling-log traps, hanging snares and footsnares, all of which are used by men only. Women and men both gather and may kill small game by beating with sticks. Men construct blinds for shooting birds and use mimicry to locate and attract birds and marsupials.

Since garden fences are rarely completed and often ineffectual in construction, wild pigs attract a dual attention as despoilers of crops and as game for hunting. Baktaman men seem to regard themselves as involved in a continuous war with the wild pigs; they spend hours in the men's houses describing their depredations in detail, discussing their habits and individual idiosyncrasies, speculating on their location and next move. Their tracks are closely observed and often identified as to individual; their lairs are carefully investigated when found (they frequently build nest shelters of large leaves against the rain); fires are left burning in the gardens to bluff them into staying away. Baited falling-log traps are set for them and they are hunted with bow and bamboo-bladed arrow, the latter reluctantly as wild pigs can be very dangerous and occasionally gore and kill hunters.

The meat of wild pig sows and piglets is eaten by men from middle degrees of initiation and up; male wild pig is only eaten by fully initiated men. Both categories of meat involve other ritual proscriptions to be described in detail later, and result in a temporary taboo on entering taro gardens. Besides the meat, the front teeth are used to make necklaces, and tusks are strung into necklaces or worn as nose decorations by men in their pierced nasal septum.

A major category of game is classified in the Faiwol category *nuk* — essentially furred, warm-blooded wild animals, i.e., marsupials and rodents. These include rats, flying squirrels, bandicoots, opossums, cuscus, tree kangaroos, marsupial mice, and tiger cats. A few of them are regarded as definitely unclean, but most are edible by some status categories and many of them have crucial ritual significance. The different species are found in a variety of habitats and elevations; the cloud forest zone is particularly rich in them. Some are nocturnal and best hunted in the moonlight, others are diurnal and hunted by day. Animals to be used for rituals must be taken on special, secret hunting expeditions by authorized personnel.

Nuk are shot with a bow and a hardwood-tipped arrow, the smallest ones also with a multi-pronged arrow. As well as providing meat, their fur is used for head decorations, and the hairless curled tail of the larger cuscus (*kwēmnok*) is often used in the pierced earlobe of men or women as a decoration. Finally, the mandible of several rat species, with its very hard enamel incisors, is used as a chisel and knife for fine carving.

Cassowary are large, ostrich-like flightless forest birds. They are caught in large snares, set for them especially where they come to feed off the fruits of various pandanus and other trees. While setting the snare one wears a small string bag suspended over one's breast-bone; it contains the red, chestnut-like seed (*byā-kīn* = cassowary-eye) of an unknown tree, obtained in ceremonial trade from the south. This red seed is supposed magically to blind the cassowary so that it will stick its head into the snare.

Like male wild pig, cassowary can only be eaten by fully initiated men and various other taboos and proscriptions surround them. They are also valued for their feathers, which are used in senior male headdresses and decorated string bags, and their quills, which are used as nose ornaments. As among many other New Guinea people (Bulmer 1967) cassowaries are not regarded by the Baktaman as birds but classified in a special class of their own and regarded with veneration.

The bird fauna of New Guinea is spectacularly rich, and a great variety of species are found within Baktaman territory. Birds receive endless attention from the Baktaman — their presence is always of interest, their flight observed, their calls mimicked, their behaviour interpreted both for evidence of other animals and for foretelling future events or simultaneous distant events. Flying free in the sky and largely perching in trees they epitomize ritual purity in terms of basic Baktaman criteria, and they are with few exceptions permissible as food for all categories of person. Birds are also valued for their feathers, which are used in a variety of male decorations, and the brilliantly colourful birds of paradise are especially skinned and prepared, and traded as decorations.

Birds are shot with a bow and a multi-pronged arrow or a stunning blunt arrow, usually from ambushes or blinds built high in the trees. Some varieties are also caught in foot-snares, or in hanging snares. Nests are also robbed for eggs and immature birds when the opportunity arises.

Most bird hunting, and the hunting of other animals not mentioned above, such as snakes, lizards, frogs, etc., are not directly connected with ritual performances, though some may provide incidental ritual equipment.

Fish are caught, whenever opportunity arises, by shooting with multipronged arrows in shallow water. More important, fish may be poisoned as a collective operation when a spell of dry weather has reduced the flow in the streams. The poison is obtained by crushing the stalk of the *mait* plant — a vine that does not occur naturally in Baktaman territory, but is cultivated in the lower gardens. The poisoning operation is surrounded by various taboos and special magical procedures to assure its efficacy; ancestors are also called upon in ritual to support the operation. The poison has the effect of stunning all fish so that they float up and are carried by the current to the banks and shallows, where they are gathered up by eager participants.

Beyond this, there is also active gathering of crayfish (*tayōk*), and a wide variety of insects and other invertebrates, including spiders (*ēngabúm*), praying mantis (*fõgiok*), grasshoppers (*kwieŋ*), beetles (*umin*), wood-boring grubs (*yerōp*), and larvae (*ŋap/munsur murum*).

A very wide range of vegetable products, too extensive to allow even a summary review, are also gathered from the jungle. Walking with the Baktaman through the jungle, one's progress is constantly impeded by their attention to these resources, either to note their presence, amount and degree of readiness for use, or to utilize the opportunity for minor gathering. Thus, a few edible leaves will be plucked here (to be wrapped in a larger containing leaf and tied in a bundle with any convenient vine), a ripe fruit or two will be taken there. Of foods of scattered occurrence there are leaves, edible ferns, mushrooms, and wild yams (*dayás*), which also serve as a harvestable famine food. The occurrence of suitable building materials is noted; a more frequently recurring need is that of bark materials for string production, all-purpose rattan for rope and fire-making, and of course firewood. Nettles are gathered for medicinal and ritual purposes, bamboos for water containers, etc.

Of particular interest and importance are certain trees which fall in an intermediate category between wild and cultivated, especially breadfruit, pandanus of several varieties, and sago. The nut-bearing pandanus (*seid*) occurs in groves at higher altitudes; these groves are owned by individuals and saplings are planted to supplement natural reproduction. The breadfruit (*sayon/yoŋabip*) occurs especially in fallow gardens at middle and lower altitudes, where such trees

41

belong to those who last cultivated the site; when found in unused jungle the trees are claimed by the finder. Many trees go unclaimed, however, and the rights are those of first rights to major harvesting, not exclusive monopolies. Baktaman will often attempt to plant such trees by scattering their nuts in suitable places; according to general belief fruit-bats perform this service regularly by carrying nuts with them, and losing them. Breadfruit have an elusive symbolic significance, perhaps hinted by one of the terms used for them (*yoŋ-abip* = garden-village?).

The red pandanus is rarely planted, but always claimed by anyone who finds a new tree, and the rights to harvest it are quite jealously guarded. The red, phallus-like fruit is highly valued as a ritual food, and this and related wild pandanus species appear in numerous ritual contexts.

Finally, sago trees are definitely individually owned. They are planted in sago swamps and other suitable places, mostly by fathers for sons; as with the other trees mentioned above, rights are inherited patrilineally and held by men only. Sago palms take about 15 years to mature, and are a highly valued resource to fall back on when the production from taro gardens fails. Located mostly far from the Baktaman village in the southern part of the territory they are worked from temporary shelters close to the swamps for periods of 10–14 days. Sago is worked collectively by related or friendly households together, directed by the male or males who own the resource; the techniques used appear to be those common to large parts of New Guinea. Though sago keeps well, its production is so time-consuming and the product so bulky and heavy in relation to its nutritional value that it is not much valued as a food and only used to delay harvesting in taro gardens for stretches up to a fortnight, to allow the root crop to mature more fully before harvest. It is thus avoided as a staple for longer periods by the Baktaman.

To complete the sketch of the Baktamans' dependence on the forest outside their village and gardens, mention should be made of the the collection of water. Preferred sources of water are natural springs, where they emerge from the ground. Most streams are also regarded as adequate; some are taboo for drinking as being ritually unclean. These streams are associated with death pollution from having had corpses thrown into them or from flowing close to the places where the bones of the dead are deposited; others arise or pass through taboo areas. The main impure streams of the Baktaman are the Kātor and the Waŋōp.

Water is collected by any person, but particularly by children;

it is stored in bamboo sections or gourds and used for drinking and minor washing, never for boiling as no suitable containers are known for that purpose.

Normal day routine. Around these subsistence activities, a general pattern of life forms which can seem rather monotonous and eventless to the Baktaman as well as to an observer. Before contact, the main incursions into an unremarked flow of time were provided by warfare and ritual. With total pacification and the probable future diminution of ritual as a result of mission and administration influence, there may be little to break up a rather dull routine in the future.

At the time of my fieldwork, the once careful observation of security measures had been essentially discontinued. Till recently, the Baktaman maintained defensive towers against the border of their most aggressive enemies, the Seltaman. In the village, there was also a functionary, referred to as *leibom*, who arose before dawn every day to inspect the area and paths around the village for footprints and other signs of strangers and ambushes. This duty rotated among the adult men. Women and children were not allowed to move away from the settlement except in large groups, and men preferred to scatter in the surrounding forest before allowing them to move far, and to accompany them to the gardens and other regular places of work. Today, only the most timid express any fear of attack, though men never move far without their bows and arrows, including one war arrow in the arsenal; and stronger reluctance is felt about visiting areas close to the Baktaman boundaries. Indeed, it should be noted that the Baktaman environment is remarkably benign as far as natural dangers are concerned: there are no large carnivores, few poisonous snakes or insects, no danger of exposure or freezing to death. Though largely uncomfortable, their habitat is in no way threatening — only the danger of violence from neighbours, or from a range of spirits and ghosts that inhabit the forest (cf. pp. 123 ff.) can cause serious fear.

Having reassured themselves that all is peaceful in the morning, people will take some food, generally from what was baked the previous night; the women will send the pigs away from the houses for the day, friends and spouses will exchange some tentative remarks about what plans they have. As the mists rise and the first proper sun breaks through, women gather in groups composed of those planning to spend a full day's work in the same garden; piglets and children may accompany them or other arrangements are made for them. When unexpectedly refused permission to accompany mother to the garden, a child may throw a screaming tantrum, while spectators

43

snicker prudishly at what they suspect is an arrangement for marital intercourse. Finally, these groups of women move off, conversing and calling others left behind in the village till they are out of earshot.

Men generally disappear more quietly, singly or in small groups, and their schedule is more irregular since their activities are more varied. They also often linger longer, and it is not till 10–10.30 a.m. that most people have left the village.

During the day, some information about the activities of others tends to spread by word of mouth or from tell-tale signs such as smoke from garden fires, cooking fires, etc. People start filtering back to the village by early afternoon; around 5 p.m., the most hardworking women will return from the gardens, generally carrying harvested taro; cooking fires will be lighted up in all the houses and by dusk everyone prefers to be safely in the house. The main meal is cooked at that time; occasionally men will move between nearby men's houses, or groups of men will depart for moonlight hunting, or an occasional dance will start to the light of torches; but most people remain in their houses with their doors boarded up, as they fear spirits prowling in the dark.

An alternative routine develops in the garden houses, or in sago camps, where families live in closer intimacy away from the main public arena. Baktaman spend at least a third of their time in such residences away from the village, and individual preference influences their choice considerably. It is particularly my impression that some older couples, more in love and at ease with each other, choose to spend more of their time in this more intimate setting; on the other hand, their children generally object to garden house residence as being very dull and eventless. There seem to be no direct sanctions against mature men who adopt this pattern, as there would be against young men who associate too much with women; but frequent absence from the village inevitably reduces the active influence of such men on community affairs.

Normal routines are occasionally interrupted by the visits of ceremonial trading partners from other communities — they will often spend a full day or two in the men's house, there may be some slight feasting, and a group of men will congregate around them to exchange news. Irregular periods of taboo on garden work and sometimes hunting, following a variety of ritually significant events, will also impose occasional periods of leisure. Finally, the preparation and performance of major rituals restructure the pattern of life drastically for periods of time in ways that will be detailed later.

PART II

The initiation rites

CHAPTER 3

General features of
the system

In this part of the monograph, I shall attempt to give an account of
Baktaman cult activities, and an explication of the meanings of these
idioms and acts and the messages they are used to express. I wish to
provide a substantive documentation of the forms of Baktaman ritual
activity, and as far as possible establish not only what may be understood and intended by the leaders of these cult activities, but also
what is actually received as messages by audiences and participants.
In this way I shall try to establish a body of data from which we may
ask questions both about the structure of ritual activity as a medium
of communication, and the nature and extent of the knowledge and
insight which is transmitted in this medium. The simplest and truest
way to go about this is through a presentation of the initiation rites,
in sequence.

Among the Baktaman, all men must be initiated if they are to
attain manhood, normal social recognition, active participation in
any religious affairs, and any kind of sacred knowledge. The initiation
rites also constitute the major cult events of Baktaman religion, and
contain among their constituent parts all the elements and ceremonies
practised at other times in the cult houses. They are thus both the
authoritative models for all other cult activity and the only entry to
participation. Only one male over puberty — a feeble-minded deaf-
mute — is not enrolled in the initiation system at present. The justification for this is, somewhat incongruously in his case, that he might
tell the secrets to the women — a conventional phrase, emphasizing
the trust and responsibility imposed on initiates and their differentiation from the irresponsible and dependent women. The view thus
seems to be primarily that men are saddled with a responsibility, on
behalf of the community as a whole, to assure prosperity by achieving
ritual purity and performing the cult; it is not a male cult but a

communal cult performed by men. However, since the conventional blessings enumerated as springing from good cult practice include the growth and strength of sons, and there is some public concern about the low reproductive rate of the Baktaman population, I did once suggest the possibility of a parallel female cult to assure the growth and strength of women. This elicited a warning that such a cult would make women *too* strong, if they had initiations in addition to their natural fertility they would want to be on top when copulating; and this led further to the telling of myth no. 3 (see Appendix III). Despite this sexual dichotomization and rivalry, recognizable as a persistent secondary theme, the main focus is none the less on the rites as a cult for the whole congregation of the Baktaman nation, or its component clans.

The total sequence of initiations is composed of seven degrees, each separated by an indefinite time period from the next. They must be done in the correct sequence but can take place in the cult houses of neighbouring groups, not necessarily in those of the Baktaman themselves. Other groups of Faiwolmin have in part different names, different sequences, and different total numbers of initiations; but the relevant equivalents are known by the fully initiated. I will not elaborate on the names and interrelations of the different grades but rather present them in sequence to simulate the progress of a novice through the series; indeed the fact that there are a total of seven is not known to a man until he has reached the fourth or fifth grade.

It quickly became clear to me during fieldwork that the formal initiations were the key to all participation and knowledge about ritual matters. I consequently invested all possible thoughtfulness and effort in gaining confidence and admission to such activities, and ultimately succeeded in overcoming deep-seated distrusts and suspicions, and the fundamental reluctance to give information that must be associated with a secret cult. These, I think, could only be removed by initiation. My materials are consequently composed as follows: (i) I have observed parts of 1st degree initiation among the Baktaman, as they were taking place during my residence there. (ii) I have observed the 4th degree as done in Kasanmin, the closest north-eastern neighbours, as co-member of a group of Baktaman seniors who visited Kasanmin for the occasion. (iii) I have performed the essentials of the 5th degree in a private ceremony in the *Katiam* of Feisabip hamlet, so as to be qualified as (iv) a novice participant in the 6th degree initiation performed by the Baktaman 27/5 —4/6 1968. (v) I have participated in a series of minor cult activities im-

48

plying these initiation statuses, and also some requiring 7th degree initiation. (vi) I have detailed verbal accounts and descriptions of all the initiations from several informants, both cult leaders and fully or partly initiated members.

All initiations among the Baktaman are collectively held for stably constituted sets of males. These sets form at the bottom of the ladder through the accumulation of a new 'generation' waiting to be inducted into the system. Upon jointly entering 1st degree initiation as novices they are constituted as a group. They may refer to each other as *fik-kumēr* (brother-in-initiation), and will move up jointly through all subsequent initiations. Indeed, if one member for some reason is prevented from participating in a particular initiation, he is still regarded as having moved up together with the rest of his set; and when the set makes use of the initiation rites of neighbouring groups to move up the ladder they may frequently decide to send only part of the set, to represent them all in the ritual. In such cases, those who have not participated in the formal occasion will be instructed somewhat as to its contents at a later, more ad hoc occasion.

Depending on the number of young boys available, and the impatience of their fathers to start them on the path of social recognition, a new set may be formed shortly or a longer time after the previous one — and indeed the Baktaman have no way of measuring the time elapsed. Judging from the apparent differences in physical age between members in a set, I think that the average span is of the order of 10 years, but that it may vary considerably.

The initiation sets emphatically do not constitute an age set system; the seven grades are steps in the advancement of any one group of initiates and not positions that have to be filled at all times. Among the Baktaman in 1968, 6 sets were found. Set (a), with 9 members, was in the first degree. Set (b), with 28 members, passed from 5th to 6th degree. Set (c), with 15 members, was in the 6th degree, while sets (d), 7 members, (e), 3 members, and (f), 1 member, had all been initiated into the 7th and highest degree.

The sets follow each other in unchangeable sequence, but their respective rates of progress through the grades are essentially independent. Each set has special functions in the initiation of the next junior set. Thus, when the (c) set move up into 7th degree they will be 'shown' the ritual by the (d) set, assisted by the seniors and particularly the cult house master; when the (b) set in turn moves on to 7th degree, the (c) set will have to 'show' them the ritual, in the capacity which has then been passed on to them and which they then hold. Apart from the first and the last grades, (respectively *laqsalman* and *tamboylot*) there are no names for occupants of the various degrees of initiation, except for the collective term *kimitōk*. This may be translated as *kimit* = those who know/are allowed, and *ōk* = water, i.e. those who have completed the post-initiation fast of refraining from drinking water, i.e. have completed an initiation. Senior sets call junior sets *neŋ-kimitōk* (= younger-initiate) and the juniors call the seniors *lil-kimitōk* (= elder-initiate).

The different stages of initiation are directly related to first entrance into formerly taboo houses, or deeper levels of participation in the cult activities that take place in them. In order of sacredness, these are (1) the men's house (*Kawēram*) with minimal ritual activity (2) the *Katiam:* the clan cult house for taro and hunting, (3) the *Yolam:* the communal cult house for taro and warfare, (4) the *Amowkam:* the communal cult house for taro. The native terms for these latter three kinds of cult houses will be used in the subsequent text. The names for these houses or temples are familiar to the uninitiated population, but nothing about their contents or interior — they merely stand there as forbidden places, on pain of death, in which important and unknown rituals take place.

Indeed, the secrecy in which the temples and the ritual activities are shrouded, and the actual ignorance of the contents and purposes of initiation that obtains among non-initiates and novices, should once more be emphasized. Boys and young men approaching an initiation may occasionally be teased and frightened by their elders with lies about the terrors they will have to go through, but even that is generally frowned upon as an indiscretion. The unpreparedness and ignorance of novices are a persistent theme of initiation, and emphasize the character of Baktaman religion as a true mystery cult, the mysteries of which only slowly and opaquely come into focus.

CHAPTER 4

First degree initiation

The first phase

The precipitating events that launch young boys on initiation should fall upon them with unexpected suddenness, though both fathers and mothers may indeed have hinted to the child that some such thing is approaching, to avoid too poor a showing when it takes place. The staging is dramatic. The boys, ranging in age from as low as five and up into their teens, have been children to this point, eating and sharing food with their mother or foster mother and sleeping in the women's hut with her, possibly other women, sisters, and pigs. Suddenly in the small hours of the night the men of the village, adorned with feather head-dresses and pigs' tusks, sweep into the house, tear the boy loose from the protesting and beseeching mother, and drag him off into the dark, frightening forest where till then he has not been allowed to go at night for fear of spirits and ambushes. Progressively, a group of shivering, frightened age-mates are collected there, herded by their elders. If some break down too badly, they will be consoled by a father, elder brother, or uncle; but a fair level of subjective terror is created and maintained for them by their seniors.

In the forest, they are made to collect dew from the leaves and rub themselves all over their bodies with it, particularly on the chest, upper arms, and thighs. Thereupon they are led back to the village, and for the first time, into the men's house. Inside, they are shown pork fat which has been stored in bamboo containers, told its secret taboo name *fir*, and made to rub themselves with the fat, starting with the forehead at the hairline and proceeding to face, chest, arms, and legs. Their seniors thereupon smear red ochre on them in the same fashion, emphasizing the hairline and face. They are instructed to repeat these dew and fat rubbings every morning, and never to divulge the secrets of the identity and sacred name of the pork fat, or they will have

51

their throats slit and their corpses thrown in the river. The novices are then given the special insignia of the 1st degree initiation: *minīk* — two 1–2 cm broad bands tied from string and formed as loops, to be worn crosssed diagonally across chest and back — and the *laqsal* — a small string bag constructed over a U-shaped cane and decorated with feathers, to be worn on the back. Having obtained these secrets and items of ritual equipment, the novices must observe an absolute taboo on drinking water for two days and nights. From this point on the boy will be called a *laqsalman* — a child-of-the-*laqsal* — for as long as he remains in the 1st degree of initiation.

As dawn appears, the new set of *laqsalman* are led away secretly into the forest, so their mothers do not see them. There they are taught and helped to build a small communal hut, designed exactly to accommodate them, raised off the ground on poles, and very tightly thatched and walled with leaves so that it will be rain- and wind-proof, with a small entrance and no fireplace. They are also made to construct a special structure — a low slanting leaf awning covering the length of a log which has been cut and placed in a slightly open area in the forest.

The *laqsalman* are then instructed in the prescriptions and taboos which now obtain for them. Every morning before dawn they must wash themselves with dew, except in the face. At night when they hear showers of rain coming, they must lie down on their backs with their heads on the log under the sheltering roof and the rest of their body exposed to the falling rain. When dry from the rain and dew in the morning, they must rub themselves again with pork fat. In the daytime they must roam the forest and hunt; at night they must sleep together and keep each other warm in the cold brush hut. They must further observe a number of taboos: never wash in running water; avoid water on the face; not eat during the day; not enter the village except at dusk to fetch cooked taro; not enter the gardens; not eat pork fat; not eat certain specific kinds of game (see below); and not approach fire (except, as a special dispensation on cold nights, the *laqsalman* are allowed on request to enter the men's house and sit by the fire for a short while to 'thaw out' before returning to the brush hut). If these rules are closely observed, a *laqsalman* will grow quickly and be strong and healthy, whereas breaches will cause weakness, sickness, and even death.

The launching of the 1st degree initiation has been under preparation for some time before the novices are seized. Firstly, public opinion is built up that there is a need for initiations: the parents of sons who are growing up will be impatient, whereas ambitious fathers with very young sons will try to delay the event so that their child will be big enough to be included in the set, and not have to wait another indefinite period. Differences in influence between fathers, depending on personality and vitality and not directly on ritual status or material assets, thus to some extent affect the life situation of novices. Once the necessity of the event is more or less established, the problem of obtaining pigs for pork fat arises: there should ideally be 4 pigs slaughtered, though generally two or three will do. These pigs are secretly slaughtered and their fat stripped and stored in bamboos in the men's houses.

Meanwhile, the women make string and tie the *laqsal* bag and the breast bands. This is normally done by a mother or senior sister of the novice, who are thus inevitably parties to the forthcoming events. Making the breast bands has a particular significance in asserting a close personal bond between the woman and the boy: when he wears them, she will 'see' him more readily, with the connotation of stronger awareness of his presence, anticipation of his arrival, emotional confirmation that he 'belongs' to the woman. Some men wear these bands throughout life, and have them renewed from the same woman as they grow out of them or wear them out. In return for receipt of the bands, a *laqsalman* should present the woman with an item of fresh game, preferably a brush turkey — taboo to men because of its unclean habit of foraging on the ground (but note later its ritual significance, revealed in the highest initiations). Of other emblems, the only common but optional one is dried shredded leaves of the *saksēk* cane, worn in the boy's (secular) arm band and supposed to further growth.

The context for some of these major idioms:

The *lāqsāl* netbag, normally tied by the mother, is subsequently decorated with feathers by the father, or his functional equivalent. The feathers used for the *lāqsāl* are those of the tail and wings of the great cuckoo-dove (*Reinwardtoena reinwardtsi*, native term: *moin*). As noted, birds are generally regarded as ritually admirable; certain species are particularly used as emblems and are associated with degrees of initiation (cf. the man-bird identity expressed in myth 5, Appendix III). The association of 1st degree novices with the cuckoo-dove starts them at the bottom of a sequence of man-bird equivalences: the cuckoo-dove is a medium large, peaceful, and gregarious bird.

Third degree initiates are similarly allowed, but not required, to wear a string bag decorated with eagles' feathers; the eagle is also associated with 3rd degree initiation in other ways and 3rd degree qualifies the initiate to participate in warfare. Fourth degree novices are required to wear the white tail-feather of the otherwise all-black male hornbill (*Aceros plicatus*, native term: *kawēr*, cf. p. 50, *kawēram* = men's house) — a large, heavy bird with a phallus-like enlargement of its upper beak. They also may wear a net bag decorated with its black feathers. Fourth degree initiation has a number of features indicating its association with adult male sexuality. Finally, 7th degree initiation gives the right to wear a decorative net bag covered with cassowary feathers and is associated with the cassowary in other ways; it also seemed obvious to me, though denied by informants, that male dance (and only 7th degree initiates can play the drum used for that purpose) mimics the cassowary. Though not a 'bird' in the Baktaman sense of *awon*, I think the cassowary can legitimately be included as the culmination of this series of bird emblems for bird-man equivalences.

The significance of fire in this as in other initiations is far from clear; one aspect of its prohibition, however, can be emphasized, viz. the discomfort of doing without it. The drinking taboo is similarly a hardship; in connection with some later initiations there is direct torture, and the pain involved is emphasized by the initiators. The major discomforts characteristically follow immediately after the revelation of major secrets, and are consistent with their forbidden and esoteric character: penance must be done for the knowledge obtained.

The significance of water is much clearer: whereas dew and falling rain accumulate, running water washes away. Growth and retention are like dew and rain, but inimical to water. So boys should not wash away their substance, or the strength received in ritual; special powers are retained through the period of abstinence from drinking. In later initiations such power is then deposited in the gardens before drinking is resumed. Water, even in the form of dew or rain, is also inimical to fat; thus the parts rubbed with fat should not be rubbed or exposed to water of any kind. Therefore the need for the face-sheltering awning when exposing the body to rain.

The pork fat (and red colour) will recur in a series of contexts. Likewise the action of rubbing: with stinging nettles to 'fight' the pain of sickness, with the red falling leaves of the *dubkōn* tree to strengthen the adult male body. These red leaves are also used to polish the skull, particularly the forehead, of the ancestor in the *Yolam*. Most directly analogous to the *laqsalman*'s rubbing with (white) pork fat is the rubbing of pigs with sacred white earth in the evening, to further their health and growth. The precariousness of health for both animals and men must be remembered.

The secrets and objects shown the *laqsalman* at initiation would seem to be entirely new to them, and shared only between initiates. Thus, though female relatives may be aware of the approaching 1st degree initiation they seem in truth to be ignorant of its content. Thus even the key secret of the identity of the pork fat seems to be unknown to them: one woman, in discussing the increasing maturity of a young man commented to me in all earnestness that he had 'had glistening sweat on his face for a long time now', rather in the way mothers in our society will associate a tendency towards having pimples with puberty. Certainly, the fear of mishandling their newly-won sacred knowledge is such among novices that they are fearful and evasive in their response on such matters to seniors, and reportedly unwilling to discuss them among themselves.

After these precipitating revelations there follows a liminal period of considerable duration, ideally two moons. During this period the novices must observe all the prescriptions and taboos very carefully, avoid the proximity of women as much as possible, and avert their faces from women so that the fat cannot be identified. The cult master shows some attention to their training — mainly admonishing them to observe the taboos and accompanying them in their hunting and foraging.

The *laqsalman* of set (a), however, spent only 3 weeks in this liminal state, since shortly after constructing their brush hut they started being disturbed by a spirit/ghost (*sabkar*, cf. pp. 127 ff.) who rustled the leaves, shook the hut, and generally frightened the boys. Several fathers became concerned that the hut might be unwanted by the ancestors in its present location, and that the novices might be struck by illness. They therefore decided to bring the boys back into the village.

This involves a small ceremony of aggregation in which the novices are brought into the men's house, and the physically more mature of them taught/authorized to cook taro, till then forbidden to the boys. This is done in the lower-ranking of the two men's house fires and involves steering the boy's hands by holding his elbow as he goes through the operations of pushing aside the fire, burying the taro in the ashes, and covering it over with embers, then (after a slow period of baking) extracting it again. The novice is further instructed that he must never do this with pork fat still on his hands from rubbing his

55

face and body, i.e. he must wait till evening before cooking. The taro is then eaten by the *laqsalman* set, and they spend their first night ever in the men's house. The fear associated with this occasion is indicated by the breakdown of one of the *laqsal* boys, who in his fright was incontinent and defecated on the legs of one of the sleeping men. Further terrified, he ran away and hid. The men were furious when they woke up and understood what had happened; they searched for him and finally found him hiding in his mother's house. For this total breach of taboo, he was stripped of his *laqsal* and bands and expelled from the set, to wait till the next set forms to start his initiations.

The second phase

The inconvenience of having young novices living in the men's house is considerable: numerous matters involving secrets from the higher initiations cannot be discussed, their juvenile interests interfere with men's house peace, etc. So they are generally moved as quickly as convenient into a vacant house to fend more for themselves. They must continue to wear the *laqsal* and observe the major taboos. Eating taboos include: pandanus, fresh bananas, fresh greens, snake, birds, certain kinds of marsupials, and pork fat. The taboos on washing, mixing fat and water, and entering gardens are maintained.

The next ritual activities are organized in a phase of 1st degree initiation sometimes referred to as *imenban* (lit.: 'taro-explanation', though taro is not explicitly mentioned and the explanation remains obscure). These events are organized by the next senior set. This set goes off on a secret marsupial hunt,[1] of the kind required to provide sacramental food, without any knowledge among the *laqsalman* of the event or its significance. The senior hunters must secure one or several of a series of marsupials till now forbidden to the *laqsalman*, (cf. ch. 20). The game is brought secretly into the men's house, and cooked with hot stones in a leaf oven. Thereupon the meat is stripped off without breaking any bones, and the novices are brought in to eat the meal, being instructed not to throw away a scrap and not to break any bones they might find. Unbeknown to the novices, all the bones

[1] As will be seen later, only men who have passed their 5th degree initiation can take part in such a secret hunt. Thus, unless the preceding set has reached this point before the next set reaches second phase of 1st degree, special arrangements must be made. In the course of the average 10 years that separate the sets, I suspect that the necessary progression through the grades has usually been achieved; if not, I would suppose the sacred meat to be provided by other, more senior hunters.

will later be taken to the clan ancestors in the *Katiam*, presented to them, and burned — whereby the novices will unknowingly have participated in a sacramental meal.

Having eaten the meat, the novices are then taken to the nearest cave. The prohibition of their entering caves is thereupon removed, they are shown into the cave by their seniors. Upon emerging, the novices are attacked by the senior set with branches and viciously whipped, while the seniors cry *kwei* — the secret, taboo word for stone. After this, the novices must again separate themselves from profane life and reside in their brush hut in the forest for a long time, preferably more than two moons.

The final phase

The reaggregation centres on defining the novices' status in relation to their female relatives, and their public status as males, and it terminates the *laqsalman* stage. A pig must be obtained from the mother of one of the boys. It is stripped of its fat, which is cooked in the men's house, while its meat is taken elsewhere and slowly cooked in an earth oven. The novices are brought into the men's house; there they break their fast on pork fat by eating it ceremonially, rubbed with trade salt from Oksapmin. This is significant in terms of colour symbolism: most of the small quantity of salt obtained is today white industrial salt. Traditional salt obtained from ceremonial partners and known to be originally produced in Oksapmin is black; and in all contexts where salt occurs ritually the colour appears to be so important that the qualitatively greatly preferred white salt cannot be used.

The novices then leave the men's house and are made to pass between two lines of the senior set, who whip them with branches, much as was done after visiting the cave. They then return in a line into the men's house, where in turn they are fed a piece of the *weimkūn* pelvis cut of the pig, allowed only to men. These pieces of meat are passed into their mouth through the arch of a pig's tusk, held and administered by a senior man; alternatively it may be passed to them under the left armpit of the giver.

The rest of the pig's meat is given to the women, who cook it and cook taro, while the novices are sent back to their forest hut. When the cooking is completed, the boys are called back; each is equipped by his seniors with a raw taro. He is then sent to his mother, whom he confronts for the first time since the initiations started; he gives his mother the raw taro, and in return she gives him a cooked taro and (some of) the cooked pork she has. With this he returns to the men's house to eat there with his set. From this point on he is allowed to live a normal secular life in the village as a man, speaking with women including his mother but not sleeping in her house, and observing the other taboos encumbent on ordinary male status. He discards the *laqsal* — though he may still use it occasionally — and rubs himself with pork fat only irregularly, with dew more frequently.

CHAPTER 5

Second degree initiation

Shortly after the completion of the 1st degree initiation, the 2nd degree is generally performed. It is connected with the *Katiam* cult house and called *katiamban*, i.e. '*Katiam*-explanation', and is a small and brief affair. I have evidence from several informants that the initiation by this name follows much later in the sequence elsewhere — as fourth degree in Abolgobip and perhaps sixth degree in Bolovip, only two days' travel west of the Baktaman. However, such information is always grossly unreliable because of deception as well as confusion, and the difficulties of equating ceremonies.

Among the Baktaman, the initiation entails the sacrifice of one pig, and two days' taboo only. On the day of the ritual, all people other than the senior sets are sent away from the village; the novices must accompany the women to the taro gardens, where they harvest taro and bake it in earth ovens. The seniors then slaughter a pig, on the ground in the village circle close to the *Katiam;* this is steam-cooked with red-hot stones in a bracken and banana-leaf wrapping. The cooked pig is then divided lengthwise along the middle, but with the pelvis area (*weimkūn*) attached to one half and the head (*gbōwmkūn*) attached to the other.

This way of dividing the pig recalls the ceremony of establishing bond friendship (*tayon*), where a bird or a small marsupial is divided in similar fashion between two boys or men who promise each other eternal friendship. Though a relationship which is familiar from young boyhood, no one enters it lightly and many men have no *tayon* at all. It thus provides a powerful idiom for friendship and obligation between the two sets.

When the other villagers return from the gardens with their cooked taro, the women and children are made to go directly to their houses and close up their doors. The novices are then taken to the *Katiam*, to enter it for the first time. As they approach, they are frightened by a warrior, with pig's tusk in his nose and black head-dress, flashing a threatening face in the door. They climb into the dark interior and see fires burning low in the fireplaces; walls heavily adorned with pigs' mandibles, pigs' skulls, and cassowary pelvises; and between the fireplaces, a sheet of dark cloth with a small collection of human bones, painted red. The novices are told they are the ancestors, and further frightened by threats that if they look closely at the bones, the earth will tremble and the mountains crack. As the novices flee from the *Katiam* in fright, the seniors tramp on the floor and make the whole structure shake.

The novices are then taken to their normal residence in the young men's house, where they eat the taro they have brought and their half of the pig. They remain in the men's house, and they observe a taboo on drinking water through the evening and night. Next morning their lips are barely moistened with drops of water given them by the next senior set; thereupon they are sent to a garden where planting is taking place, and they each plant some taro sticks. On their return to the village in the afternoon, the seniors give them ample water, which completes the ritual.

The *Katiamban* initiation exemplifies perhaps most simply of all the initiations the two general features of incompleteness and falseness of information obtained, and the partial and conditional character of the rights gained. First, the information: the novices have been introduced for the first time to a previously forbidden temple, and the very name of the rite indicates that some explanation of its contents or function has been given. Let us look, with the wisdom of higher initiations, at the nature of the *Katiam*.

The temple itself is often known in ordinary speech as *yēnām* = 'big-sister's house.' in contrast to the *Yolam*, which is called *neɲām* = 'little-sister's house,' though the latter is in fact the more sacred and powerful of the two. Inside, a *Katiam* should preferably contain two fires — of the two *Katiam*s found among the Baktaman today, the larger and focal one in Feisabip hamlet has this character and my description will concentrate on it. It is a large, very dark house, blackened inside by years of smoke and soot, and used as a residence by 7 fully initiated men plus 3 men of the (c) set, long since initiated to the 6th degree. Its leadership is dual in that ritual authority is vested in Kwonkayam, the only surviving member of initiation set (f) while practical leadership is in the hands of Namraeŋ of set (d). These two use the floor by the sacred, right-hand fire as their living space, while the other eight group themselves around the left-hand fire. However, the area between the right-hand fire and the wall is sacred, and not for living use. This wall is covered with trophies of sacred animals caught by the hunters: above, three tiers full of cassowary pelvises, below, one tier of wild pigs' mandibles, and on the floor a row of pigs' skulls — male to the left and far right, female in the right/centre. Most significant of all, the wall contains five ancestral shrines and some ritual equipment; the opposite wall contains one ancestral shrine and a recently established small collection of pigs' skulls and mandibles.

The shrines are composed of select bones of clan ancestors, and the cult of the *Katiam* is strictly a clan cult. The complete list of clans represented among the Baktaman is found in the census lists of Appendix II. In the Feisabip *Katiam* are found: (1) the mandible of Laqbūyok, a major Minkarin clan ancestor, stored in a string bag decorated with feathers because of the importance of the bone. This shrine is attended by Kwonkayam. (2) The right index finger and collar bone of another Minkarin ancestor, stored up on the wall in a pandanus leaf and attended by Taktien (set e), who would not divulge to me his ancestor's name. (3) The right index finger of Bōyaŋ, the most important Yeni clan ancestor, stored in a string bag and attended by Namraeŋ. Further are two shrines containing collar-bone and right 3rd finger respectively belonging to a Minkarin ancestor and the ancestor of a small clan which has no fully initiated member; Kwonkayam attends both as a holding operation till authorized clan descendants can take over their own shrine. On the facing wall are the right index finger bones of Mútim, the Yabik clan ancestor attended by Taneŋ (set d). The other *Katiam* of the Baktaman is in the hamlet of Kamsurbaŋ and contains the bones of the third finger of the ancestor of the Wanfaɏir clan, attended by Yawksɏam (set d).

Briefly, these clan shrines receive offerings of bones from all wild pig, cassowary, and a considerable range of marsupials killed by a member of that clan; this assures the fertility of taro. They are independent shrines, each associated with a group of members of one clan; and the initiates explicitly conceptualize the distinctness of clans through the separation of the identities of these ancestral relics. The idea of mixing them up when showing them to the *Katiamban* novices is a conscious hoax to prevent them from knowing the practice of clan cult or interpreting any other aspect of their significance — the information communicated to the novices is thus limited to (a) the crucial association bones — ancestors — red, and (b) the appearance of the *Katiam* temple: its black interior, sacred fire, and display of pig and cassowary remains. The fruitlessness of speculating further on the significance of the *Katiam* and its sacra is complemented by the threats and fears associated with examining them more closely: a realization of their importance and power is closely associated with their danger and destructiveness. The significance of the taro-planting visit to the gardens after the view of the sacra and the communal meal, but before the breaking of the water taboo, is thus probably not apparent to any novice; though the bases for a dawning association of temple and garden are doubtless being built up. The fundamental character of mystery cult is thus emerging — the fearful awareness of a vital, unknowable and forbidden truth behind the secret and cryptic ritual acts. But this is created at the cost of trust between novices and initiators, where the former will become increasingly aware of the deceptions and hoaxes presented as revelations by the latter.

The other general feature of all initiations is the loose connection that exists between initiation as a rite-de-passage and the actual practice of the new status and capacities. Many of the rights codified in the initiations are in fact also conditional on physical development, social maturity, or the whim of one's seniors. Thus in the 1st degree initiation boys are separated from their mothers and brought into the men's house, but clearly do not belong there yet; improvisations are made and for a long time they will continue to be excluded from what they have been ritually inducted into. There was a rite of authorization to cook taro; but only those novices of the set who had reached considerable physical maturity were so empowered. In the *Katiamban*, the whole set is taken into the temple, only to be again excluded from entering it for a long time. Justifications for such exclusions are generally phrased with reference to the health of the person: he would become ill, his body would wither away, etc. Where physical and social maturity is present, but ritual authorization is absent, on the other hand, the impediments relate to garden conditions: the taro plants would die, the tubers would not form. In every case, *both* ritual and secular qualifications are required to effect a status transformation, and the incongruity and mild limbo that is the result of fulfilling one without the other is a not infrequently recurring experience.

CHAPTER 6

Third degree initiation

The next step in initiation involves a long and dramatic ritual and introduces the novices to the *Yolam* temple. It is called *Wunmalal*, literally 'arrow-demonstration,' for reasons to be discussed later. As in the cases of previous initiations it gives some sacred knowledge while withholding other; it includes explicit and covert deception and subjects the novices to more trials and mistreatment than previously experienced.

The *Wunmalal* follows an irregular unspecified period after *Katiamban*, and does not seem to be triggered by any particular cyclical event. In the case of set (b) less than two years seem to have elapsed between 2nd and 3rd initiation; in the case of set (c) four to five years. Ideally, 6 grown pigs are needed for completion of the initiation; but fewer will clearly do if necessary.

The decision to hold the initiation is made by the *Yolam* cult leader (*Kamoyam*) and the senior, initiating sct. Invitations to participate may or may not go out to friendly, neighbouring groups. A fair amount of equipment must also be procured: besides the pigs, a male dog must be obtained. A special variant of taro, with a dark core in the tuber, is collected and cooked; the dog is fed on this for several days. Finally, firewood and stinging nettles are accumulated as well as certain other shrubs (see below).

The first day of the ritual opens with an incident in connection with the slaughter of the first pig. Before the assembled crowd, this pig is shot at with a small bird-stunning arrow (*yōl*). When this proves without consequences, a senior man emerges from the *Yolam* carrying a quill-decorated string bag; he shoots the pig with a proper bamboo-arrow. This may connect the blunt *yōl* arrow with the *Yolam* — an etymology never confirmed by informants. It may more probably connect the *Yolam* with war and efficacy in battle. The string bag in question, decorated with quills of the *sisim* bird, is used in warfare to carry the mandible of the *Yolam* ancestor. The *Yolam* is also referred to by initiates as the 'house of warfare.'

After this incident, women and children, and the set of novices, are sent to the mature gardens to harvest, bake in earth ovens, and eat taro; the novices are particularly admonished to eat much. The seniors then take the dog, and several live pigs, into the *Yolam* to slaughter and cook. Uniquely in this rite, the pigs are not shot but suffocated by a complex operation: the black palm (normally used as material for flooring) grows from a central, light-coloured shoot (*kaban-dēm*, lit. black-palm-baby); this is forced into the pig's mouth, which is then held or tied shut around the palm rod. Further, the stems of a small bush (*sanōkiok-weim-ŋerín*, lit. bandicoot-tail-bush) are rammed into the pig's nostrils, causing it to bleed and suffocate. No explanation could be provided for this manner of killing the pig, except that it keeps it from shrieking and thus assures secrecy. The fat from the flanks of this pig is then cut loose; it is heated in the fire and mixed with the black contents of the dog's intestines (fed, we will remember, on black taro cores) and some additional black taro; this mixture is steam-cooked in leaves, together with the dog's penis. This work completed, the seniors make a sacramental meal of the pig's meat, presenting pieces to the ancestral sacra and praying for strength and health for the novices, the women, the pigs; for much taro and other blessings.

In the afternoon, the non-initiates are fetched back into the village, returning in single file with the women, their net bags loaded with cooked taro, in the lead. There follows a communal taro feast; the meat of the first slaughtered pig is distributed to the women; the war shields are brought out and there is dancing and hand-clapping; then the novices enter the *Yolam* for the first time. As they grasp the outer, central post to climb into the temple they suddenly shake with fear; inside they see the sacred fires burning, the skull of the ancestor on the far wall painted with a red stripe across his forehead, and a confusing variety of other sacred objects partly visible across the small but overcrowded room. Immediately, the ritual proceeds. The cult leader places the novices in a compact group between the two sacred fires; he encircles them with a blackened string loop (made for the purpose by a very old woman who keeps it secret and knows it is for initiation, but has no knowledge of *how* it is used) and admonishes them never to stray from each other when in danger and always to remain together and defend each other. Each novice in turn is then held and has his elbows pounded with sacred black stones. Though

64

referred to by the taboo word for stone, *kwei*, these should specifically be what is known as *náfitūm*, literally 'stone-from-Nafi,' a tributary of the Murray River close under the Hindenburg range. These stones, however, were lost by the Baktaman when they moved the *Yolam* to its present site; they now use two stone adzes in their place. The beating, though painful, is beneficial in that it makes your arm strong when pulling the bow. The novices are also assured that this is the only hardship they will suffer.

As soon as this is completed, however, the seniors grab bunches of nettles and whip the novices over the face and chest, causing them great pain. They are then presented with the leaf package of the dog's black gut contents and cooked penis. They are forced to eat the black mixture and at least lick and suck the penis; this makes them brave in battle, and they are encouraged by the assurance that this is the very last trial they must endure. The remains of the dog's penis is subsequently burned.

The next senior set thereupon lines up with spread legs around the *Yolam* fires, led by the cult leader. The novices are made to crawl on their hands and knees between the legs of the line of men; each man they pass under whips them with the burning nettles over back, legs, and particularly the genitalia. This is supposed to make the novices big and strong. Red and blistered by the nettles and terrified by pain, the novices are then assured that this completes their tortures and are ordered out of the *Yolam* to show themselves before the happy, feasting women and dance briefly for them.

They are then brought back into the *Yolam* and made to sit around the two fires. Wood is piled high on the fires, and the next senior set sits behind them, crowding them closer as the flames grow hotter. This starts a four-day ordeal: blistered and burned by the fires they are now kept continuously awake by shifts of the senior set, they are not allowed water or moisture in any form, and they are constantly forced to eat dry taro (increasingly difficult as they become dehydrated). Every night, there is feasting and dancing outside by the rest of the population, which the novices can only watch through the cracks in the *Yolam* walls. At irregular intervals they are again forced into the fires and burned. On the morning of the fifth day, seniors open the *Yolam* door and insert a sugar cane; the novices are fearful of doing something wrong but desperate for moisture, but when they grab to catch hold of the cane it is jerked away. In this way they are teased for some time, before being given each a small amount of sugar cane to suck; later they are also allowed out of the *Yolam* briefly and wet their mouths with banana sap. The following night, the ordeal by fire culminates; on the subsequent morning they file out of the *Yolam* and are given water by the senior set as they pass through the door, presented to them under the left armpit of the giver. As they come down from the house on to the ground in this decrepit state — weak, emaciated, and dehydrated, mouths stinging with sharp water, bodies blistered and burned — they are exhibited to the assembled women and made to dance for them. Subsequently, they go to a new garden and plant taro. Until this taro develops large leaves — probably several months — they are subject to a number of temporary taboos: They must not eat together with any less initiated person than themselves, they must not eat pandanus, pitpit, fish, or snake of any kind. The completed 3rd degree initiation gives the right to certain emblems: pig's tusk in nasal septum, cassowary quills in nose wings, eagle-feathers on your net bag. With *Wunmalal* they are also authorized to be members of ritually prepared raiding parties.

Let us consider some of these idioms from the novice's point of view: what has been clarified for them? The ritual uses of fire and water seem largely consistent with previous initiations. The liminal forest is separated from fire, whereas the *Yolam* is too close to its source. Water washes away ritual strength as it washes away material things (though some drinking was interjected between the *Yolam* rites and the taro planting, probably from physiological necessity). So far, these two elements seem to be utilized fairly directly for their inherent properties. Temple and garden activities have become connected: while both are forbidden at the inadequately sanctified *laqsalman* 1st degree stage, both 2nd and 3rd degrees had the initiates carrying sacredness from the temple to the garden (while women carry earth-cooked taro, epitomizing plenty, back from the gardens to the village.)

Water and fire are also used for torture, reinforcing the basic messages of earlier initiation: that these forces are powerful and dangerous; sacred knowledge is costly and must be paid for with hardship and its value thus confirmed. The exhibit of novices to the women further publicizes the value, cost, and danger of sacred knowledge.

Colour symbolism would seem to be clarified and extended somewhat for the novices. Red is probably the only colour with an even moderately explicit symbolic valency to the novices: it was applied to them in the first initiation, ancestral bones are red and the skull has its red line of decoration; they have also seen individual healing sacrifices (cf. pp. 139 ff.) with use of blood as paint on the forehead, and they may have noted the red-leafed *kasok* bushes planted in front of the *Yolam*. It thus seems fair to expect them to have an awareness of the association of red and the ancestors. The other colours in the sacred tricolour (exemplified on the decorated shields, and the ancestral figures on the *Amowkām*) are black and white. White occurs naturally only in a few contexts, notably shell valuables and cooked taro; its ritual use has been limited to the white earth with which pigs are rubbed, and the whiteness of pork fat with which one has daily rubbed oneself during the many months of being a *laqsalman*. Its importance is also negatively signalled by the whiteness of most of the marsupials tabooed with entry into initiations; but I doubt that it has taken on any conscious symbolic meaning for 3rd grade initiates. Black, however, has clearly been manipulated in this initiation — it was a feature of the loop that ties the set together, the stones that give them strength, and, most elaborately contrived, in the repellent sacred 'food' to be eaten for courage in war. Its 'normal' context is in the blackened ceiling of houses (particularly the temples, where black pigment is obtained) and in the cassowary feather bags and drums of the fully initiated old men. Perhaps an association has been created of black with male solidarity, warfare, courage, and virility.

The rebirth motif immediately recognizable to the anthropologist in the idiom of crawling through the spread legs of the next senior set need not be denied; but a more generalized significance may be more accessible to the novices. A recurrent theme in much private and public ritual is how a person's spirit (*finik*) clings to objects associated with him and thus threatens and attacks others through these objects. Senior men, most concerned with their personal sacredness, are constantly and visibly practising precautions to sacralize objects and rid them of such pollution. This may be done by rotating the object a few times round your head, thus tying or lashing it to yourself; more commonly by passing it under your left armpit and thus driving away the foreign spirit — conceptualized as a smell, i.e. intangible substance — with your own smell. Passing through a gate controlled by a strong spirit may also have the same effect. The banal and obvious significance of crawling between the seniors' spread legs is thus one of sacralization, of ridding the novices of polluting spirits and making them ritually fit partners for their seniors. In this, it belongs with the previously described idioms of sacralizing water by passing it under the left armpit, or food by passing it under the arm or under the arch of a pig's tusk. In fact, the right to wear such a tusk in your nasal septum provides the 3rd degree initiates with just such a sacralizing arch over their mouth.

The use of the *left* armpit may be an artefact of right-handedness, or it may be felt consistent with the partial right-left dichotomization, where right is the ritually purer side of the body and therefore the left side, which is more polluting, is also the more threatening to other spirits. It will have been noted that ancestral sacra are from the right (and central) parts of the body and never from the left. But the dichotomy is not systematically utilized, e.g. in ranking the degree of sacredness of the two fires in men's houses and temples — there, which will be the more sacred is fortuitously settled during the building of the house and is sometimes right, sometimes left.

The question inevitably arises why this initiation is called *Wunmalal*, 'arrow-demonstration.' The answer, in characteristic Baktaman fashion, is because of a focal ritual act — a sacrifice performed with arrow — which is associated with the initiation but which is withheld from the novices (as it has been in the two last performances of 3rd degree initiation). The Baktaman cult leader, however, described it as an optional element and I know that it has in one case been incorporated in the initiation itself elsewhere (in Abolgobip around 1958). Sacrifice by arrow is the central ritual act in *Yolam* cult, and thus constitutes a natural focus for initiation into the *Yolam*. It takes place frequently, independently of initiations, in the form of the *Wonsā* (lit.: 'arrow-ritual'). I have attended two such rituals, and the problem seems to be that their performance requires a secret marsupial hunt, to which novices should not be initiated until the 5th grade. Showing them any part of the *Wonsā* could easily give them foreknowledge of the mysteries of the hunt and its accompanying sacrament, as well as certain reclassifications of marsupials that are associated with these mysteries (cf. p. 82); and such knowledge on the part of 3rd degree initiates is regarded as mortally dangerous to them, and destructive to the taro. I shall, however, describe the *Wonsā* ritual in the form it takes when incorporated into 3rd degree initiation, thereby hoping to indicate what this initiation 'is really about' to the informed seniors, in contrast to what the novices are supposed or expected to recognize.

In the case where the arrow ritual is incorporated into initiation, the next senior initiating set proceeds on a secret marsupial hunt while the novices are interned in the *Yolam* for their ordeal by fire and thirst. The hunters must secure a particular small marsupial,

68

called *eiraram* (a marsupial mouse?), as well as a few larger marsupials of the cuscus/opossum group, preferably with long fur. *Eiraram* is normally classified as vermin, and never eaten by Baktaman; after 5th degree initiation it is revealed that this small marsupial is in fact the most sacred animal of all: it belongs entirely to the ancestor and must be consumed in its entirety by him. These game items are wrapped in leaves and brought into the *Yolam* on the day of the novices' breaking of the water taboo and planting of the taro. The *eiraram* marsupial is hidden behind the shield, leaned against the wall beside the ancestral skull. In preparation for the rites, bamboo-bladed arrows used for pig-hunting (and also for killing people; war arrows with heavy hardwood barbed points may also be included) are leaned, points upwards, against the face of the fighting shield (with its design representing an ancestor). A black, double-ended ritual arrow is then brought out: it is the sacred arrow (*won*) which has been hidden elsewhere while the *Yolam* has been occupied by the novices.

On their return from the gardens, the novices are brought back into the *Yolam*, where they find the arrangements completed. They are seated as spectators along the wall with the door, facing the skull. The cult leader is seated by the skull; he fetches the *eiraram* out from behind the shield, punctures its abdomen with the sacred arrow, and pulls out the entrails. These are hung on the high strut between the fire posts of the most sacred fire (point d in the diagram p. 114) where they are left indefinitely to dry and shrivel up. The cleaned *eiraram* is then wrapped, with a preheated stone, in the red leaves of cordylene bushes (*kasōk*, the sacred bush that grows outside the *Yolam*) and placed in the ash of the sacred fire to cook. No word is spoken by the cult leader or congregation; while they wait for the offering to be cooked the cult leader may rub the ancestral skull and mandible with the red, fallen leaves of the *dubkōn* tree. He likewise turns to the sacred fire post (point d in the diagram); it is made of hardwood and attached to it is a container made of pandanus leaf. Some of the contents of this container — the right-side long bones of the ancestor — are taken out and similarly rubbed with *dubkōn* leaves. The part-cooked, steaming *eiraram* is then retrieved from the fire and rubbed against the bones while the cult leader cries '*Ba-ba-ba-ba*'[1] and then briefly prays and entreats: 'protect us from sickness; bring us wild pigs in our snares; make the taro grow large.' The long bones are then re-wrapped and put back in the pandanus leaf. Thereupon the *eiraram*

[1] These exclamations are paralinguistic.

69

is rubbed against the skull and mandible while similar prayers are said; it is then placed in the mouth of the ancestral skull with the cry '*Fip-fip-fip-fip*.'[1] The used leaves of *dubkōn* and *kasōk* from rubbing and cooking are finally hung in a crack in the wall above the skull, completing the phase that gives the ritual its name.

In the next phase, a second marsupial is used, which may belong to one of several sacred but edible species. The cult leader fetches out this second marsupial (which, like *eiraram*, but unlike all game otherwise brought home from hunting, is furry and unsinged); he breaks the hind legs of the animal (magically to prevent the meat from disappearing down the thin end of the leg); swiftly turns and passes the animal between his legs (cf. the creeping of the novices under his spread legs) and into the sacred fire. At this point the seniors rise, and make the novices do the same; they tramp on the floor and make the *Yolam* thunder and shake. The cult leader grabs the burning, smoking carcass, holds it horizontally against the points of the hunting arrows that are leaned against the shield. He sings a cryptic chant, in which he is joined by the senior set:

O wō	*burusyáyai*	*won sōy*
Oh he calls	(the secret name for *eiraram*)	the arrow's edge
warābare	*balám sōy*	*warābare*
cuts him	the knife's edge	cuts him
baruseksek		*wō*
(a mimicry of the call made by *eiraram*)		he calls
burusyáyai	*wō*	*āē, — āē.*
eiraram	he calls	yo — ho.

This text is definitely not understandable to the novices, though they may understand from context that *burasyayai* is the sacred name for *eiraram*. The song is only gradually learned from repeated participation in *Wonsā* arrow-rituals; it is characterized by seniors as a hunting song about *eiraram*, which pleases the ancestors.

The cult leader then prays to the ancestor: 'May they (the hunting arrows) find the wild pig; may they fell him surely.' Thereupon he rubs the still smoking marsupial down along the arrow shafts, shouting '*Khē-khē-khē-khē*' ending up in a squatting position; all the congregation follow his movement and collapse on the floor.

This is the maximum of what the 3rd degree novices must see; and

[1] These exclamations are paralinguistic.

the hope is that they have not understood, or will not speculate over, the use of verminous *eiraram* in a temple offering to the ancestor. At this point, however, as I understand it, a dilemma arises: on the one hand the novice set must observe a strict three-day isolation and water taboo after their first arrow-ritual, and should remain throughout this period in the *Yolam*. On the other hand, the seniors have a sacramental animal on their hands which they should immediately proceed to cook and consume in a joint meal with the ancestor (this refers to the larger marsupial, emphatically *not* to the *eiraram*, which must be left untouched). But the 3rd grade set is not qualified for participation in, or any knowledge of, this — if they ask they are supposed to be told that all sacrificial meat is eaten by the ancestor, and that no food cooked in the sacred fires may be eaten by men. I do not know how the Baktaman solve this dilemma, except perhaps by imposing a liminal period in the forest on the novice set and thus getting them out of the way, so that the sacramental meal can proceed.

One further problem confronts the seniors who must stage-manage this performance: how to secure the appropriate female participation without divulging any crucial secrets. After the *eiraram* sacrifice, a communal taro feast should follow next day, where the whole population cooks taro in earth ovens in the gardens, exchanges food, and is generally euphoric, while the 'smell' of the drying *eiraram* spreads to the farthest gardens and pleases the ancestor. Though the women know that there is activity in the *Yolam*, they are supposed to think this to be quite secondary to their own part of the festival, which is publicly known as *Imen-dāp*, 'taro-festival.' This is readily arranged in connection with irregular 'arrow-rituals.' but more difficult to integrate at the end of the six-day marathon feast for women which is associated with the *Wunmalal* initiation; and this also favours a separation of the two.

In the recent two initiations, in other words, novices passed through 3rd degree without obtaining any knowledge of the sacred arrow and the sacrifice to the ancestors which it allows, nor did they hear prayers addressed to the ancestors; their new knowledge and insight was limited to the items described in pp. 63–66 and explicated in part in pp. 66–68; and in this way the major functions of the *Yolam* remained unknown to them.

CHAPTER 7

Fourth degree initiation

With an age span of perhaps more than ten years, the members of an initiation set cannot reach physical maturity at the same time; yet the Baktaman explicitly connect 4th degree initiation with the appearance of beard on the novices' faces. The association probably reflects the major theme of the initiation rather than the age of the novices, and some candidates certainly pass through without having reached this stage of physical maturity, corresponding probably to the early twenties in this population.

The name of 4th degree initiation, *Mafomnaŋ*, refers to its association with pandanus rather than the development of the novices: *mafom/ māowm* is a name for a wild pandanus, also known as *sēr/sēl*. The second element, *naŋ*, may indicate 'mother' or more generally 'teacher'; obversely, the novices may be referred to as *mafom-man*, i.e. '*mafom*-children.' The ritual contains two major phases in which the second largely repeats the first; uniquely among initiations, previously initiated persons may join the novices as equal participants in the second phase, or the ritual may be performed entirely without novices, in which case only the second phase takes place.

The characteristic sequence is as follows: The senior set procures an ample number of pigs, as well as the other equipment required, in great secrecy. They then wake up the set of novices one night, and take them out into the forest to build a hut shelter. In the morning, fires are built, stones are heated and earth ovens dug, and the seniors bring great amounts of taro that are baked in the ovens. The seniors then fetch their drums and the other equipment, and join the novices in the taro meal. Both sets wear pigs' tusks in their nasal septa.

An elaborate hair-tying ceremony then takes place, in which the novices' hair is lengthened with the shredded leaves of the *sēr* pandanus and ultimately collected into two long pigtails, requiring two hours

72

for several men to complete for each novice. Unknown to the novices, these pandanus leaves have been collected and dried, and shredded with the use of a flying fox's claw — an animal which the novices, till completion of 6th degree initiation, are supposed to regard as polluting. The hair-tying is performed as follows: one by one, tufts of hair are separated out from the curly mat on the head. A wisp of pandanus fibres, nearly 1 metre long, together with one stiff fibre, are pressed into the curly tuft. Then a long 3–4 mm broad strip of pandanus leaf is wound around starting with the tuft of hair and proceeding in a tight spiral down the pandanus fibres for at least 50 cm. Thus a roughly 5 mm thick, pandanus-covered rod or cylinder is produced, which hangs from the hair-roots and down below the novice's elbow, with a free tassel of pandanus fibres at the end. This is repeated again and again till his head is covered with such pendants — slightly lighter material being used in the triangle above his forehead, slightly darker over the rest of the head.

The tying is done by seniors, who work, sing, and shout frantically, the endlessly repeated words of the song being: 'We tie his hair, we tie his hair.' Meanwhile there is a pandemonium of drums being beaten, the novices help prepare suitable wisps of fibre while sitting still, the seniors shout for more fibres of lighter or darker variety, which must be kept strictly separate, etc. Food is distributed irregularly, and cooked ginger is constantly eaten and blown over the group — to drive away malignant spirits with its 'smell'. The noise and music surrounding this phase of activity form a consciously contrived part of the performance.

Once the whole head is covered with such hair-and-pandanus pendants, the drumming subsides. The light straws over the forehead are thrown forward; all the darker ones are collected in a tight pigtail down the back. Spools of ordinary string (secretly made from the appropriate kind of bark) are brought out, and this string is wound close in a single thickness around the pigtail so as to form a continuous covering. When about 10 cm of pigtail is covered, a strip of bark-cloth is added to the pigtail, and wrapped around it to strengthen it. The string covering is continued down the slowly tapering pigtail; after another few centimetres, some pandanus fibre is wrapped around a length of the string, so that when it is wound around the pigtail, a narrow belt of pandanus in a transverse pattern is produced. This is repeated several times down the pigtail. At the end, a bit of bark cloth is allowed to show, and small stick, incised with a V pattern (called *inaŋ* and inexplicably emphasized by the initiators) is tied to the end. Thereupon, the same operation is performed on the lighter 'forelock', which is shaped and tied to follow the line of the head backwards and lie on top of the lower, bigger pigtail. This completed, the novices are told that the upper, smaller pigtail is *imúk*, and that this is a secret, sacred word for 'male', and the lower larger one is *yaŋús* and that this is a secret word for 'female'.

To their relief, the novices are told that this completes the initiation. They are led away to the thunder of drums and told to sit down with their backs against a split log. The senior set then grab bunches of nettles they have left in readiness and beat the novices' faces till they swell up. Meanwhile, fires are revived and bamboo containers placed along them; these contain a pre-made mixture of pork fat, red pandanus juice, and the red-staining juice of the *berbēr* tree. A clean sheet of bark is stripped off the tree and shaped into a trough; red ochre is crumbled into the trough and the melted fluid from the bamboos poured over it and stirred in with a spatula made of eagle's bone. As the red colour flows, the men break into the standard war cry of '*wus-wus-wus*' and stamp the ground.

The resulting paint is applied to the novices by the senior set. They start with the hairline above the forehead, and as they paint they whisper hoarsely: 'I shall make you very red; you must be strong red, etc.'. The whole body is thus painted a brilliant red, as is also the 'male' pigtail, leaving only the 'female' one unpainted. Finally, the white tail-feather of the otherwise all-black male hornbill (*kawēr* — cf. *kawēram* for men's house) is stuck into the top of the head, and the novice is ready to return to the village.

This takes place in a triumphal procession, for which the women have been waiting: senior men, dressed with white shell bands on their forehead and head-dresses of red parrots' feathers, precede and follow the brilliantly painted novices, thumping their drums and yelling '*wus-wus-wus*'; women and children line the path at the entrance to the village and cheer the procession, the women embracing each other in congratulation for the beauty of their sons or brothers. An entirely apocryphal, but intuitively suitable piece of secret religious knowledge is current among the young boys: if you are able to join that procession for a while, then run by back paths and sneak up behind the admiring women and strike a girl over her rump with a banana, then that girl will surely love you for the rest of her life.

With the entry to the village, a water taboo sets in. The procession breaks up before the *Katiam;* some seniors enter it while others continue the drumming; the novices start singing and dancing, each leading the singing in turn while all present join in the choruses. The songs include all the known songs in the normal dance repertoire, including war songs, love songs, and some profane hunting songs. Only one theme is special for the occasion, in which the singer entreats the sun to 'go down, sun go down'. The context for this is the fact that the heat of the sun spoils the tone of the drums by slackening the drumskins — as a result the drummers retire to the shade, and shortly give up to take their drums back into the *Katiam*; a less exciting dance continues to the rhythm of handclapping. Not till sunset do the drums emerge again, and the dancing quickens.

The dancing continues all night. Next day, the women go to the gardens to harvest and cook taro in earth ovens; the novices persist in a slow shuffle dance in the glare of the sun, individually breaking off to rest in the shade of a house but under a taboo against entering any house. The return of the women, laden with cooked taro, is greeted with drums and more forceful singing; all thereupon join in a taro feast, and then resume the dancing all night. On the third morning pigs are slaughtered to sustain the festival mood before the women again proceed to the gardens to harvest and cook; the novices continue their dance. In the evening when the women return, they receive pork, while the senior men take their cuts of meat, and the fat. The novices are allowed taro rubbed with pork fat and no other meat, and they may not drink.

Their marathon dance continues in this way through a fourth day; a senior is always present to prevent them from falling asleep while individually resting; they support themselves each with a long stick (also painted red) and approach complete exhaustion — grimy, only half conscious, shuffling round and round in an eternal circle, but still vividly red and striking in their pandanus wigs. On the fifth day the novices are finally released; they are given water by the senior set, offered them under the left armpit, and then sent back to the hut shelter in the forest for a seven-day period of rest and isolation.

The second phase of initiation largely repeats the first. First a pig is slaughtered (which provides fat for new paint), the women are sent to the taro gardens to harvest and cook taro, the novices return to the village in the afternoon and join a taro feast (corresponding to their initial feast in the forest with the senior set) where they refrain from meat and fat. They sleep in the forest hut at night, and redo their pandanus wigs in the morning; senior men may now join them and also have their hair braided. The *mafomnaŋ* are painted with the red colour, but not tortured this time; they return in a triumphal pro-

75

cession to the village and enter upon a new 5-day dance marathon. On the fourth day of this, the water taboo is eased to allow them to suck banana sap and sugar cane; on the fifth day they receive water from their seniors and return to the hut in the forest. The ritual is then completed, and they re-enter the men's house after sunset of the following day. The first night after entering, they must sleep along the walls with seniors between them and the fire; after this night they remove the pandanus wig.

The taboo on eating pork fat persists for some days, till it is clear that the novice has fared well during these trials and revelations. While the colour still shows on the novice's skin, or perhaps for a full moon, he may not enter the gardens and observes a taboo on pandanus fruit (since he has it on his skin his meat would disappear if he also ate it), snake (or his meat would disappear), pit-pit and leaf cabbage (or he might get ring-worm, belly-ache, and die), and fish (or the taro would be damaged, grow all leaf and no tuber). On the completion of this period, the initiates go to plant in a new garden, and then are released from the taboos. The senior set, on the other hand, make a point of planting while the novices are dancing, to utilize the good will of the ancestors during this period.

Though partly composed of familiar elements, the cluster of idioms constituting the *mafomnaŋ* initiation seems to have a special character, different from all previous and subsequent initiations. Especially the pandanus wig, clearly central to the 4th degree initiation, is unique. Nor is a search for analogues in daily life successful: while various feather head-dresses are used, any other form of wig is unknown, and the attention given to hair is limited: it is cut according to each person's preference, generally short; it is not shorn at mourning, not coloured or decorated.

As with so many idioms of ritual, head decorations similar to these pandanus wigs have been reported ethnographically from other parts of New Guinea. Photographs from linguistically related peoples in the Star Mountains to the west, and various lowland south-western peoples including Asmat and Merind-Amin, show pigtails of various shapes, often moulded with mud. However, it seems doubtful that reports from elsewhere could elucidate a meaning that remains obscure where the idiom is observed in full context.

Alternatively, one may be struck by the presence of symbols familiar from psychoanalysis, like the opposition between (male) sacredness and (female) water, the taboo attention to snake and fish (also in connection with pregnancy, cf. p. 138), or the association of hair and sexuality, and its braiding and tying with controlled assertion. However, our intention is to develop an understanding of the Baktaman system of communication and messages; and whatever understanding of meanings we achieve should arise from their didactics and knowledge, and not from external schemata.

What can we achieve within these constraints? Clearly, a message is being communicated about sexuality. It has reached the little boys, who subscribe to the fantasy about the girls and the banana (p. 74); to the novices it should be relatively clear in terms of the phallic features of the pandanus fruit, the remarkable protuberance on the hornbill, and the overt sexual symbolism of the male and female pigtails (in above-below positions corresponding also to the only accepted Baktaman positions for copulation). Translating the further message to a verbal code — as no Baktaman does and as I doubt that they would ever be able and willing to do — I think it is correct to say that the novices' sexuality is being authorized and sanctified by the ancestors. This emerges most explicitly in the use of the colour *red* in the rite, in conjunction with the Baktaman theory of conception. According to this, the child springs from male semen as from a seed; it grows in the mother's belly and is nourished from her blood, which is why menstruation stops, but has none of her substance; it shares its substance only with the father and his clan, and can marry people from all other clans.

Now red colour has been consistently associated with the ancestors: as a blessing of growth from the fathers in the 1st degree initiation, as a signal of the ancestors and their strength and authority in 2nd and 3rd degrees. In this 4th degree, the whole novice is anointed with red in his sexual capacity (including the male pigtail but *not* the female one); he is one with the ancestors and the clan in his procreative ability. It is also fitting that the rite is directly associated with the *Katiam* and its clan sacra. My literal mind was vaguely disappointed when I noted the seniors' failure to pay any special attention to painting the genitalia of the novices; but Baktaman are in most ways very prudish and I do not feel this falsifies the interpretation. The admiration of the women, their constant presence in their female role as reapers of taro in plenty throughout the rite, and their continual participation in all-night dances with their songs of male valour and of love (cf. song texts, pp. 146, 203 f.) are all highly distinctive and unique features of this one initiation. Such a continuous presence of women cannot but affect the novices' experience of self in the situation, and thus contribute to raising the messages they receive about their own male identity and capacity to a reasonable level of awareness and explicitness.

The other aspect or idiom cluster, connected with *hair* appears to me less explicit and definite at this stage. Admittedly, one may expect the universal experience of puberty to provide a basic key to understanding for each individual novice. But more precise connotations have certainly not been built up in previous initiations — the only clues were in the treatment of fur in the *Wonsa* ritual, which novices have probably not attended. But we may also give some attention to the meanings entertained by the seniors who tie the pandanus wig on the novices — they have been through 6th degree initiation and know the meaning of hair as the essence of potency and growth (cf. pp. 92 f.) in a cosmic analogue between hair on the head, the roof of the temple, and vegetation on the earth's surface. To them the association of the novices' hair with the phallus-like pandanus which feeds the sacred cassowary, contains the ancestral sacra and harbours and produces fire (pp. 187 ff.) may provide moving and enlightening imagery.

Finally, an additional element which we may carry one step further: the prevalence of drums in this initiation. A dichotomy has thereby been signalled which is entirely consistent: rites associated with the *Katiam* and *Amowkam* temples are generally heavily characterized by drumming; those of the *Yolam* are specifically characterized by a taboo on drums. Some of the implications of this dichotomization will be explored later.

CHAPTER 8

Fifth degree initiation

The secret hunt, which has been a hidden part of several of the earlier rites of initiation, is finally the focus of attention in the 5th degree. This initiation is called *sēban*, from *sēp* = 'forest' and *ban* = 'explanation.' According to the senior men, this initiation is performed if the taro tends to produce much stalk and little tuber. I take this to mean that such signs indicate the displeasure of the ancestors because the new set of men have been kept too long from contributing to the meat offerings in the cult houses.

Having decided to hold the initiation, the senior set secretly prepare taro for provisions. Then they wake up the novices and lead them off into the forest to an area where the hunting should be good, preferably up towards the cloud forest belt. In this perennially foggy, damp, and gloomy environment, among trees grotesquely festooned with moss and lichen growth, they build two brush huts, one for the seniors and one for the novices. The seniors explain that the object is to hunt game of the *nuk* category (i.e. hairy mammals) and divulge the sacred taboo name *awēm* for this category. They may also provide an incomplete list of the particular species sought (cf. chart, p. 182).

The whole group then goes off to hunt, seniors and juniors mixed. As soon as anyone is successful this is called out, and all abruptly return to the brush hut of the seniors. The animal that has been shot is then singed over the fire, as would normally be done with game; thereupon it is firmly lashed to a stick, which is planted upright in the ground inside the seniors' hut. Spells may be mumbled as this is done, but no explanations are offered. The seniors then declare that no more should be done this first day.

For the subsequent 3 days, all the hunters are active, trying to secure as much game as possible. If the novices kill *eiraram* (the secretly most sacred marsupial mouse used in sacrifice to the ancestor)

79

they are made to throw it away and to continue to believe it is disgusting; a senior man will then later sneak back and collect it, to carry it to the *Yolam* for sacrifice in due course.

On the fourth day, the seniors fetch quantities of raw taro; an earth oven is dug and stones warmed, and much taro is prepared. When it is ready, the seniors take it into their hut, and wrap it with the game in large leaf packages, which are loaded into the carrying bags. The novices are then called into the seniors' hut and each given a small portion to eat. When they have tasted it, they are attacked by the seniors and beaten with nettles. The seniors then suddenly leave them, and hide in the surrounding forest. After a while the novices timidly emerge, looking for them — finally the seniors make themselves seen, and call the junior set together. They are given the carrying bags with all the game and cooked taro to carry, and all return together to the village. There they proceed directly to the *Katiam*.

In the *Katiam* they have the simplest version of a sacramental meal of the marsupials they have brought. This means that all the food must be meticulously kept within the *Katiam* and none removed, and that everything should be consumed by them or by the fire: all bones, wrapping leaves, skins, claws, etc. are burned, as are all edible parts that the novice might not wish to eat. The seniors will doubtless dedicate the meat to their clan ancestor and pray to him, and they may instruct the novice to do the same, but this is not necessary.

There are no taboos subsequent to this initiation. Indeed, whereas there is generally a taboo on entering a garden after eating marsupials, this prohibition specifically does *not* obtain after completion of this meal in the *Katiam*.

When the seniors have finished the sacramental meal together with the juniors, and have assured themselves that the prescriptions regarding the burning of bones, etc., have been observed, they do nothing further to explain the sacramental character of the rite. Normally, they will retire to the *Yolam* for further, exclusive rituals. Thus in the case of the last *sēban* initiations held by the Baktaman, the (b) set, who were the novices, had a summary meal in the *Katiam* after their return from the hunt, and then went to their normal men's house. They saw the seniors go into the *Yolam* and saw smoke rising as from a meal being cooked in it, but by their own reports they thought this must be some kind of ritual where a whole animal was burned as an offering. Nor had they properly understood the special nature of the meal they had eaten in the *Katiam*: that they had participated in sacramental commensality with the ancestors. The

80

Plate 9. A set of 1st degree novices wearing laqsal netbags and other 1st degree insignia. Wopkeimin village, SW of Baktaman.

Plate 10. 4th degree novice with pandanus wig. Other decorations are optional: forehead bands of small shells (bonaŋ) and cowries; nose decoration of cassowary quills and white tailfeather of hornbill; plaited neck, arm, and leg bands; pig incisor necklace; diagonal breast bands; twined armband of rattan. The large string bag is utilitarian, while the rattan around the waist, the waistband for the suspension of the penis gourd, and the penis gourd itself are conventional items of male clothing.

Plate 11. 7th degree initiate on his way to the garden. He is wearing a cassowary head-dress of the short variety, a rattan loop for climbing trees, and carries an axe (of steel, traded in from the west) rather than the normal bow and arrows.

Plate 12. Kimebnok in the entrance to the Yolam. Note the central post before the door, with its bark muff covering the sacred portion that might otherwise be touched, also the sacred cordylene bushes in the left foreground.

Plate 13. Taro garden during maturation. Note the contrast to normal jungle, as in the background on Plate 1, and the analogue of the shade trees and the fireposts of Plates 17—19.

Plate 14. The Amowkam of the Seltaman, the closest extant temple of this kind and the most likely place for the next 7th degree initiation which the Baktaman (c) set may attend.

Plate 15. Men cooking breadfruit in a new garden (the shorts worn were a gift from me!). Note how the smoke looks, and the possible analogue to sacrificial smoke in Plate 17.

sacred character and use of *eiraram* (pp. 68 ff.) was similarly unsuspected. This was first revealed to them at the first *Wonsa* rite that I attended myself, at least a year after the completion of their *sēban* initiation. The only regular ritual activity that immediately resulted from that initiation was their presence in the *Katiam* on occasions when female or infant wild pig was eaten.

The other activities to which the initiation is a ritual authorization are only taken up slowly and stepwise, at the pleasure of the senior set. By stages, the juniors thus enter into a fuller and fuller participation in ritual life after the 5th degree initiation, involving minor offerings to the clan ancestors in the *Katiam*, secret hunts and sacramental meals in the *Katiam*, secret hunts to provide game for *Yolam* rituals, and finally participation also in these rituals. The larger schema that connects forest, village, and garden in a causal chain of, respectively, secret hunt, temple sacrament, and taro growth through the intervention of the ancestors, who release the wild game, share in the sacramental meal, and cause the taro to grow — this larger schema is far from clarified by the initiation. But the 5th degree does allow initiates an active part in procuring the ritual material; and since their participation in the later phases of most ritual sequences has already been authorized in principle through 2nd and 3rd degree initiations (to *Katiam* and *Yolam* respectively), the road is open to participation as a congregational audience in most of the major rituals. How quickly and clearly a deeper understanding will develop depends mainly on two factors outside the formal framework of initiations: the frequency of intensity of ritual life (which is highly variable, cf. pp. 119 ff.), and the extent to which seniors are willing to explicate sacred knowledge in everyday conversations and novices to communicate such insights to each other (and both these kinds of communication are strongly inhibited by the emphasis on taboo and secrecy.)

Another major feature of Baktaman religion is made more explicit, though perhaps no clearer in its implications, to the novices in the 5th degree initiation: the nature of secrecy, taboo, and 'true knowledge.' A recurrent theme of previous initiations has been that of *deception*. Sometimes, statements and promises have been made that were immediately exposed as lies by the next ritual act; sometimes information was made vaguely suspect by hints or evidence that it was rendered false or grossly incomplete by further secrets. Even the central revelation of one initiation — e.g. the showing of the bones to 2nd degree novices — was shown to be largely a hoax in a later initiation. The justification for this edifice of deceptions has been the imperative of taboo: *Eim*. To the uninitiated and to novices, this has stood for a concept of 'forbidden' only, sanctioned by threats, danger, and fear. Progressively, some elements of what used to be forbidden have been revealed to the young men; but for each item of such knowledge they have been punished with torture and hardships. With the secret hunt, a new dimension of taboo is revealed: it is its very secrecy that sanctifies; some animals of normal use achieve new properties through the men's observation of secrecy; some dangers otherwise created (such as the threat to garden fertility after profane eating of marsupials) never arise in the context sanctified by this secrecy.

Not only that; it also emerges that animals otherwise inedible or harmful become good and sacred through the agency of the secret hunt. Boys grow up with the knowledge that some animals are allowed as food for some status categories and are forbidden to others. They allocate the fruits of their hunt accordingly: some items forbidden to them they give to their female relatives, others are forbidden to all but the senior men, etc. With changing statuses, their own permitted diet changes. But now it is revealed to them that behind this system of categories lies another, 'truer' set of categorizations and distinctions. The list of sacramental animals includes members from categories (1) allowed only to women and children, (2) allowed to all, (3) forbidden to young men, (4) allowed only to senior men. And the insignificant little *eiraram* is removed from the category of disgusting vermin and elevated to a sacramental category all of its own: privileged food monopolized by the ancestor. This whole set of crossing classifications is summarized in the chart on p. 184.

The observance of taboo and secrecy thus takes on a new meaning, together with a restructuring of categories of purity and pollution. But this is not without profound epistemological consequences: deceit is not just an expression of opportunistic self-interest, or the supremacy and whim of senior men. It is shown to be a means to generate deeper truth. And some time, the question seems inevitably to arise: where does this end? Are there not secrets withheld in the 5th degree revelations, that create deeper knowledge for others by virtue of being withheld from me? And what about 6th, and 7th degree? Pursuit of true knowledge becomes like peeling the layers of an onion, or exploring a set of Chinese boxes: information on one level may be the deceitful cover that creates another kind of truth at a deeper level. How and when such doubts set in is hard to tell; but their eventual presence can be demonstrated and some implications of them will be explored in a later chapter.

CHAPTER 9

Sixth degree initiation

No Baktaman initiation rite is accompanied by the telling of myths; and in the small corpus of myths that I found current among the Baktaman there are none that show any connection with any major segment of the initiation rites described so far. There is, however, a myth in existence which specifically should not be told before listeners who have not passed through the 6th grade of initiation. Kimebnok, the cult leader in the *Yolam*, who told me the myth, also clearly felt that it is a rendering of some of the same messages as those contained in the initiation rites. It runs as follows:

First there was a dog — he came down, went to the base of very large trees, bit off the roots, dug a hole under the tree; out of such holes he pulled the first men, many places. [These holes are now limestone sink holes, at known and named geographical locations. When told to suitable audiences, the myth may incorporate a considerable sacred geography at this point.] The men were very glad to be out of the ground, and they danced and sang. But these first Baktaman had not carried any taro with them; the dance made them hungry and they wanted and needed food. *Awarek* [the secret name for *kwēmnok*, a large, long-furred, grey cuscus marsupial. This cuscus forages in the trees, eating leaves and fruit, during the night, but sleeps all day in a burrow under the ground or in a hollow trunk. The secret name *awarek* also means grand-father/ancestor] remained below ground in his hole, clutching the taro and would not release it. Neither dog nor man dared go down into the hole to fetch the taro. Finally the swallow [all black except for a white patch under its tail; its nests are tunnelled into the ground in steep hillsides] volunteered. He flew down into the hole, but was frightened and turned back. He tried again, but again

83

turned back in fright. The third time, he managed to snatch a little bit of taro, he flew out of the hole and into the air, and he deposited small bits of taro high up on the white tree trunks, and on the white cliff faces of the mountains. The men fetched down the taro and made a big feast. Then grandfather cuscus came up out of its hole bringing plenty of taro with him. He lined up the people by clans, according to which hole they had come out of, and named them, making the clans of Yeni and Minkarin and Murukmur and all. Then he went down under the ground again.

An interpretation of the myth can more usefully be done after a description of the ritual that is supposed to render a related message.

The 6th degree initiation is known as *Amkōn* (lit. house-roofing) and involves the rethatching of the *Yolam* roof. The physical state of this roof has no relevance to the performance of the initiation, since normal maintenance may be done at any time and rebuilding is possible independently of the initiation of novices. The performance among the Baktaman in May 1968 took place for a number of reasons: a few of the oldest and most able of the (b) set were becoming impatient; the cult leader was in need of asserting his authoritative position; and the event offered an opportunity to induct me into the system, which I had been requesting and manoeuvring for during the preceding months. The critical point in the decision-making process was the pledge of the requisite minimum of three pigs. Once this was clear, the rest followed with apparent inevitability. In the following description, I shall give an account of the particular performance as it took place at that time — since no one was willing to give any generalized description beforehand, as this would spoil the secrecy and effectiveness of the performance; and discussions after the event were of a special character, since I had 'seen it all.' I took part as an ordinary novice through the preliminaries and the first major day of ceremonies. On the second day I was transferred to the status of member of the (c) set, and accompanied the cult master through his activities.

The first phase of initiation involved a short secret hunt. A few representatives of the (c) set left during the night; as soon as a suitable marsupial was obtained, the hunters returned to the *Katiam*. Others then went in secret to fetch a 1–2 m section of rattan of the type (*mōt*) used to encircle the walls in housebuilding, and a creeper/weed (*wareŋamnoŋ*) which commonly invades the taro gardens. Both these items were elaborately wrapped in leaves so that they could be brought

84

into the *Katiam* unseen. The stage thus set, the novices were called into the *Katiam*. There, a representative of the senior set unwrapped the marsupial. Its guts were removed and hung on the fire posts, its hind legs were broken; it was then placed on the more sacred *Katiam* fire and thoroughly singed so that no fur remained. The cane was then unwrapped and its taboo name (*fionēm*) spoken. The marsupial was placed with its back against the cane and tied firmly with the creeper, which was also referred to by its taboo name (*ŋebnok*) in the context of a short spell: '*ŋebnok*, tie him firmly; look, I am tying him firmly.' The marsupial was further fastened with ordinary string, made on the spot from bark fibres, and the cane with the stretched-out marsupial was hung over the sacred fire. The cult leader instructed the novices to collect ample firewood to keep the fire burning for the subsequent days to smoke and dry the marsupial — if they fail in this, their taro will be poor and their wives will abandon them. They were warned of a one-day taboo on water and an indefinite taboo on fish, and sent out of the *Katiam*.

On the subsequent day, men from both sets accompanied by women went to the sago swamps to fetch leaves for thatching materials. This is not secret, and the women were informed that the roofing materials were for the *Yolam*. Simultaneously, secret provisions were prepared for a big secret hunt, and on the following night a large number of men, representing both sets, went off on such a hunt. Though the whole variety of sacred edible animals may be collected, it is essential to obtain one *kitēm* — a long-furred, dark grey cuscus — on this hunt. Others went out with invitations to the neighbouring communities of Seltaman and Kasanmin to join in the rites on the day appointed, 3–4 days hence.

The main phase started when the hunters returned, discreetly slipping their leaf-wrapped packages into the *Katiam* and mixing unacknowledged with the other men as if they had not been away. The women were sent to the gardens to cook and fetch taro; there was an atmosphere of suspense. Incoming visitors were individually greeted with care and formality, but there was general unease and self-consciousness. The return of the women in the early afternoon was unsignalled, but triggered the performance. Groups of men formed in each hamlet and men's house and swept into Feisabip hamlet with '*wus-wus*' war-cries. The *Yolam* cult master entered the *Katiam*, with all the seniors and novices for whom there was room; the rest crowded around the door. He cut loose the marsupial that had been drying over the sacred fire, and wrapped it in bark cloth; the dried intestines that had also been hanging there were thrown on the fire; then he departed, hiding the package against his body. Other seniors came and fetched some net carrying bags, presumably containing the catch from the secret hunt; the novices were left behind in the *Katiam* or adjoining men's house, waiting in silence, occasionally speaking to each other in hoarse whispers.

Finally, the novices were called into the *Yolam*. As they entered, they saw the senior set standing in a packed crowd, all reaching up and covering an object with their right hands — the effect is a pyramid of arms and hands rising above their heads from the middle of the crowd. In the midst of this was the cult leader, growling. Suddenly all the hands were withdrawn, revealing a furry, unsinged *kitēm* marsupial tied or lashed to a bow with white, shell-decorated forehead-bands (*bonaŋ*) festooned with red feathers. The seniors shouted '*wus-wus!*' and stamped on the floor; the cult leader holding the lower end of the bow jabbed it, with marsupial and all, into the roof while he yelled:

> *Awārek, āwārek,   awon-bugōr   kin-ba-ba-ba*
> ancestors   bird-eagle   help us!
>
> i.e. 'Oh ancestors, help us overcome the eagle!'

He then climbed the fireposts of the holy fire and slashed the fastenings whereby the roofing is attached to the roof beams, repeating his cry for help from the ancestors. After a brief effort at this he came down again, whooping and yelling the war cry and stamping the floor, then running between the two fires and out of the door. The seniors among the congregation yelled, stamped, and rushed after him; and the novices followed suit and circled around the fires and out, along the central axis of the temple. While the group hesitated outside, the cult-leader slipped back into the *Yolam* and shortly emerged with a quill-covered net bag; by careful contrivance the naked curled tail of the *kitēm* was looped over the edge and visible, while the body of the animal was hidden so that women and children as distant spectators would see nothing. He led the men in a dash around the *Yolam*, then madly started tearing up grass from the ground yelling:

> *Nebereber,   awārek nebereber*
> hair   the ancestor's hair!

The seniors did the same, and the novices were made to join in, crying 'the ancestor's hair,' tearing up grass and shrubs from the

86

ground around the *Yolam*, and throwing them down so that they formed a big pile. Then the whole group was led in a rush to the central clearing of the hamlet, where the audience of women and children stood, to shout war cries in triumph and wave their hands in the air. This climax would appear to be particularly expressive in the eyes of the audience; several women afterwards commented how moved they had been to see me as one of the congregation at this moment.

This completed novice participation on the first major day of *Amkōn*. In the course of the evening, further preparations were made for next day by the very senior men, including the complete cutting of all the roof lashings. There was also activity in the *Yolam* during the night, but I was never able to ascertain what it involved.

The second main day of rituals started immediately at dawn, when groups of novices and seniors again swept into Feisabip shouting war-cries. This time, freshly retouched shields were carried, and all participants were dressed in the very best they could muster. Even Kimebnok, the cult leader, who normally does not wear any decorations even when officiating, had on a cassowary head-dress, with a single white hornbill-feather in front, a white forehead-band of cuscus fur, and a white shell ornament. In his nose-wings were cassowary quills, bone splinters from a tree kangaroo curved forward from the point of his nose, and through his nasal septum was a big pig's tusk. On his back was the quill-covered bag, with the cuscus-tail showing. In this regalia he emerged from the *Yolam* and faced the assembled crowd of seniors, novices, and — at some distance from the *Yolam* — women and children. One by one, he called the clans: 'Oh women of Yeni clan, will you give a pig for the initiation of our men? Oh women of Mankarin clan, will you . . .' etc., etc. until he reached the clan of the wife who had by previous arrangement pledged a pig, who then spoke up affirmatively.

Wife and husband fetched the pig, which was tied to the sacred, central front post of the *Yolam*. Meanwhile, Kimebnok returned into the *Yolam* and, as the initiates would see only later as they entered the temple, painted the ancestral skull with a *red* and a *white* line on its forehead. The crowd of men was divided, so that the women could see the slaughter, and Kimebnok danced, kicked the pig to make it squeal, shot it and then withdrew the arrow, to dance back and forth before the *Yolam* brandishing the bloody arrow and crying the war cry. The novices were meanwhile assembled some distance away, while senior men blew aromatic bark and ginger at them. Kimebnok ducked into the *Yolam* to deposit his bow and arrow and fetch a bamboo knife and the dried marsupial wrapped in bark-cloth. Carrying these, he climbed a preconstructed flimsy scaffolding up onto the roof, followed by a dozen men of the senior set, all of them dancing as they waited and climbed, and spreading out along the roof-top. Kimebnok took up position above the point where on the previous day he had pierced the roof from the inside; he forced the cloth-wrapped dried marsupial through the hole so that it dropped through, and down in front of the ancestral skull. Thereupon the seniors on the roof all peeled the old roofing off so that it rattled to the ground, and came down themselves. Kimebnok then reclimbed the *Yolam* with a few symbolic new sago leaves, to lay them over the ridge-pole while crying for the ancestor's blessing. After that, the spectators and the novices were sent out to the gardens to harvest and bake taro in earth ovens.

With novices and spectators out of the way, the seniors set about their various tasks more openly. The pig lay where it had fallen, and two of the most senior men set about butchering it. Some of the less senior ones worked on the rethatching of the roof, firing their own enthusiasm with war cries; occasionally they would break off for a drink of water from a gourd in the *Katiam* — this was special water collected from hollow trees and cup-shaped leaves, and thus not forbidden. The moment the new roof was finished, everyone broke out in war cries, and then collected all the old roof materials, and the grass and shrubs that had been torn loose to the cry of 'the ancestor's hair' the previous day, and threw it all on pre-lighted fires to produce thick, grey, billowing smoke as it burned.

Kimebnok collected a few select pieces of pork fat from the pig and entered the *Yolam* for a small sacrifice. The left, most sacred fire, which had been burning continuously since the men set out on the secret hunt five days previously, was used for the sacrifice. Later Kimebnok was joined by the two seniors, who had finished butchering, and they transferred fire to the right fireplace and used it for a similar rite on their own behalf; these special morsels of the sacrificed pig are the perquisites of the most senior participants. A second phase of feasting involved the whole senior group. Those who had stripped and relaid the roof received meat from the rib-case and fat from the ribs and shoulder; the rest shared a big slice of belly fat and meat from the head. The fat was melted in the right fire, and dripped on taro from the previous day; taro, fat and meat were shared and exchanged dyadically in a constant criss-crossing of gestures of friendliness, but the cooking of these bits of food was individual. No attention was given to the ancestor in this phase — it is a feast for the living. Kimeb-nok instructed all to rub their fatty hands on legs, chest, and arms for strength after eating.

The *Yolam* contains special cooking stones for pig and marsupial (different from those for cassowary and pandanus); these were heated on the less sacred fire, and a division was made of the game available from the secret hunt: some was given to visitors for subsequent subsidiary rituals in their own temples, the rest were for the present event. These latter were wrapped, with pieces of the sacrificial pig and some taro, in a leaf oven with the red hot cooking stones. During the hour or more this takes to cook, the men dispersed. Reassembling when the meal was ready, the atmosphere of this incident of feasting was rather different from the previous one: participants were quiet and restrained in contrast to the easy individual activity of frying pig morsels. They spoke in whispers only, but the same dyadic redistribution of the allocated food pieces took place. When the meal was nearly finished, the novices and women could be heard returning from the gardens. At this, the door to the *Yolam* was quickly closed, and all the seniors sat completely quiet. The novices swept into the hamlet clearing with a great flourish, carrying a shield and shouting war cries; finding a quiet, apparently empty village their cries died down and they started roaming aimlessly. At this point the seniors shouted and dashed out of the *Yolam*; the sets joined in dancing and hand-waving and a great festival feeling was generated.

After some preparation inside the *Yolam*, a line was formed of the initiating set and some select, senior, and prominent novices, whereas most of the novices were excluded and retired to the men's house for a feast of the taro they had brought. One by one, the select line entered the *Yolam;* there Kimebnok fed each a piece of pig's liver, a piece of pork, a piece of marsupial, and a piece of taro — all fed through the arch of a pig's mandible. As the food was swallowed, each was also struck on the back with a fist-full of cooking leaves and taro. When the whole line had entered, the door to the *Yolam* was closed. Behind Kimebnok, the novices could see the ancestral skull decorated with a red and white line painted on its forehead.

Kimebnok thereupon brought out the furry *kitēm* marsupial he had been carrying. He held it up before the shrine of ancestral long bones on the corner post of the sacred fire, then placed it on the floor below the post and started beating it with a stick, saying: 'I give you this, I cook it for you. Give us many pigs! Strengthen our taro gardens, make the taro tubers grow large! Look after this set of men, give them plenty of food so they will be strong!' Having broken all the bones in the animal this way, he threw it in the sacred fire, turning it to singe the fur. The seniors scrambled forth to secure some of the charred fur, wrapping it in leaves they were holding in readiness; some recriminations and adjustments were made before the participants accepted the distribution of charred fur relics to the different persons and groups of participants. (These relics were later burned in the taro gardens, to further taro growth.) The *kitēm* was then cooked with stones heated in the sacred fire, while the congregation waited in respectful silence. Once it was cooked, Kimebnok dedicated it to the skull and to the long bones, praying again for plentiful taro. Then followed a distribution of the main cuts of pig, and the remaining marsupials, among the persons and groups present. The cooked parts of this were consumed immediately (after much dyadic exchanging) and the bones offered to the ancestors and thrown on the fire; the uncooked parts were for taking away to the *Yolam*s of other communities. The *kitēm* given to the ancestor was subsequently dried by Kimebnok over the sacred fire and fed in small portions to that fire over several subsequent weeks, as he had already started doing with the first marsupial that was dried over the *Katiam* fire.

Finally, on the morning of the following day the *Amkōn* initiation was completed with the slaughter of two pigs in the early morning hours. There should have been more pigs, to assure plenty for all, including the uninitiated population; under pressure of these expectations Kimebnok promised to give one (large) pig to the Baktaman women, so the two (small) ones that were already available were mainly given to the visitors.

A telling incident happened at the end. All the initiates and novices assembled outside the *Yolam*, where they danced together before departure (to handclaps, since drumming would drive away the goodwill of a *Yolam* ancestor). As the group broke up, the Seltaman contingent departed in a solid phalanx; after a moment, they started dancing and singing and handclapping down the main path. This caused consternation among the Baktaman seniors, who quickly got the Baktaman dancing and clapping — otherwise, the *Yolam* spirit would have left with the Seltaman and given all the taro blessing to them alone. Indeed, the taro of the Seltaman did much better than the Baktaman taro in the subsequent months and Seltaman seniors had to come on several goodwill visits to the Baktaman, bringing gifts of pork, to re-establish amity after this deceitful trick.

On each evening during the ritual and the subsequent three days, till the novices went to the gardens to plant, there was dancing (without drums) in the hamlets by both men and women.

Certain taboos accompany and follow the ritual, as was also observed after previous initiations. The participants must not drink or wash in water for three days. On the day when the novices go to the new garden to plant they may suck sugar cane and banana sap, but may not drink till the fifth day. The theological refinement that allows participants to drink *stagnant* water, as noted above, is not explained to the novices. A taboo of several months' duration is placed on pitpit, leaf cabbage, pandanus, snake, and fish. The restrictions on dividing an item of food — a taro, a bunch of bananas, a bird, but not a pig — is also strengthened vis-à-vis persons who have not passed through 6th degree. Nor must the participants have any part in funerary rituals for several moons. A few other taboos, on the other hand, are lifted as a result of the initiations, specifically by virtue of the items eaten through the mandibular arch on the second main day (cf. p. 89). These included (i) liver from a pig raised outside Baktaman territory, together with a piece of an immature *kitēm* marsupial — thereby lifting the ban on receiving pork gifts from foreign communities and thus implicitly qualifying the initiates for an inter-community political role. (ii) A piece of meat from the lower jaw of pig was included — to remove the taboo on this part of sacrificed and of wild pigs. (iii) A piece of first-fruit taro (*yoŋabip-imēn*) was also included, to authorize the initiate to make decisions about starting the harvest of taro from a new garden: this first-fruits harvest must only be eaten by a senior man, and no one else can harvest until this is done. (iv) Finally, the blow with steam-cooked leaves on the back of each participant lifts the taboo on eating fruit bats, including flying fox.

Preceding this *Amkōn* initiation was a heated debate among seniors as to which form it should take. A contrast has obtained for some time between Baktaman custom, which has been conservative, and a 'new style' of performance spreading from the west and adopted by, among others, the neighbouring Seltaman. In the end, the Baktaman followed suit and the ritual described above is in the new style: traditionally the novices have participated in a larger part of the events, notably in the fur-burning and subsequent meat distribution on the second main day. This change was not introduced without resistance: Kimebnok argued persistently that he wanted to 'show' the novice set as much as possible, while most of the seniors strongly advocated the more exclusive style. In fact, their main motive seems to have been the ulterior one of securing more marsupial and pig for themselves, and not a theological argument about the nature and need for secrecy. The ranked commensal groups constitute, in this aspect, an incipient system of graded feasts, and it seemed that petty greed arising from this was decisive for the change. But one should not exaggerate this, since the extent of privilege obtained by the change is negligible (1/2 kg of meat per senior man once every ten years!), and it is only its feasibility and consistency with hallowed values and principles of secrecy and exclusion that make the new style acceptable at all. Kimebnok, as cult leader, in fact chose a course that achieves both ends by doing *Amkōn* in the new style but following it with a secret hunt, fur-charring, and a sacramental meal for the novices at the end of their taboo period, i.e. after two moons.

Let us now pass to an attempt at extracting some major aspects of symbolism. *Amkōn* initiation is a large and complex ritual which combines many themes and is complicated by its elaboration of levels of audience segregation. I shall have to switch somewhat in explication of meanings as between novices, first repeating set, and fully experienced seniors.

A central message is clearly the close connection between marsupials, ancestors, and taro, which is given in various permutations. The myth at the opening of the chapter, in which a marsupial named 'ancestor' holds and finally comes up from the ground with taro is a further indication of the validity of this interpretation. Here, the novices see it expressed by a variety of idioms: the first sacred marsupial in the *Katiam* is tied with the *wareŋamnoŋ* creeper while drying/maturing, just as the taro maturing under the ground is tied by the same creeper weed as it spreads over the garden; the next marsupial is tied with white shell bands, like the white of taro. That same sacred marsupial is later carried in a quill-covered net bag, such as those used only to store and carry the focal sacra (mandible and skull) of ancestors. The next senior set repeating the ritual, who are allowed to enter the *Yolam* on the second main day of ritual, see the ancestral skull for the first time decorated with a red *and* a white line on its forehead, thus finally bringing white colour into symbolic focus. The seniors know, and say, later, that the new set *looking* at that white line cause the taro to grow.

The most vivid imagery, and the most essential message directed at the novices is no doubt the explicit analogue that is exhibited between skull, temple, and earth, and the central theme of fertility mystery that thereby starts emerging. Fourth degree initiation, and minor incidents in other rites, may have codified hair as the sign and essence of potency and power. Now, the structure of the rite together with the cryptic key in the cry 'the ancestor's hair' should establish the homologies hair : ancestor's skull = roofing : temple = fur : cuscus body = vegetation : earth. The miracle of old men's hair turning sacred white belongs as an elaboration of this, and appears as a theme in Myth 2 (cf. Appendix III). The repeaters of the ritual see another evocative permutation of this homology: just as the ancestral skull feeds upon the smoke and odours of the fire, so the strength of the temple's roofing materials and the ancestor's hair is carried as thick, billowing smoke over the land, and the blessing of the marsupial sacrifice in the sacred fire is repeated in the blessing of the taro when the charred relics of marsupial fur are burned and spread as smoke over the gardens. Perhaps even the absence of the novices during the rethatching is part of a contrived 'miracle' of regeneration based on the same imagery: the first marsupial from the *Katiam*, prepared for ancestral consumption, is secretly (i.e. wrapped in cloth and known only to initiates) introduced into the physical structure of the temple, 'causing' the old hair/vegetation to be shed and a new foliage to have appeared when the novices return from the garden. It must facilitate this understanding that there is one basic concept, *kōn*, for hair on head and leaves on trees, including the sago palm fronds used for thatching.

If we turn briefly to the interpretation of the myth of grandfather cuscus (pp. 83 f.) in these terms, it may be seen to be mainly structured around an above ground/below ground dichotomy with a series of special agents mediating between the two. This theme, which emerges as a major paradox — and thus a focal mystery — for root crop cultivators who define things below ground as polluted, underlies much Baktaman thinking on fertility and is also expressed ritually (cf. chs. 18, 26). But the myth also very clearly expresses the ancestor-marsupial identity and the role of marsupials in providing taro. Briefly, these themes in the myth may be summarized as follows: The dog as an agent from above brings man up into purity, but separates him from taro. The swallow (black as courage and white as taro, who flies in the air and nests below ground) mediates and sanctifies some taro by carrying it up. The feast and dance bring the ancestor/cuscus (who eats in the trees and sleeps under ground) up from the ground with taro plenty. Thereupon a covenant is established, based on the rules of clanship, whereby the ancestors approve the extraction of taro from the ground, as mediated by the cuscus. The mythical rendering in no way parallels the ritual, but clearly contains the same basic message as one of its constituent themes.

I was puzzled why the particular marsupial of the myth, secularly known as *kwemnok*, was not preferred as the offering in the *Yolam*. The species favoured, *kitēm*, does not show the particularly suitable behavioural peculiarity of eating leaves and sleeping under ground — it both eats and sleeps in the trees (and is consequently unambiguously clean). Kimebnok readily understood my question; but pointed out that the myth is an *old* story, from the ancestors. In those days, *kwemnok* may have been the strongest for the taro; now it is *kitēm* that is strongest.[1] I think the use of *kwemnok* would provide better imagery for the rite, but that this difference does not appear to be important. Indeed at several such points I have a feeling of one, less precisely suitable species substituting for a related, more suitable species in the Baktaman system of idioms. The reasons why such secondary symbolizations may occur at crucial points will be discussed later (cf. ch. 24).

---

[1] It might be noted, however, that though *kwemnok* is permitted food for both women and men, Kimebnok and some other very senior men choose *not* to eat its meat — supposedly as an individual idiosyncrasy.

CHAPTER 10

Seventh degree initiation

The seventh and final formal initiation is called *Amowk*, and is performed in a separate temple, the *Amowkam*. This temple was destroyed and the ancestral sacra lost during warfare with the Seltaman, around 1958; since then the Baktaman have been unable to perform 7th degree initiation themselves and the (c) set has been waiting, with growing impatience, to attain the status and privileges of fully initiated seniors. A few of these privileges have been tentatively and reluctantly extended to them as a stop-gap solution; sooner or later a formal initiation will have to be arranged, either by participation elsewhere or by the reconstruction of a Baktaman *Amowkam* temple.

Most senior Baktaman have no suggestion as to the etymology of the name of the temple and the initiation. One of them, however, gave as authoritative the derivation 'house of mother, from *am* = house and *owk* = mother (cf. *emowk* = his mother; *owkneŋ* = mother's sister). This connected it in the series *Amowkam* ~ mother, *Katiam* ~ big sister, and *Yolam* ~ little sister (cf. p. 60); and a widespread myth, not particularly apposite to most Baktaman conceptions (Myth 3, Appendix III) was cited by the informant in support. Others remained unconvinced by this but contrasted *Yolam*, as being masculine in its essence, with *Katiam* and *Amowkam* which are female in character, since they allow the eating of male pig. An alternative term for *Amowkam* is *Imenam*, i.e. Taro-house.

The *Amowkam* was decorated with painted ancestral figures similar in design (and in name: *eiskom*) to the fighting shields. Seniors agreed that this way of decorating a house façade was a recent introduction from further west. The initiation named, and corresponding to, *Amowk* in these western areas (e.g. *Bolovip*) comes earlier on the series, reportedly as 4th degree.

The following account of 7th degree initiation is based on three informants: the man who by normal succession would have been cult leader in the Baktaman *Amowkam* after his father, the present cult leader of the *Yolam*, and a Seltaman, then resident in Feisabip, who is now cult leader in the Seltaman *Yolam*. The three versions are very close; they complement each other in detail but contain hardly any contradictions.

The initiation is launched by the pledging of a minimum of two pigs for a first sacrifice, and the departure of members of the next senior initiating set on a secret marsupial hunt. Meanwhile the cult leader keeps the *Amowkam* fires burning and paints the ancestral skull with a line of red ochre on its forehead. On the return of the hunters, two pigs are slaughtered — one inside the temple, one outside on the ground. The novices (it should be remembered that these 'novices' are by now generally in their thirties, and thus leading members of the community) attend the slaughter and wait outside, helping to cook the pig, while the other pig is cooked on the sacred fire within the temple. When the meat is ready, the novices are called to enter the *Amowkam* for the first time, bringing the meat with them. Each set feasts on its separate meal, and there is no offering of meat or fat to the ancestor.

After the meal, one or several *kitem* cuscus (cf. 6th degree initiation) obtained on the secret hunt are brought out. The senior set instructs the juniors in the cooking of this sacred marsupial; that is, the juniors touch the elbow of a senior while he singes the marsupial and then wraps it with hot stones from the sacred fire in a leaf steam-oven.

The two sets sleep together in the *Amowkam*. Next morning the cult leader unwraps the marsupial, places it on a piece of wood, and with a stone adze severs the head and chops the body up in small pieces. Each piece is wrapped in leaves and tied with *wareŋamnoŋ* creeper (cf. p. 92) and placed over the sacred fire to dry. For five days the fire is kept burning while the novices remain in the *Amowkam;* both novices and seniors observe a taboo on water but may eat taro and pork at their pleasure. At the end of this, the pieces of marsupial, now dry and hard, are put into carrying bags and taken by the novices to a new garden. There, land is cleared jointly by the two sets and taro is planted; the pieces of the body of the marsupial are buried in the ground while the head is placed in a wild pandanus leaf (as is done with ancestral sacra in the temples) and fastened high up on a tree trunk in the garden. After this they are released from the water taboo.

When they return to the village, they send the uninitiated population away for a prolonged residence in garden houses. A group of

Plate 16. Kimebnok between the sacred fires in the Yolam. The corner post of the most sacred fire is to the left; the lashing that connects the hardwood and the normal post can be seen, but the long-bone shrine is hidden behind these posts and partly covered by a string bag, fronted with hornbill feathers, used for minor sacred purposes.

Plate 17. *Interior of the Feisabiṗ Katiam. The sacred fire in the foreground, with smoke after a completed offering. On the floor, leaning against the sacred wall, are wild pigs' skulls; wild pigs' mandibles are hung in a row above, and cassowary pelvises are barely visible in the rows above them again. Bundles of clan sacra hang among these trophies.*

Plate 18. *The ancestral skull and mandible in the Yolam. The pandanus-leaf shrine on the wall is for the remains of the other (largely destroyed) skull now hidden away in the forest. The sacred arrows may be seen, leaning against the wall just to the right of this shrine. Left of the skull, before the lower corner of the fighting shield, is the wild boar mandible incongruously incorporated among the sacra. For other identifications, see the diagram text, chapter 12.*

Plate 19. Kimebnok and the author outside the Yolam.

hunters composed of both the senior and junior sets go off on a secret hunt, and the resulting game is used for a sacramental meal, with prayers for taro fertility, in the *Amowkam*. The temple is then boarded up and closed; a gate is constructed over the main path leading into the village, closed with poles and branches, and the whole village is left deserted. The men build brush houses in the forest and stay there for 8 days — or one full moon according to one informant. At the end of the liminal period, the men return to the village, bringing taro and a pig; the pig is slaughtered outside the gate, which is then opened; the men enter the village and the *Amowkam*, cook the pig together in the temple, and have a joint meal there from one pig.

The population is then brought back into the village and the women are sent off to harvest and bake taro in the gardens. The seniors build a platform on a scaffolding over the entrance to the *Amowkam*. When the women return, there is feasting on taro, and in the evening the seniors bring out the drums. The cult leader of the *Amowkam* ascends the platform, and dances and beats the drum to the song:

Nōmō	*yiwarū*	*yebakawō*		*Dundūn*		
(place-name)	sago-sack	beat-me-with-it		(place-name)		
yebakawū	/	*usok*	*Nōmō*		*yiwarū*	*yē-i ā-ē-i*
Beat-me-with-it/		feel(?)	(place-name)		sago-sack	

No interpretation could be given for this song. I take it that the thumping of the drum is being compared to rhythmic beating of sago and the production of sago plenty; but in view of the general ritual insignificance of sago and its secondary subsistence role (though it is also valued as roofing material, in preference to the alternative pandanus leaf) I see no clear relevance for the simile in this context. The dancing continues till sunrise.

Next afternoon the women again go to the gardens, while the seniors go to the closest large stream, where they construct a platform similar to the one in front of the *Amowkam*. The drums are brought there, and the juniors are called. On the platform over the water (where the reverberations are carried away by the water and cannot harm the taro) they are taught to beat the drum, their seniors holding their elbows. Seniors and juniors then return to the still empty village and the juniors play the drums in the *Amowkam* and on the platform, but still not on the ground. Thereupon, seniors and juniors hide in the *Amowkam*, behind the closed door, except for two seniors who hide *under* the temple.

The procession of unitiated returns in triumph to the village carrying great quantitics of taro baked in earth ovens. The women sing the song:

Imēn-ō,	*awoŋimēn-ō,*		*kimimēn-ō*	*yē*	/	
Oh taro,	yellow-coloured taro,		*kim*-taro	ho		
Dim	*ŋarū,*	*Wanōr*	*tarāū*	/	*y i ā*	
(a nearby hill)	we return	(another hill)	we come			

i.e. 'carrying taro, all kinds of taro/we return from the Dīm and the Wanōr gardens.'

They are led by old women carrying big taros; these women go directly up to the *Amowkam* and attack it, beating its walls with the taro. At this, seniors and juniors rush out and down on the ground, tramping and beating the drums, while the two who hid under the temple pursue the shrieking women and children.

In the evening and all night there is dancing, with both the senior and the junior sets wielding the drums. Next morning pigs are slaughtered, in as great a number as possible; visitors from other communities are given shares and leave for home, while the local women are given plenty, which they cook and on which they feast. That evening the cult leader announces the completion of the initiation, and the competence of the junior set to play the drum and slaughter the pigs. A further night of feasting and dancing ends the celebration.

No special taboos follow the initiation; on the contrary, several important and minor taboos are removed. The new initiates may now eat male wild pig and honey as well as four small species of bird (black with red head markings) which have been forbidden till now. Most important, however, is the competence that arises from completed 7th degree initiation to slaughter pig and sacrifice animals to the ancestors, and thus to perform cult acts on one's own behalf in the *Katiam* and be in charge and lead cult activities on behalf of clan and community in *Katiam*, *Yolam*, or *Amowkam*.

A number of idioms utilized in this rite should be readily understandable from their use in previous initiations. There can be no doubt that the new set of initiates experience the progressive incorporation with their seniors from the initial meal of separate pigs (slaughtered respectively on the ground outside and off the ground inside the temple, and thus of different degrees of sacredness) to the joint slaughter and meal at the re-opening of the village. Likewise they are being progressively given responsible command of the drums in the sequence over the running water → off the ground → on the ground, where the effects of vibration are greatest. The secret hunt sacralizing the game obtained, and the subsequent sacrifice by drying over the holy fire should also be familiar and explicit to them, with its reminder of the marsupial-taro connection in the use of the taro garden weed creeper. Finally, the complementarity of male temple cult and female profane taro productivity is more explicit in the procession of women, and their attack on the temple with their taro, than in any previous ritual of initiation. And the joyful connection of taro plenty and ancestral blessing with dancing and communal celebration is expressed as vividly as in the 6th degree.

New imagery is used which reveals new homologies in the structure of the world around the initiates, consistent but not identical with those of 6th degree. The sacralized body of the *kitēm* marsupial is equated with taro and buried in the taro gardens — this time it is not its fur which is like vegetable growth, but its substance which is like taro tuber, the 'bread' of the Baktaman. Simultaneously, the marsupial's head is treated like an ancestral relic and placed in a pandanus shrine. This also very vividly exhibits the homology between temple and garden: as the ancestral sacra in their pandanus shrines are tied to the pillars of the sacred fires, so these shrines are tied to the pillars formed by the trunks of the remaining shade trees, transforming the garden into the semblance of a colonnaded temple. Indeed, these trunks are specifically of the hardwood tree, which, epitomizing durability, is used as a symbol for the ancestors: in the *Yolam*, a length of this hardwood is tied to the most sacred of the fire posts, and has the ancestral shrine tied to it again.

The other outstanding feature of the 7th degree initiation is the closing of the village during a period of liminality for the whole Baktaman population. This contrasts with all lower initiations, when liminality is imposed on the novices only, or (in connection with the sacralizing marsupial hunt) on representatives of the seniors. On other occasions when the uninitiated are sent away from the village, this is just so as to achieve audience segregation. Yet the collective liminality is not entirely without analogue: there are times when the whole population collectively occupies a sacred state. Thus, a birth or a death in the population affects all Baktaman and places them under a set of common, temporary taboos (cf. p. 162). Likewise, before the *Wonsa* taro ritual, the whole population must observe certain abstentions (cf. pp. 114 f., 163) or the efficacy of the rite will be destroyed. In all

99

other cases, the critical sacred states, and their accompanying taboos and prescriptions, are status-specific or individual.

What then can be the meaning of imposing a liminal period on the whole population? Surely, the message as expressed and understood by the initiates must be that this status change, like the events of change of group membership or the general welfare of taro, is one that concerns the whole population. Corporate authority and representation for collectivities are poorly instituted and conceptualized but not entirely absent; through their liminality the Baktaman are made to declare that it is *their* authority system, leadership, and identity that are undergoing change and thus the whole community is affected by the passage.

Finally, we are left with the place of the drums in 7th degree initiation — a feature that I am not able to explicate. Besides the cryptic exegesis suggested in the song about the sago sack, we may search for sources of connotation for the drum and drumming in (i) everyday or natural events, (ii) features of the construction or design of the drum, and (iii) contexts where drums are used, or forbidden. As for (i), pounding is a prominent feature of sago-production, and secondarily also characteristic of the production of bark-cloth — done only by women when they make their (female) rain-hoods. The vibrations of the drumskin are also reminiscent of, and explicitly compared to, earthquakes; and men trampling on the floors of the temples simulate the same. The sacred cassowary's footsteps when running make a loud, sometimes resonant thumping rhythm. As for (ii), the drum itself is constructed of light, easily-worked wood which is hollowed in a slightly swung-waisted tube; one end is covered with a drumskin. This membrane is made of the skin of the large water-lizard (*sām*) — taboo as food to all men, its mandible being used in children's amulets, and as a ritual implement in curing sacrifice (cf. p. 140). Tension and tone in the drumskin are controlled by heating and moistening it, and by manipulating four pellet-like bumps made of a mixture of beeswax and mud, fastened to the drum-skin. The skin itself is coloured black; the wooden body of the drum is carved and decorated in black, white, and red in a pattern representing the leaves of the giant fern (X-like forms) and the gizzards of birds (G-like forms). As for (iii), drums are mainly in use for secular dances and, as noted, for rituals performed in connection with the *Katiam* or *Amowkam*. Their use by unauthorized persons results in insect blights (worms) on the taro. Drums are taboo in connection with warfare, and *Yolam* rites; they are unsuitable during mourning.

100

No clear confirmation of the sago-beating reference, or any other striking association, seems to emerge from this. Nor was any more elaborate association of drum and sago made by informants. I might note a potentiality of the sago imagery which does *not* seem to be exploited. Sago and pandanus are alternative leaves for thatching roofs, the former being preferred. Pandanus is the favourite food of the cassowary, and associated with it; its leaf base is also used to contain the ancestral sacra, which give taro fertility. Anyone who has seen sago beating and washing will recognize the striking use of sago leaf bases — in form alomost identical to these pandanus leaf bases but far larger in size — as basins for washing out the sago; indeed, the edible precipitate from sago-washing settles in these leaf basins and fills them with the sago flour, which is an alternative crisis food to taro. But if these homologies are imaged by any Baktaman senior, they are expressed so diffusely and weakly that the message is certainly not received by most initiates.

A more vivid analogue is that of the senior men, dressed in casso-wary feather decorations and dancing with arms folded across the chest in a dance that to my eye mimics the cassowary, to the rhythmic thump of drum/cassowary footsteps. But my suggestion to participants that such a mime was taking place elicited nothing but puzzled denials.

Amowk comes as the culmination of a long ladder of initiation, and gives the initiate status as a fully authorized senior. But in another sense, it is still only a stage in a man's religious education — only by repeated observation and increasingly responsible participation in rites does a man become an adept who feels at ease in the temples, at home with the idioms, and confident in his knowledge of the rites. In the words of one senior: 'You know how it is during your initiation: your *finik* (spirit, consciousness) does not hear, you are afraid, you do not understand. Who can remember the acts and the words?' Most men probably never reach the stage where they would dare to lead a congregation in ritual, even if they live long after their 7th degree initiation, though most who survive eventually do assume some responsibility at least for the clan cult in the *Katiam*. But even for the cult leaders, fears and doubts remain. Initiations have revealed veil after veil covering an elusive and mysterious reality, and time and time again the same phrase crops up: 'This was all our fathers told us before they died,' Knowledge is a convention shared by a group of people; it may be powerful and dangerous, but it is not tied to any idea of absolute truth. The ancestral skull in the *Yolam* has a taboo name; you pray to him as *Awārek*, 'Ancestor', but may learn in time that he is really *Womāriᵹ*. This knowledge is fearful and dangerous; but perhaps before Kimebnok dies you will hear him, in a hoarse whisper, tell that the ancestor's even more taboo name is *Anõwieᵹ/Anamoyiᵹ;* and this knowledge you will share with only 4–5 other seniors. But how will you, or how does Kimebnok, know that there was not another, even more taboo and 'true', name for the ancestor which was *not* ever whispered to you? The initiations cannot give, and are not built on, any basic, fundamentalist premisses of confessional nature; though a major source of insights and idioms, they are constantly confronted with the pragmatic test of life and its vicissitudes, and the subjective requirement of 'feeling right' in relation to other symbolic expressions and experiences. An analytic understanding on our part of the structure of Baktaman philosophy and the codes of its transmission must therefore give full attention to all communicative contexts, outside as well as within the temples.

PART III

Other idiom
clusters

CHAPTER 11

The social context
of communication

My subject in this monograph is Baktaman culture seen as a system of communication, or a flow of messages. This requires an exposition both of the symbolism and the sociology of Baktaman knowledge; and to the extent that these are clarified we shall have given an analysis both of the processes whereby the culture is expressed or made manifest and the processes whereby it is transmitted or sustained and changed.

The elaborate sequence of initiations described in Part II is a significant part of these phenomena; and their description and preliminary analysis have explored some of the codes and idioms of communication, the forms of knowledge communicated, and the social organization of this communication. But it should be noted that particularly in the latter respect these rites, since they are organized as initiations, show some very special and simple features. The act of communication in initiations is constrained by the following set of cognitive directives: (a) it is done with the primary responsibilty of the actor committed towards the audience — it is done 'for their sake,' as indicated in the idioms of parent-child for cult leader and novices, and elder brother/ younger brother for seniors and juniors, and the emphasis on 'showing' and 'explaining' as its purpose. (b) The messages which constitute the rites are triggered or released because of the state and needs of the audience, the novices, and not of the initiating actors. (c) A single decision — to do the initiation — releases a *long* flow of communicative events, specified by pre-established conventions as to the body of symbols and knowledge they should contain. (d) The receipt of the messages entails a status change on the part of the recipient, which again (with certain delays and reservations) entails a right and a duty to participate in activities based on the knowledge they contain.

In all these respects, the initiation rites are very special, and atypical of most communicative events. These features being as they are, they have allowed us to concentrate heavily in our analysis of the descriptive material on simply discovering meanings for certain symbols, and identifying some of the themes and ideas in a Baktaman world view.

In looking at other idiom clusters, however, we need to broaden our analysis and ask systematic questions also about the sociological variables of the communication. The following chapters, therefore, will be concerned not only with the symbolic codes of messages, and their information content, but also questions such as: What triggers the release of a message? What interests is a message designed to serve? How are the form and content of a message affected by its place in a social situation and a sequence of communication — e.g. is it an expression of a free, personal inclination or a group consensus, is it part of a dialogue, is it a move in a contest? How are persons defined as actors and audiences in communication, and how are they equipped and constrained to change and control these definitions? The social facts brought out in answers to such questions are significant determinants of the flow of messages among the Baktaman and will affect the construction of Baktaman reality.

The substantive sectors of behaviour treated in each of the chapters in this part of the monograph are identified mainly by having distinctive characteristics in these sociological respects. To my understanding of the language, Faiwol is weak on semantic labels for such general categories as these sectors represent, and though I could suggest a relatively adequate gloss for some of them a complete set covering all would quite clearly be my contrivance. On the other hand, I do believe that I could readily explain my categorizations to Baktaman actors and have them accepted and understood, if there were any interest taken in them at all. They can thus be defended as major institutional complexes. But in saying this I am *not* assuming a priori that each such sector of behaviour, and its cluster of idioms, will prove to be associated with a unified and distinct code — or indeed that all of Baktaman culture is one unified system. Nor do I assume that each of the sectors of activity that I describe constitutes a separate, or unified, system of propositions and knowledge. I regard such features of consistency and integration as highly problematical, and see the discovery of their extent, limits, and fields of relative intensity as a major goal of description and analysis.

CHAPTER 12

Community and temple leadership

Leadership as an analytical concept subsumes a number of the features which were specified as sociological questions in the preceding chapter. But for our interests in the generation and flow of messages, we need to focus our analysis of leadership in a particular way. Clearly, instituted positions of authority are of central importance, since a major aspect of the role performance of incumbents of these positions is the emission of replicated messages. We can thus understand the pattern of communication in part from the construction and field of activity of such status positions. But we must also examine the communication which the presence of these positions indirectly creates through the competition they call forth among pretenders and rivals. This also generates messages: criticisms and justifications and analyses of cultural premises and valid information — i.e. 'knowledge' is created and disseminated also by these activities.

Basic cultural codifications of the nature of authority underlie the construction of instituted leadership positions. Among the Baktaman, the notion that any person should have any particular responsibility for, and accompanying authority in, public secular government is very weak; and no demands for general signs of respect and submission are made by persons in positions of authority. I can illustrate this from a hunting trip, when 5–6 men and boys were together around noon-time in the area close to the settlement. Under these circumstances one cannot expect more than a small catch of lizards, small birds, and perhaps tree snakes. Among the men was Namraeŋ — the cult leader of the Feisabip *Katiam*. He and a 12-year-old boy simultaneously heard a rustle in the low close foliage and moved towards it. The boy tried to trip Namraeŋ to get ahead of him, but failed; he then darted past him and shot the lizard they had spotted with his arrow. Namraeŋ showed disappointment, but not indignation. Yet, if the same boy shot game of the kind that is the prerogative of senior men he would never eat it himself but give it to Namraeŋ or another of his seniors, and any failure to do so would cause general consternation, as a breach of taboo. Nor can the allocations made by a father or senior brother, e.g. with respect to sago trees, be directly challenged or disregarded by junior agnates. But a father will observe his two children quarrelling and making claims and counter-claims to an object (often where justice is clearly on one side) without interfering; if it catches his attention or that of others he may comment on it, express opinions that are not listened to, but he will only impose a solution if the disturbance caused by the conflict annoys him. Likewise, a conflict between adults involves others as observers and commentators, and perhaps (if they are drawn in) as participants, but not as adjudicators.

The formally instituted leadership statuses among the Baktaman are headman in a men's house (*Kinim amsun* = big man, also used more imprecisely for any influential man) and cult leader in a temple (*Kinim eīm* — taboo man). The leader of the *Yolam* may also be referred to specifically as *Kamoyam*, though this is rarely used.

Men's houses: The men's house leaders tend to develop into cult leaders and men's house groups into closed audiences, so we need to give some attention to the emergence of both. Men's house groups are composed of relative equals and form a loose aggregation only; residence is changed at will and members are not economically dependent on or indebted to the leader; and for political purposes they function as a clique at best, and sometimes with hardly any common political stance. The cores of such groups tend to develop as friendships among boys at an early age. One among them, older or more active, will informally be in charge. During the uneasy period after their initiations have started, but before they have reached the age and maturity to stay with adult men in an established men's house, they may team up and build a house of their own. Later, the membership re-sorts itself and fuses, and regular men's house groups crystallize.

The leader of a men's house occupies the privileged area of floor between the two fires; the house is known by his name; and repairs and rebuilding of the house are co-ordinated by him. As the group matures there will be a considerable attrition through deaths (cf. Appendix II for life expectancies) and further fusion of groups as well as recruitment of slightly younger members; persons also change membership because of particular conflicts or enmities, often in connection with relocation of settlements; and in response to a series

108

of deaths in the group (with associated fears of sorcery) it frequently dissolves.

As members approach or pass 7th degree initiation, the leader may obtain some secondary relics, usually finger-bones, of a clan ancestor of his. He will not know the proper ritual procedure for this, so it is only with the aid, and authorization, of a cult house leader that such a shrine can be established. In the process he may learn enough of the ritual to repeat it, and progressively transform his men's house into a *Katiam*. More probably, an increasing amount of participation in *Katiam* rituals eventually leads to a transfer of residence to the *Katiam;* in this case, if he has clan sacra in his men's house which have served him well he will probably transfer them to the pre-established *Katiam* as well. The position as leader of a secular men's group may persist despite such a transfer. Thus Namraeŋ (of initiation set d) on moving the settlement to Feisabip decided not to rebuild his men's house but live in the *Katiam* with his group (of sets c and d), setting up his much younger brother Kaindip (set b) as leader of a young men's house. The cult leader remained Kwonkayam (set f) but none the less the men in the *Katiam* were regarded as Namraeŋ's house group; and with the debilitating illness of Kwonkayam towards the end of 1968, Namraeŋ also took over the cult leadership. But even before that, the activity and vitality of the Feisabip *Katiam* reflected Namraeŋ's political ambition rather than Kwonkayam's religious enthusiasm; so the flow of ritual messages from the temple was predicated by these political rather than religious factors.

Katiam cult: The cult leader in the *Katiam* has the following duties: he coordinates the maintenance of the temple, supervises the handling of sacra, and organizes secret hunts. When he is not in residence — e.g. staying in a garden house or in the sago area — the *Katiam* is closed and should not be opened by anyone. When it is in use, he coordinates the provision of firewood and minor repairs. Most rituals are individually performed by clan seniors for their own clan sacra; but he determines the location of the shrines and the bone trophies from sacrifices. He may also serve as steward for the sacra of clans without senior members, though some seniors have a more exclusive view and do not want the sacra to go, even temporarily, out of clan hands. Thus when the last senior of the Warop clan fell ill about 20 years ago, he carried all the clan sacra out and hid them in the forest. He failed to explain where they were before his death, and now the Warop clan is without sacra.

At irregular intervals, the cult leader may also name participants in a secret hunt, and without his word this activity, and the subsequent sacrament, cannot take place. Finally, he organizes the re-building of the *Katiam*. This involves special precautions, since any view of the inside or contents of a *Katiam* is forbidden to women and children. One may either (i) cover the building with an outer shell of tree-bark, so the work in progress cannot be observed; (ii) one may complete a new *Katiam*, then order the villagers away to the gardens for a day while the sacra are moved from the old to the new temple; or (iii) one may without warning suddenly run from the old to the new temple, carrying the objects in bundles under covering bark and shouting the *wus-wus-wus* war cry to frighten spectators away.

The major rites connected with the *Katiam*, apart from the initiations, are the individual and collective cult of clan ancestors. The idioms of these are recognizable from the initiations. The bones of all marsupials (*nuk*) eaten in the *Katiam* are carefully burned in the sacred fire after being presented to the ancestral relics; this is accompanied by prayers for hunting luck, and taro growth. As for cassowaries and wild pig, all such should be treated ritually no matter where they are eaten — and these are, of course, only eaten by initiated men. Cassowary pelvises, and pig's jaws (and sometimes skulls) are retained as trophies and stored with the sacra, while the other bones are all carried to the *Katiam*, dried, and progressively burned, with prayers to the ancestors. In the case of collective cult, all residents in the *Katiam* observe taboo on meat-eating while the secret hunt is on, and they then join in a sacramental meal of all appropriate kinds of game obtained in that hunt, accompanied by prayers to all ancestors collectively. On all occasions, the sharing of food is emphasized by distribution of meat to all present, and in the everyday setting by at least the offer of taro, sweet potato, or any other vegetable to those present at mealtimes.

What are the main messages generated by such activities?

1) The most characteristic ones concern the existence and nature of clans. The ancestral bones that constitute the clan sacra are the main emblems of clans as social groups, and the ancestral cult that links them with taro fertility leads to a constant reiteration of the existence and importance of clans. Thus every event of meat consumption triggers one or several acts of sacrifice to the hunter's clan ancestor, accompanied by prayers for hunting luck and taro. In fact, clans do not emerge very clearly in any other situation. Though some of them have a kind of joint estate in the form of separate hunting and gathering areas, these are always administered by one person, and as a rule he favours

110

his own brothers over more distant clan members, and allows affines access as well. As noted previously (cf. Myth 1, pp. 83 f.) clans are supposed by senior initiates to have come about by separate creations; and this is connected with a rule of exogamy. The explicit sanction for the exogamy is the destruction of taro growth and the earth's fertility that would result if semen from the intercourse of relatives were to spill on the ground. But the observation of exogamy also fails to define the clan, since the prohibition, and the accompanying sanction, also cover marriage and intercourse with all other, non-clan first cousins; and in a demography of many clans among a small population, relatively few mates are in fact debarred because of clan rules. Finally, the very word for clan, *naŋár* — shoulder, is a metaphor for a number of concepts (e.g. numerals 10 and 18, mountain/-ridge, shelf, etc.) and not often used in discourse in its clan meaning; nor is this meaning general in the Faiwol language: other dialects use other terms, or lack the concept of unilineal descent group entirely. Thus the cult of the clan ancestor in the *Katiam*, as the only frequently recurring occasion for the affirmation of clan identity, seems essential to the social creation and maintenance of this group.

So much for the instituted, replicated messages about clans in the *Katiam* context. But the concept of clan relics also gives rise to contingent analyses and discussion, viz: when they are absent, as in the case of the Warop clan. The question concerns Ngaromnok (set c) who has special interests in ritual and now would be regarded as qualified to attend to ancestral relics in the Feisabip *Katiam* where he lives. He was an infant when his father died; if the father informed his senior sons of the location of the sacra, they have died in battle with the Seltaman without time to pass on the information. I never had the good fortune to hear the topic arise spontaneously, but twice elicited a discussion of it by a simple question. In the one case, others in set (c) argued that bones from Ngaromnok's father might be brought in to constitute a new shrine, but Ngaromnok claimed that his father's funeral had been arranged by men who are now dead, so the bones cannot be definitely identified. On another occasion, I suggested that Ngaromnok himself might look forward to a future as a *Katiam* ancestor (he has 3 growing sons). Others of set (c) were incredulous of the possibility, but a senior of set (d) confirmed it. Ngaromnok was ambivalent, and finally dismissed the thought with blasphemous banter, saying if they brought him in as a spirit he would pester them continuously, for who wants to watch other people eat marsupial while he himself only gets the smell from burning bones? These contingent messages can be better exemplified and analysed in connection with the *Yolam* cult, below.

2) Of other replicated messages in the *Katiam*, the rites of bone offerings to ancestors also constantly repeat a general assertion of dependence and exchange between ancestors and descendants whereby men hunt game and transform their essence to the immaterial smoke and smell that the ancestors can receive, while ancestors control abstract fertility and transform it into material taro which man can receive. The cosmic tripartite division into forest/garden/village (epitomized in the temple), and the interdependencies between the forces governing these three, are also constantly restated in the relationships exhibited between game/taro/ancestors.

3) The collective cult, depending specifically on the decision of the cult leader for its activation, produces messages with a different emphasis. The major sequence (i) communal taboos → (ii) secret hunt → (iii) sacramental meal intermittently restates (i) the joint involvement of all members of the *Katiam* in each others' affairs and welfare (ii) the role of secrecy in sacralizing action and giving power to the fertility mysteries, and (iii) the communion of living and dead in these mysteries.

4) The theme of secrecy is particularly dramatized, vis-à-vis an ignorant audience, in the precautions surrounding the infrequent rebuilding of the *Katiam*. But these merely epitomize the daily experience of privileged participation of initiates in their daily entrances and exits from this secret, taboo temple.

5) Finally, the segregation of seniors that results from their residence in the *Katiam* creates a closed arena for the high-level politics and theology which pervades much of their activity as a meta-message. It facilitates the creation of joint decisions and agreements by the inner core of initiates which gain greatly in authority by being stated post hoc to an external audience that has not observed the confusions and disagreements of decision-making. The solidarity of this group is also constantly asserted by their everyday commensality and consequent food-sharing, heightened by, but not dependent on the recurrent sacramental meals.

Yolam cult: In the *Yolam*, on the other hand, we see a single temple as the focus of a communal cult to which all of the Baktaman are defined as the congregation. This has a number of implications for the

112

context and meaning of messages. It also implies that there is one exclusive position to fill as cult leader for the community; and the nature of rivalry, and its arguments, are affected by this. It is my impression that this was also so when the *Amowkam* was in existence, since it appently lacked specialized irregular cult activities and was more like a senior *Katiam*, although it was dedicated to a communal rather than clan cult.

Since nearly all cult in the *Yolam* has a communal character, the cult leader becomes a more focal status though his functions are essentially similar to those of the leader of the *Katiam*. Thus, only he can open and close the *Yolam* — and this rule is observed absolutely and strictly — and if the fires have gone cold he can only re-enter if bearing with him an offering implying a senior sacramental meal. He must also initiate all activities connected with the cult, since all of it except the collection of fire wood must be sacralized by secrecy. Not only does he depute hunters on the secret hunts, and keep the holy fire burning through this and similar critical periods; the performance of minor rituals also requires other equipment, as does the maintenance of the building itself. Thus red paint must constantly be produced, variously made of red ochre, pandanus juice, and red bark juice singly or in combination. Besides its use in various rites this is also needed to maintain the three red circles around the *Yolam* housepost in front of the entrance: a particularly sacred part of the building to which pigs are tied for sacrifice, and which must be covered with a bark muff, so men who have recently eaten fish do not touch the post and the red circles, and thus harm the taro. Inside, there are the sets of cooking stones to replenish — one set for marsupials, pig, and cannibal feasts, another for cassowary and pandanus. And every sacrifice requires the provision of cooking leaves and bracken and red cordylene in the case of special sacrifices. All these must be found secretly to be adequately sacralized, and so can only be produced by order of the cult leader. Otherwise, there is little maintenance to do. No purification rites are ever performed to the *Yolam* itself, and the requirements of tidiness within it are very lax though the cult leader occasionally sweeps dirt and debris down through the floor cracks, and the ancestral skull is required to lie on the *gāim* termite's nest, which in turn lies on a stone slab, off the floor.

The rites performed in the *Yolam* besides the initiations, are *Wonsā*, small sacramental meals, warfare ritual, and *Yolam* rebuilding. *Wonsā* follows a secret hunt during which the whole Baktaman population must observe a taboo on all meat and insect food. Unless

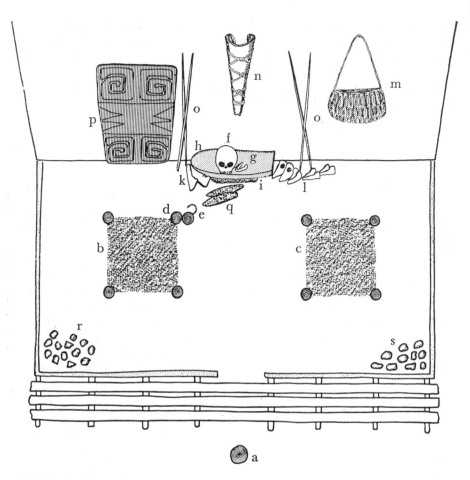

a) Housepost before door, carrying roof-beam b) the more sacred fire c) the less sacred fire d) the sacred fire post e) the long bone sacra f) the ancestral skull g) the ancestor's mandible h) the insect-nest sheet (*Gãím*) i) stone slab k) male pig mandible l) skulls and mandibles of female pigs m) quill bag for ancestral jaw n) pandanus container for bones o) sacred arrow (*bogyōn*) for sacrifices p) fighting shield q) black stones (adzes) for 3rd degree initiation r) cooking stones for pig, marsupial and man s) cooking stones for cassowary and pandanus d) strut for hanging parts of sacrifice this is enforced, the blessing sought through *Wonsā* may turn to taro blight. Consequently, the whole population is concentrated in the village for the occasion, and senior men must announce the taboo, though not the secret hunt, to women and children as soon as the hunters have left for the forest.

Two elements of the *Wonsā* have already been described: the sacrifice of *eiraram* (pp. 68–70), and the blessing of the arrows (pp. 70 f. A third element also belongs in the complex: a sacramental meal. This element may occur alone, or in conjunction with either or both of the two others. It is particularly addressed to the shrine on the fire post, containing the long bones of the ancestor and the foot of a brush turkey (*weirok, awonsunāyo*). The same animals used in 5th degree initiation are also appropriate to *Wonsā*; besides, taro is baked in the *Yolam* fires. The meat is cooked with fire-stones in leaf packages between the fires; it is unwrapped by the cult leader with prayers for taro directed to the firepost shrine. A division of the game is then made, and recipients exchange meat and taro dyadically. Each participant prays to the shrine as he presents his offering of bones and meat scraps; the juniors leave progressively as they finish. When a homogeneous core of seniors is left, they unwrap a second package of meat and have a more exclusive meal; only the most high-ranking of them use the left more sacred fire for their bone offerings. The meal is a very serious performance in which all participants are quiet and speak in subdued voices. There are no taboos subsequent to *Wonsā*, unless it has included an *eiraram* sacrifice, in which case the cult leader must observe 3 day's abstention from water.

The day after *Wonsā* may be the occasion for an *Imen Dāp* public taro festival, in which the whole population goes to the gardens and bakes taro in earth ovens, exchanging and intervisiting, while the cult leader alone remains behind and burns marsupial offerings to the ancestor. The smoke and smell from this are supposed to reach out into the gardens where the women will sense them, and the ancestors will be happy. The event has a happy, festival mood; carrying the cooked taro home the women sing what is for them a cryptic song:

Kubūri,	*dubūri,*	*ey-ā-ē* /
We load our netbags	(alliteration of same)	(exclamation on completion of something)
Awunsunāyo mundeim /	*kubūri, dubūri,*	*ēy-ā-ē*
Brush turkey wild pandanus		

115

or, freely transposed: 'We load taro, we carry taro, our work is done/ like the brush turkey eats the pandanus/we carry away the taro, we have finished our work.'

Smaller sacramental meals in the *Yolam* may be performed by the cult leader, or a small circle of persons together with the cult leader. They may consist of no more than some blood from a sacrificed domestic pig; otherwise there is game from the forest: clean marsupials, wild female pig, cassowary. Male wild pig, fish, and snake are taboo in the *Yolam*, as are bats, grubs and white larvae as justified by Myth 2 — (Appendix III). Human flesh, on the other hand, *must* be offered to the ancestor in connection with a cannibal feast. All offerings of meat are accompanied by prayers for taro plenty and the welfare of the Baktaman as a whole. Scraps of meat and fat, as well as the bones, should be given and burned on the *Yolam* fires.

The rites connected with warfare involve the *Yolam* and its cult leader, but are better described in another context (cf. pp. 150 ff.) Concluding this description of formal rites, the procedure for rebuilding the *Yolam* will be summarized briefly. First, a small house is built to store the sacra, and they are carried into it covered with bark cloth. Then at night, when the uninitiated are sleeping behind closed doors, the seniors tear down the *Yolam* walls, light a fire and burn all the bark and wood materials. Thereupon the roof is torn down, while the men sing a song, the meaning of which was cryptic to all informants:

| *Fārārok* | *āmonē,* | *dirilok āmonē* | / | *fārārok* |
| Swallow | enter house | bat enter house | | Swallow |

| *Awom* | *tum-tēm* | / | *fārār* | *ā-yō-yōōōō-ōē* |
| Strickland River | cave | | Swallow | (chorus) |

— as the roof is thrown on the fire.[1] At dawn the uninitiated go off to the gardens to harvest and cook taro. The seniors slaughter a pig while rebuilding the *Yolam* from pre-collected, hidden materials. A fire is lighted on the ground close to the new *Yolam*, and marsupial

---

[1] I have an incomplete description of rebuilding the *Amowkam* wich closely parallels this, but uses the song:

Usok	*kāt-e*	*mour-am,*
Notice	blackbird	woodpecker (parrot?)-house
fīr buku,	*fīr-e-ī,*	*fīr-e-ī*
Red we make,	red,	red

i.e.: Come and notice, blackbird; your house, woodpecker; we paint it red, red, red!

(from a secret hunt), taro (secretly obtained), and pork are cooked in this fire. When the fireplaces in the new temple are ready, the cult master fetches the sacra, puts them in place, sacrifices the pork fat on what thereby becomes the more sacred of the two fires and shares the pork fat with the ancestor. He then calls the others to bring in pork, marsupial, and taro, which he piles in layers between the two fires: first taro, then pig, then taro, then marsupial, and then taro; from this all the seniors have a sacramental meal. Then, when the women and children return from the gardens with oven-baked taro, all join in a public feast. This latter phase, connected with the re-introduction of the sacra to the new *Yolam*, also constitutes the ritual for the introduction of new ancestral relics into an existing *Yolam*.

These various rituals centring on the *Yolam* communicate to a wider audience the importance of cult for the taro, the importance of taro, and in the various collectively imposed taboos both the importance of taboo and the communal nature of the rites. In the *Wonsā* and temple rebuilding they also reiterate male-female complementarity in taro production. For the initiates, the messages produced are clearly of the same general kind in their idioms and content as those first seen in the initiations, and also practised in the *Katiam*. The importance of *Yolam* activities is the opportunity they provide for constant repetition and reiteration, supplementing the partial and reluctant insights gained in the initiations, and through variations and modulations of the same themes clarifying their contents. Thus, it is probably only through participation for some time in *Yolam* activities that an adequate awareness emerges of the mystery of ancestral control of taro, the positive sanctifying effect of secrecy, and the collective obligations and fate that tie fellow members of the community together. A few special idioms also emerge that should be noted: Those who know the creation myth (pp. 83 f.) hear the swallow commemorated in the *Yolam*-building song. The black-and-red taboo birds are connected with the *Amowkam* temple and colour symbolism. Most importantly, the brush turkey emerges as a mystery: tabooed because she is dirty and ground dwelling, she is yet a sacrifical animal; the women are unwittingly made to praise her in their song on the taro festival; and familiarity with the *Yolam* leads to the discovery that her foot is part of the sacra in the long bone shrine. No clear key is given to this mystery; I shall return later (pp. 235 ff.) to a possible interpretation.

Temple politics: The unique position of the *Yolam* cult leader, however, also gives rise to rivalry and intrigue through which concepts, values, and principles are expressed in other ways, both verbally and otherwise. Through these messages the relations and responsibilities of the cult leader towards the congregation, his relations to the ancestors, and the nature of ancestors are articulated. Addressed to an audience of partly less-informed persons in an effort to rally their support, these communications also serve to transmit the values to them and thus to perpetuate the tradition.

The recent history of the *Yolam* temple may be summarized as a background for the rivalry between Kimebnok, the present incumbent, and Taneŋ, the challenger. Roughly 15 years ago (when the village was located in Weitembip) the *Yolam* contained two skulls, one of the Yeni and one of the Yabik clan, and was under the cult leadership of Buryēp, Taneŋ's father, a Yabik clan member. Kimebnok (Minmurup clan, initiation set e) worked as his assistant. Because of the death of his brother in battle with the Seltaman, Kimebnok withdrew to a garden hamlet. An accidental fire broke out in which Buryēp only managed to save the Yabik ancestor — they found only charred bits of skull and part of one arm bone of the Yeni ancestor in the refuse, wrapped it in pandanus and put it away in a cave. Buryēp died and several relatives who took over as cult leaders became sick or died — the Yabik ancestor is generally recognized as strong but vindictive. In due course Taneŋ (initiation set d) succeeded as cult leader; he also became sick, and largely discontinued the cult activity. He put the skull away in a hollow tree in the forest; a wild pig came upon it and ate much of it, leaving only the occiput and part of the parietal bone. The taro became poor; so Kimebnok chose this point to reassert himself; he pointed out that as member of the senior set he had 'shown' Taneŋ what he knows of ritual, and thus should be cult leader; he fetched a new Yeni ancestor from the ossuary (cf. p. 125), introduced him into the *Yolam*, and took over as cult leader, allowing Taneŋ a subsidiary role vis-à-vis his Yabik skull. On the approach of the annual patrol shortly before I settled among the Baktaman, the sacra were stashed away in the forest. When retrieving them, Kimebnok brought back only the Yeni skull, thus outmanoeuvering Taneŋ.

In describing his own role as cult leader, to show how he fulfils it, Kimebnok explicitly emphasizes his responsibility to the young among the Baktaman, that he must 'show them' and finish transmitting his knowledge before he dies. After the re-thatching of the *Yolam*, he also expressed his duty as one of as quickly as possible 'blackening the *Yolam* ceiling' — i.e. maintaining a high frequency of *Wonsā*

118

rituals. He also feels responsible for the progression of sets through initiations, and for governing the effective participation of persons in the rites. Faced with the absence of an *Amowkam* temple for 7th degree initiations, and under pressure from the (c) set for drumming and pig-cooking privileges, he has come under criticism from some Baktaman and Seltaman seniors for granting drumming dispensations to them. Towards the end of 1968 there were rumours that an *Amowk* initiation was being planned in Bolivip (two days' travel westward, at the edge of the known world). Kimebnok decided he would send both sets (c) and (b) to participate. When I questioned the theology of initiating two sets simultaneously, he answered that this was the Baktaman's last chance — that he would paint the *laqsalman* and babies red and send them too!

Obversely, he expressed dissatisfaction with the cooperation he received as cult leader: people were unwilling to provide firewood for the *Yolam;* they did not always share wild pig, or give an adequate share to him (this is a common accusation among senior men); they never gave him taro. Being a long-time widower, he also pointed out how much better he could look after the *Yolam* if he had a wife, and made it understood that he was thinking of a certain youngish widow. This was not taken very seriously by anyone, as no one can impose marriage on a woman; and he was made the butt of occasional ridicule behind his back for this attempt.

The major criticism of his role performance served to hold up and articulate in part different aspects of the role. It is dangerous to cultivate the ancestors, then ignore them: they are angry at unfulfilled promises. The cult leader should be an old man but act like a young man: be active and strong, hardworking and consistent. That is how the community is kept healthy: regular cult leads to much taro, satisfied women, and no hunger. Kimebnok was widely criticized for his inconsistency: at the end of *Amkōn* he pledged a pig to the women, then procrastinated, and the women became angry (which served as a alternative explanation of the poor taro results after the initiation, (cf. p. 90). The leader of the Kerabip hamlet men's house finally stepped in and slaughtered his pregnant sow — which to his distress turned out to be carrying 12 unborn piglets — after a public oration on the nature of *Amkōn* and the importance of collective euphoria. This shamed Kimebnok into also slaughtering *his* pig. Among seniors, the criticism increasingly focused on the irregularity of cult intensity, and the dangers of his occasional threat to close the *Yolam* and discontinue the cult altogether.

119

Reasons for such behaviour on his part were brought out in his self-defence, and reveal the character of ancestors. They are very much like live old men — capricious, petty, and sometimes vindictive, and being more powerful they are less controlled in their reactions. As a result, they are handled with care. Kimebnok was having constant discomfort from yaws, which he interpreted as the effects of the Yeni ancestor scratching him at night; he also developed a swollen foot. His threats to stash away the skull in the forest were as much directed towards the ancestor as towards the congregation. There is a general consensus among seniors, in which they instruct their juniors, that one should withdraw from the presence of ancestors when one is sick and weak — you do not sleep close to the sacra, you do not perform cult, you remove your pigs' teeth and other decorations so as not to cause irritation by hubris. Kimebnok's relation to the ancestor is particularly precarious since he belongs to another clan. At other times he tried to placate him by giving him cult attention. After deputing hunters on a secret hunt for a *Wonsā* ritual who came home wearing their netbags turned with the feathers towards their back — the secret sign that they come empty-handed — Kimebnok claimed he had put the ancestor to the test; when he would not release game for a sacrifice, he deserved to be put away. But others said Kimebnok had failed to keep the sacred fire burning continuously. And a recent experience of the Seltaman was cited: they had opened a *Yolam* after a long period of discontinuing the cult, and when they prayed for taro at their first *Wonsā* the skull just whistled absent-mindedly and would not listen — but with the patient repetition of rituals, relations improved.[1] A disused and tumble-down *Amowkam* among the Seltaman, with its skull still in place, and several disbanded *Yolam* buildings that I have observed in other villages indicate that this kind of situation can deteriorate to the point where all cult activity in the temple is discontinued.

The two competitors in the present contest show weaknesses, so that this might be the outcome among the Baktaman. Taneŋ is an indecisive and unsuccessful person: when the large, joint gardening area was opened (p. 31) he continued to go crashing through the bush, unable to decide on a plot for himself, long after most people had settled for their places; to the last *Wonsā* rite he brought a taro so large that it was still half raw when the time came for each

[1] This was incidentally accompanied by an inconclusive discussion of whether it is possible to whistle without lips — i.e. could the skull have done this or were the Seltaman lying.

to divide and exchange taro. Conversely, Kimebnok has been a forceful person, but is growing old. His favoured successor is Ngaromnok — a candidate also well spoken of by the Seltaman seniors — but Ngaromnok belongs to the unfortunate set (c) who were still waiting for 7th degree initiation in 1968, and he also expressed fear of what the reaction of the Yeni ancestor might be if he, a lonely Warop clan member married to the widow of dead Yeni, took over the cult. The tactics of the rivalry towards the end of 1968 were as follows: Taneŋ accused Kimebnok of sorcery, burning the former's hair in the *Yolam* to cause sickness. Kimebnok was incensed at the accusation, arguing (i) he knows no sorcery, as his father died without teaching him (ii) he is a brave man and fights openly when he is angry; he has killed 3 Seltaman. He tries also to involve Taneŋ in a secondary cult role and force him to cooperate by naming him to lead secret hunts. Taneŋ in turn criticizes Kimebnok for not doing rituals, then refuses to return from his garden house for the taboo period preceding the *Wonsā*, thereby blocking the performance of that rite.

These various verbal formulations of beliefs and principles, and the various ritual conundrums that the rivals attempt to construct for each other, are broadcast as messages to audiences of various sizes. It will have been noticed that some are made known to the population as a whole; the majority of them, however, are contained within an audience of *Katiam* attendants. This defines an inner circle of 21 men including all members of sets (f), (e), and (d), and a few of (c). Some of these are weak and old, some of them are marginal and will remain insignificant because of deficient personality or intelligence. Essentially, six men in sets (e) and (d) are addressing the five most competent and assertive members of set (c) to rally them for alternative solutions to these political problems and in the process training them in the intricacies of belief and structure. Some few Seltaman cult leaders enter into this dialogue as significant others; but essentially the transmission, and thus persistence, of central features of Baktaman culture hang on this thin thread.

Cult life and gardening: The wider implications of these rituals for other sectors of life should also be recognized. Perhaps the greatest indirect significance of ritual activities is the output of gardening interests and decisions which they generate. The recurrent consequence of rites is to propel groups of men to the gardens to perform agricultural tasks with heightened significance, often in preparation and nearly always in conclusion of rites. The most striking case is that

121

of the Seltaman community. Struck by an epidemic in late 1967 which killed about 20% of the population, when I first saw them in 1968 they were a listless and broken population. One of their main cult leaders, Kaÿimkayak, had for some time resided among the Baktaman. In June 1968 he decided to return and open a long inactive *Yolam*. By the end of the year *he* was transformed from a passive, although highly interesting and perceptive, old man to a forceful, active leader; and the Seltaman community was a prosperous, successful population of cultivators clearing forest, planting gardens, completing fences and engaging in ceremonial trade, while steadily performing *Yolam* and *Katiam* ritual. Their corporate spirit and vitality, proverbial from the days of warfare before pacification, were visibly reconstituted.

Both they and their neighbours recognized this as the direct results of ritual on taro, health, and prosperity; and a pragmatic proof of the efficacy of rite was thus provided. Two things, however, are important to note in this connection. Firstly, the confirmed awareness of this success made the Baktaman no more able to break out of their relative impasse: the prerequisites of active and assured cult in terms of personalities and the mechanisms of secrecy, confidence, and revitalization of the mysteries were no more available to them than they had been. Secondly, there is little technical programming of production implicit in Baktaman, or Seltaman, cult. Problems of pig management are not significantly involved, as has been indicated in some other parts of New Guinea (e.g. Rappaport 1968), and land use cycles, size of gardens, organizations of labour, etc. all remain as decentralized, technical decisions to be made by households and coalitions. It is the heightened significance, the symbolic collectives that are created, and the occasional ritual requirement of a new garden — of any size — that together provide the elements which an awakened enthusiasm puts to work. Neither a religious nor an adaptational teleology can provide an adequate picture of the processes whereby these consequences are effected.

CHAPTER 13

Spirits and the dead

The Baktaman have beliefs and rites whereby they conceptualize and express man's spiritual nature, his soul and its fate after death; and their world is also peopled with other invisible things or spirits with which they interact. Without prejudging the extent to which these conceptions form a single system of knowledge in an analytical sense they may be treated thematically as a cluster of idioms.

It is important to acknowledge our basic rationalist position that such supernatural beliefs and projections are the product of other men's imaginations. In a superficial exercise of relativism we might otherwise be tempted to treat such spirit beliefs with the make-believe concreteness of a fairy-tale, and then subsequently focus our attention merely on how they reflect Baktaman values and ideas. But this would prevent us from asking the more useful question of how they serve Baktaman as conceptual tools — what they enable a Baktaman to think, feel, and understand. After all, in their man-made character these constructs are merely like all other concepts and constructs of a culture, and we should ask of them, as of the others, how they make a person grasp aspects of his life situation and reality, and what consequences they have for the form which a person's reality takes. In these respects, supernatural constructs in general may show some characteristic features; one frequently has the impression that the construct itself, e.g. the ghost or spirit, is considerably elaborated and specified, whereas the sensory events which are related to it as its expressions are variable and the criteria for relating them imprecise. If so, the constructs would be little amenable to falsification by confrontation with reality. These questions can be explored by investigating the following themes: What is the character of events which are interpreted by means of such constructs? What action or response does such an interpretation release, and what are the consequences of the response, particularly with respect to the possibility of falsification and learning? What communication takes place in which the appropriateness of using the construct is questioned, providing opportunities for social confirmation or disconfirmation? The answers to such questions should provide an understanding of the aggregate, cultural agreements that are generated; and the following material is presented with these questions in mind.

As noted previously, every person has a *finik* — a spirit, soul, or consciousness, which is his real self, in contrast to the body. In the living person it is located in the solar plexus, or behind the breastbone; in ancestral representations on shields and temple fronts it is often marked as an inverted triangle near the middle of the torso. Dogs, pigs, cassowaries, and marsupials (*nuk*) also have spirits; people are unsure as to birds, but definite that other animals, or plants, do not have them. A person's spirit clings or spreads to his belongings and his food; it may attack others and then it tends to ride the victim's back.

With death, the spirit becomes separated from the body — a condition that also subsumes unconsciousness. As a result, Baktaman believe it to be reversible; if one acts quickly and many persons dance, holding the dead person's limbs, he will be revived.

Mortuary customs both express certain features of people's attachment to each other as living persons, and codify the nature and relationship of the spirits of the dead. Grief at death may be very strong among the Baktaman; convention stipulates that Br, Si, Hu, Wi, Fa, Mo, So, Da must wail and lament and that the women among them smear themselves with ash or mud. Other persons may join them in this. A number of other expressions of grief are optional, but in part common among close relatives: breast bands like those worn by 1st degree novices, but with tassels, are made and worn by close relatives; daughters often hang a couple of their mother's taro scrapers (*yom*) on the tassels so that the musical sound of their striking together will 'remind' them. Women are known to commit suicide on the death of a husband or child. Men also grieve for their wives, but more commonly for a very dear brother.

On the occurrence of a death, the whole Baktaman community is affected by death pollution for four days and may do no gardening or hunting. The garden of the dead person is ravished by the population in general, his or her pigs and dogs killed and eaten, their garden house burned down, all in 'anger' for the death. These reactions may not be entirely dominated by anguish. Thus when the

124

two-year-old child of one relatively unpopular woman died, the other women of the village raided and destroyed her garden, much to her chagrin.

The dead body is stripped except for basic clothes (grass skirt or penis sheath), the wrists are tied together with a string, and the corpse left in the house where it died to be visited by mourners. After some hours close cognates, primarily of a dead person's clan, wrap the body in edible ferns (*abār* or *sīk,* the same kinds as those used when steam-cooking pork) and carry it to an unfrequented place, away from habitation. There a platform is built up in a tree, sheets of bark are laid on it, and the fern-wrapped corpse is placed on top. It is covered with bark, the sago-like leaves of the *tarís* tree, and tied fast with cane. The group then disperses and returns to the village by separate routes, so the dead spirit will be confused and not follow them home again. After a day or two the closest relative revisits the corpse, speaks comfortingly to the dead and fans away flies and other insects. Thereupon the body is left to decompose for some months, and the area is taboo to all.

After a sufficient time, so that there is no smell in the area, two or three close relatives go to complete the final step of disposal of the dead. They enter the taboo locality, and build a fire on the ground beneath the tree platform. One of them climbs up and hands down the skull; it is warmed over the fire and the dead person's spirit is invited to enter it; then it is put in a net bag. Next, the mandible is similarly treated, sometimes also the right-hand radius, ulna, and fingerbones, clavicle and breastbone. These and most other larger bones of the skeleton, especially of the right side, are all collected together in the net bag and carried to a limestone cave to be deposited. The main Baktaman necropolis is in a rock shelter in a ravine near the juncture if the Byoŋ and the Kātōr streams. It is subject to constant rock-falls that bury the bones, and yet 15–20 intact skulls and a jumble of bones are visible on the surface. The place where each particular skull is put is remembered by those who put it there, and the names of some of the visible skulls are occasionally identified on such visits; thus the identities of some of the dead are retained and they become potential candidates for supplementing the ancestral population in the temples. At all other times the place is avoided; and a visit to the ossuary by any Baktaman imposes a one-day garden taboo from death pollution on all members of the comunity.

This proper and complete procedure is not followed in all cases: unimportant persons may just be buried in the ground for convenience, and small infants are sometimes carried to the ossuary directly, without the intervening exposure on a tree platform. If, on the other hand, a person drowns in a river and is carried away by it, or a corpse is thrown in the river, that person's soul or spirit disappears and ceases to exist.

Some features and implications of these idioms stand out. The collective taboos connected with death express and impose a collective relationship of all Baktaman to their dead, and are the counterpart of the collective cult of one or a few ancestors in the *Yolam*. The particular clan and individual involvement is strictly subsidiary to this. One informant thus explained the 4-day garden taboo at mourning: 'We stay away from the gardens for two days because we are sorry, then two more days so as not to harm the taro.'

The use of cooking ferns to wrap the corpse creates in Baktaman spectators a direct association with cooking — perhaps not unreasonably in a population accustomed to cannibalism. The implication of a transformation into spiritual form, like that which takes place with sacrificial meat, would seem to be easily accessible to seniors who know the sacramental mystery. This takes place in the purifying environment of the trees, before a final return of the bones to man's point of origin inside the ground in a cave. The fact that the dead thus retrace the steps whereby taro came to man (cf. Myth 1, p. 83), did not, on the other hand, seem to be perceived.

It makes little sense for us to elicit inventions from informants by putting questions that they may never have asked, or to deduce logical implication of the views that they do express in their various codes. But we can learn more about the transformation from living to dead through the events that are regarded and interpreted as information about the spirits of dead persons. It would seem that whereas the essence of the spirit is transformed upon death and subsequent to it, many character traits remain unchanged. Thus, eleven days after the death and tree exposure of the old man Fiŋerok, my notes contain the following item:

Nulapeŋ arrived in great excitement at dusk — he had been out hunting birds with his wife and was attacked by Fiŋerok's *finik*. He saw him plainly, standing by a tree trunk; then the figure rushed him. His wife turned tail, he managed to raise his bow and jump aside — the figure rushed past him and then suddenly disappeared. He was recognizable as Fiŋerok, but red skinned. He left no visible footprints. If Nulapeŋ had been alone, he would have been killed.

[In a discussion between the four men hearing this news with me, the interpretation was that] Fiŋerok is angry about the slaughter of his pig — he wanted his share. Tepnok had been sent, together with Burutar, with a leg of the pig as a gift to [the neighbouring community], and this caused his anger to boil over. Fiŋerok was no doubt waiting for Tepnok and mistook Nulapeŋ for him.

Indeed, while we were talking, Tepnok and Burutar were seen returning. They could report that on the way, Burutar had died/ fainted, and was revived only by a life-restoring *singsing*. Later, they also added the claim that on their return they had heard someone rushing around the forest crying *wus-wus-wus*.

The mortuary practices are also seen as a way to prevent such troublesome spirits from hovering around the neighbourhood and to move them along to the land of the dead.

What becomes of the soul, however, also depends on the circumstances of death. Only persons who die a non-violent death go to the land of the dead and thus become *sabkār* = dead spirits; persons who are killed in battle or by violent accidents become *nawn* = tree spirits, regardless of the form of funeral, and roam in the forest. Only those who become *sabkār* can be used as ancestral spirits in the temples — but once they are brought into the temple they are no longer *sabkār* but revert to being *finik* spirits.

The land of the dead is where most souls go and stay. It is rather like the Baktaman village, except the houses are somewhat bigger, there are more of them, there are many people and many pigs. The *sabkārman* look like people but are generally taller, and red or black in skin colour. Their village is not very far away; it may be reached through one or another of the taboo, haunted areas in Baktaman or adjoining territories; some of their houses are also in these areas. Whereas most *sabkārman* live in the land of the dead permanently, some visit the live world for particular purposes, and some constantly haunt the taboo areas, or the ossuary caves, or even other places, where they may attack people.

These belief constructs are communicated in myths (cf. Appendix III), often as the experiences of particular persons. But their everyday reality as part of the Baktaman world is most apparent in how they serve to identify current events. In the course of my less than a year with the Baktaman, a number of persons suffered sporadically from having been entered by a *sabkār* who was slowly eating away their flesh. Several sightings of *sabkār* were reported, of which the above-mentioned one of Fiŋerok was the most dramatic.

127

Three months later, Tepnok, a man in his late twenties, was believed to have made a visit to the land of the dead. During a lonely afternoon hunt he put down his bow to pluck a bird he had shot. Retrieving the bow he could not pull it loose: a *sabkār* was holding the other end. The *sabkār* took him home to his village where Tepnok attended a 7th degree initiation (cf. the problem for the Baktaman of holding this initiation) before returning home after sunrise next day.

But the most extraordinary adventure, in that it involved a number of participants, was that of Ngobis, an 18-20-year-old girl, who disappeared in the forest without trace one day. Her father was very distressed, and groups of men roamed the area for three days searching for her. On the fourth day she suddenly appeared in a sago area where people were working, as if she materialized in the wake of a falling sago palm. She was unable to account for how she got there or what had happened to her, but agreed that she had been carried off by a *sabkār*, as is known to occur not infrequently. Not being able to identify the spirit by name, all her relatives could do was to rotate her bark cape (which hangs from the woman's head down her back, where the spirit would still be clinging) three times around her and then burn it. Had she known its name one could have whispered this name into water, and then thrown the water on her. She remained disoriented for some days, but then returned to normal. There was no evidence of doubt in anybody's mind that these were indeed the concrete, literal circumstances of the case.

Tree spirits, *nawn*, are more elusive; though numerous they provide fewer unequivocal signs of their presence. The one myth I found about them (Myth 4, Appendix III), gives the paradigm for their nature and powers and is told with reluctance and in secrecy, whereas the associated *iben* song is used for hunting magic. Though many men hope for the blessing of a *nawn* hunting assistant, act in ways to encourage them, and do not mind others wondering whether they have succeeded, I know of no one who claims to actually have a *nawn* confidant.

More common in their effects on people are two other kinds of spirits: *bisŋam* and *sarop*. These are of the same basic substance as those discussed above, but probably the spirits of *living* men, temporarily disembodied. The latter are the simpler: a *sarop* is a stranger who lurks invisibly on the edges of the village and shoots men with an invisible arrow in the heart as they come out of the house in the morning; they fall ill and die next night. The imagery is vivid, given the life context: in a world of constant ambush fear you wake up in the

128

grey of dawn and need to go out to urinate; as you emerge from the men's house door, holding on to the central post as you lower yourself from the veranda platform to the ground you mimic the position of a pig at sacrifice, foreleg extended to expose the heart, tied to the very post that you are holding. The interpretation placed on this graphic situation is revealing: *sarop* are sometimes specified as the spirits of trading partners who have not been reciprocated for their trade gifts of axes or other valuables.

Conversely, *bisŋam* are small, visible man-like dwarfs that attack you in the forest, and they are sometimes said to be the spirits of living men of your own village. Being only 2–3 feet tall they prefer to ambush you, only attack when you are alone, and there must be five of them to overpower you. The battle with them is a physical fight which you may win; if they overpower you they puncture you with sharpened fibula splinters from bones of the *left* side of dead men, piercing various terminal points such as top of head, corner of neck and shoulder, base of palm, ends of fingers, small of back and soles of feet. They then scratch your tongue with the dried foot of a brush turkey (*Wierók*) so you cannot report your experience. You return home and fall ill, and die after 2–3 days. *Bisŋam* are often observed fleetingly in the forest, and sudden illness elicits discussions of them.

Finally, one further kind of spirit exists which is uniquely *not* derived from the *finik* of a living or dead man: *olip* mountain spirits. These live in the high, wild rock formations of uninhabited mountains, often behind sheer rock faces oozing red ochre colour from iron oxide. *Olip* spirits sometimes cause possession, but then become benevolent, when they are used as spirit familiars in curing (cf. pp. 139 ff.).

In summary, we have covered in this chapter some highly segmented fragments of knowledge: about death as it affects the essential identity of oneself and those closest to one, about ancestors and the multitude of dead strangers, about immaterial agents of various kinds. These different fragments are only superficially connected by the fact that some of the idioms are common, or recognizable from the main tradition of cult, even when given a twisted form: cf. the role of left-side longbones, the foot of the brush turkey, etc. The striking feature is rather how *empirical* these spirits are, how they seem to appear as very concrete observable objects *in* the world, rather than ways of talking *about* the world. They are 'real' in a way that such constructs do not seem to be quite real in other cultures that I have known.

So our understanding of them can best start with the experiential contexts in which they arise: sensory experiences of moving figures in the forest; fear combined with the symbolic exposure of flank and heart to an unknown threatening world; the haunting presence of invisible danger in taboo places; supernatural ambushes and abductions. The fantasy constructions over these experiences achieve some degree of order and design, but remain loosely integrated because they need hardly ever be acted on. In conversations when they are socially confirmed, they also retain their ad hoc character: the actor recounts his observations, as if he were speaking of some relatively poorly known species of animal; all contribute their bits of knowledge, and no individual or joint further act is triggered which would require an evaluation or authoritative summary of the knowledge. Thus, for example, in the case of sighting a *bisŋam* there is no attempt to identify the person whose spirit it might be, there is no use of these constructs for witchcraft or sorcery analysis or accusations. The indefiniteness and inconsistency of these fragments of knowledge clearly reflect a situation where they are not used as a framework for action.

CHAPTER 14

Sorcery

The spirits discussed in the previous chapter are treated by the Baktaman as independent actors, and are not used to associate other persons with an event. For this purpose, other constructs are used which may be grouped under the analytical label of sorcery. By sorcery I understand: constructs which persons use to identify intentional social actors behind calamitous events; the construct includes a set of magical procedures which they also may attempt to use on occasion to cause such events. Two clusters of ideas serve the Baktaman this way: *kimōn*, or male sorcery, and *tamām*, or female sorcery. We need to give attention first to the specific features of each, and then to their communication, and effects on social life.

Kimōn is the name for a body of techniques and procedures, at best imperfectly known by the speaker, whereby men cause harm to others. It utilizes objects surrounding a person to which his spirit (*finik*) is closely connected, though I have never heard it generalized in that way. The basic technique is described as follows: the sorcerer obtains some fragment of hair, or of nails, the person's grass skirt, carrying bag, or other wearing apparel, alternatively a half-eaten item of food such as taro, meat, sweet potato, or breadfruit shells. This item is taken home or into the forest, placed on a stone and buried deep in the ash under a fire. Alternatively, it may be placed inside the skull of the *Yolam* ancestor. As the item burns or dries up, the person is seized by sickness and fever, and then dies. Though this is the prototype for male sorcery, other forms are also known to exist: some men are able to 'tie' snares and traps so that they are not released and fail to catch the game, and the hunter remains unsuccessful; or they may smite a man's taro field so that the crop is destroyed.

Tamām, female sorcery, utilizes a different range of techniques. The sorceress attacks at night when her victim is asleep, or in the day when you do not notice. Or perhaps if you go hunting alone, you will see a cassowary and approach it — but it is really a woman doing *tamām*, so it turns on you and attacks you. The sorceress strikes you with a stone adze; when you fall down unconscious, she eats your flesh, then leaves you. You wake up, remembering nothing, and go about your activities as usual — then you become ill, and die. When your corpse is put out on the tree platform, the sorceress will come and eat you; she cuts out your heart and rubs her stone adze with your blood before hiding it away carefully. The heart she cooks out in the forest; she brings it home in a leaf, and eats it in her hut. If someone looks in, they will think she is just eating taro, but it is really human flesh. A vivid alternative is for the sorceress to obtain the leavings from food you have eaten; she catches a soldier ant, wraps it with the food scraps in a leaf package which she stuffs up into her vagina. The ant bites away at your food in anger and desperation, and your insides are torn to pieces and you die. After your death, the sorceress comes to the tree platform for her necrophagic revels.

The idioms employed here are readily understood. Male sorcery works with the elements most emphasized in ritual: hair, as the essence of growth and fertility, and food as in the central sacrament. Female sorcery uses the trappings of male power and rank: she fights with an adze (a purely male act), she appears in the guise of a cassowary (the symbol of fully initiated males), she paints the adze red with blood. Alternatively she misuses her female organ as male sorcerers misuse fire and the ancestral skull. Finally she negates her role as the giver of life and taro by cannibalism.

The problems of diagnosis, identification of sorcerers, and attempts at treatment are best discussed in connection with sickness in the next chapter. Here, we may rather focus on the way these constructs affect the conceptualization of human relations and constitute a working 'Theory of Man,' with profound implications for social life.

Firstly, even though most Baktaman probably know no sorcery, and certainly have no illusions of effective control over such powers, there is no doubt in their mind that sorcerers exist. Thus only a few years ago, a believed large-scale operator of *tamām* was finally executed. She had practised it a long time and killed many people; finally she was surprised while actually engaged in the magical acts by a mother whose child she had killed previously; the mother gave the alarm and one of the seniors of that time, Gobomariok, caught her, passed a rope around her neck, and while she screamed and fought, tightened the knot and hoisted her up over a branch, while her two daughters watched, crying. They threw her body in the already taboo Byoŋ stream and she was destroyed. Her two daughters, now married, are both lonely and isolated persons and are readily mentioned in private when the fear of sorcery arises; but essentially men expect any woman, and certainly all older women, to know the techniques.

The prototype male sorcerer at present among the Baktaman is A., a widely feared and disliked person. A strong personality with a violent temper, he also seems a singularly spiteful old man. In confidence, a small group of men characterized him to me as follows: A. was born among the Seltaman; he has always been a difficult and cantankerous person. When he finally got a wife he quarrelled with her all the time, and finally beat her to death. Her kinsmen were angry, and wanted to kill him in revenge, but nothing came of it. Having lost his wife and alienated his affines, he became a wanderer, and is constantly looking for a new wife. But no woman will have him, since he is vicious and old and known to be a sorcerer. A series of deaths are traced to him, in a repetitive pattern: he starts cultivating a man with a marriageable daughter, gives him taro and pig and sweet potato. Then he asks for the daughter. The parents are hesitant; the girl refuses. He then kills them by sorcery. One of the informants claimed to have escaped death under these circumstances because a named friend saw A. put the food remains he had obtained into the fire with intent to kill; the friend managed to sneak in as soon as A. left and retrieve the food, and throw it into the river, thus saving the informant's life. Several men have had similar narrow escapes. A. is arrogant and stops at nothing. For a while he was committing incest with his sister; when she finally categorically refused he killed her with an arrow and threw her into the I river. He also copulates with dogs and pigs. The Baktaman finally became so incensed with him that he returned to Seltaman in the spring of 1968. Shortly after that, Taktieŋ, in the company of his wife and two children, met him on the path, confronted him and abused him, telling him to go home to Seltaman. Two days later the whole family came to me for medicine: Taktieŋ had fever, his wife and son acute diarrhoea, while the daughter seemed to be suffering from an acute allergic attack, with swellings and blisters all over her body.

The fact that sorcerers exist in an actor's world, indeed that he is prepared to believe that every alter in a relationship may command such powers, has a number of profound consequences for the nature of social relationships.

Firstly, it encourages sensitivity to others in everyday life. If you think that irritation or anger in alter may lead to acts that cause sickness and death to yourself, it makes good sense to be observant of the other's moods and wishes and to be considerate of his interests. Baktaman do in fact largely act this way towards each other and also did so towards me; it is important to recognize that such tact is an aspect of the *exercise* of relationships without being conceptualized as a basic positive morality of social relations. The apparent discrepancy between their sensitivity in daily events — the genuine pleasure of their company — and the insensitivity and violence of some of their acts then disappears.

Secondly, their codification of the nature of obligations in a relationship becomes more understandable. Thus for example, in my attempts to ingratiate myself with ritual leaders so as to be admitted to the cult occasions I long worked according to an ethnocentric plan of building up debts in alter which would serve as a justification in due course for demands for counter-prestations. But prestations in a relationship are not overtly conceptualized in terms of a ledger of fairness and mutual consideration, despite the tenor of everyday relations: rather, prestations are used to pacify anger and dissatisfaction in alter. As long as amity is preserved all is well, regardless of the objective balance or imbalance that may obtain in what has been given and received over a longer period. My attempts on a few occasions to confront friends and try to press them into making relatively simple and fair commitments for the future always resulted in a scramble to find some insignificant immediate prestation that might please; and once that was accepted by me, any imbalance in our relationship had been eliminated.

Finally, the way in which a 'Sorcery Theory of Man' affects moral debate may be noted. The way we in the West conceive of morality is very closely tied to the notion of impartial judgement: my action may be right even though all others believe it to be wrong. The simplest, and perhaps commonest, way to conceptualize this idea of impartiality is by means of an almighty and all-knowing god. Our moral discourse obliquely refers to this: what were the objective circumstances, what ought a person to do in such a situation regardless of the particular pressures that might have been exerted on him. The Baktaman, on the other hand, have only their ancestral spirits, which are entirely human in their capriciousness and subjectivity. And when the ultimate sanctions on a social relationship depend on the anger or pleasure of a sorcerous neighbour, the exploration of the objective circumstances becomes irrelevant at best. Moral discourse will concentrate on discovering the bases for *affect* and the easiest way to rectify it, and secondarily to generate public opinion to frighten and make him step carefully. Once relationships deteriorate from their everyday praxis of tact there is nothing incongruous in turning to a grotesque theory: e.g. that your neighbour's wife, because the piece of pork you gave her was smaller than she had hoped, is angry enough to perform cannibalistic sorcery-murder.

We may note that these orientations are also in harmony with Baktaman conceptualizations of time. In an existence where the flow of time is not adequately objectified (cf. pp. 21 ff.) it seems reasonable that the present should dominate over a kaleidoscopic past and an unspecifiable future. It is certainly true that past events are organized in terms of *where* they took place and not their temporal relations (cf. pp. 18 ff.); that strategies involving successive steps are rarely explicated verbally; that joint action (a hunting trip; collecting materials for house building) involves constant evaluation and inter-communication rather than the unfolding of an agreed master plan; that temporary and relatively minor afflictions have a devastating effect on a person as if they made his life not worth living — as indeed it might not be, if he were to suffer this affliction for ever. So also in social relations: prestations in the past and promises for the future are secondary to desire and performance in the present because a trans-actional ledger is technically difficult to specify and conceptually elusive without the framework of a sound chronology. Current affir-mation of a relationship, on the other hand, is a tangible and dominant experience. Without the buffering effect of temporal embeddedness, relations become precarious and volatile; and so they are more adequately conceptualized by a sorcery-based theory of social rela-tionships than by one based on righteousness.

If by witchcraft we mean a covert, often subjectively unacknowl-edged force that springs from envy and hate and slowly destroys its object, we can also understand why Baktaman conceptualizations lack this character and cluster around sorcery. Witchcraft is the effect of gnawing, suppressed resentment. It thus thrives best among people who take a long-term view and see subjective injustices accumulate. This presupposes a time dimension and an evaluation of human rela-tions in terms of a cumulative ledger. It is also aggravated by a social organization that imposes the contradictory demands of mem-bership and interests in several distinct corporations. These con-ditions are just not present in Baktaman life and I cannot see that the Baktaman could develop the passions, and the concept, of pure witchcraft. Where envy and resentment appear, they appear strongly and immediately; persons do not have, or conceptualize, the constraint of corporate membership. Resentment may be hidden for tactical reasons, or for fear of alter's anger and sorcery, but is not suppressed; and the subterranean force of envy is not generated. With Baktaman time concepts, it must either be acted on or forgotten; and so the action which they can conceive will have to be the positive action of sorcery, not the slow disembodied threat of witchcraft.

CHAPTER 15

Sickness and curing

The Baktaman are at present in a tragic phase of early contact when the population declines rapidly because new communicable diseases sweep through the area. However, the demographic material that can be constructed for them (cf. Appendix II) indicates that disease was also a common cause of death in former times; and they are chronically troubled by minor ailments of various kinds. At one point in 1968, for example, after a very long period of excessive precipitation, about one fourth of the total population was so troubled by skin infections and tropical ulcers that they were entirely incapacitated for work. Sickness in its various forms is thus a field of knowledge to attract their interest and ingenuity.

We have seen in the previous two chapters that sickness is thought to be caused by both spirits and sorcerers; likewise it will be remembered that various forms of sickness were also thought to result from breaches of the post-initiation taboos. But Baktaman also operate with a concept that seems close to a Western pre-scientific notion of 'disease' — a condition, often communicated or initiated by a particular incident, causing discomfort of recognized kinds and even death. Thus, for example, one man who developed a cold chastised another for having been spitting and blowing mucus all over the place when he had been sick; this had been eaten by the pigs, stored in their fat, and communicated to the patient when he ate the pork. Pressed to explain the nature of what is communicated an informant will fall back on the idiom of a spirit; but it makes sense for him none the less to declare that a particular condition of being sick is caused not by sorcerers or spirit agents, but is 'just sickness.'

The sick state can thus be brought about by a number of causes; a complete list would include the anger of ancestral spirits, various spirit attacks (*sabkar, nawn, sarop, bisŋam*), male sorcery, female sorcery, breach of taboo, menstrual pollution, and plain sickness. Rather than try to synthesize a schema for these by applying a systematic logic that Baktaman actors never seem to have applied, let us look at the acts, and conversations, that are triggered by sickness. We may distinguish preventive action from attempts at treatment and cure, and look for the particular features of a situation that can be identified as triggering an act (and this will include diagnoses), and the idioms incorporated or expressed in these acts. In this way we may approach an understanding of the classification, conceptualization, and theory of disease as it is applied as an operational system for action.

Prevention: The simplest preventative aid is the amulet; this is particularly used for children. It is composed of a small bundle of items worn in a string around the neck, usually a selection from dog femurs, water-lizard mandibles, cassowary claws, and ginger wood. It is called dog-bone (*mān-kun*) or lizard-tooth (*sām-keir*) after its main component. The spirits of these animals are supposed to guard the child from spirit attacks, while the smell of the ginger wood acts more mechanically to repel foreign spirits.

Adults, on the other hand, protect themselves by making their amulet secret, i.e. secreting it in a small, finger-sized bag suspended from the neck so that it hangs over the breastbone — the seat of one's spirit consciousness. Such bags may contain idiosyncratic items; at fateful times men may also put the finger-bone of an ancestor there. Otherwise, ancestors are appealed to in prayer and sacrifice to protect life, health, and property. Certain cautionary taboos are perhaps best understood in the same context: a pregnant woman must not eat watersnake (*woktun*) or bandicoot (*kayār*), normally allowed to her; her husband must not eat dog or tree snake (*dī*), or work with fish poison. A woman who has lost many infants may finally attempt to protect her last-born by mutilating it — chopping off the terminal joint of the left little finger. She will wear the cut-off joint in her small amulet bag till the baby cuts its first teeth, then hide it away in a tree in the forest.

When the whole community is threatened, as by an approaching epidemic, responsible seniors may build a spirit gate to control the approaches, either on the territorial boundary or by the village. In late 1967 word reached the Baktaman that an epidemic was approaching from the west. Kainen (set d) then built a gate over the western entrance to the village, one post of which was made of hard-

138

wood. He sacrificed a pig and rubbed the hardwood with the pig's fat, made a shrine of a pandanus leaf and placed a dog's skull on it. The skull he painted red with ochre and pig's blood, and on the pandanus leaf he painted five red lines. He also constructed an ancestral monument on the nearby site where the village had stood in his early childhood: he raised a hardwood post and painted three red lines around it praying to his ancestors to protect the community. Again, these idioms are clear: the hardwood and the red colour stand for the ancestors, the sacrifice pleases them, the pig's fat and the pandanus leaf sanctify, the dog spirit stands guard against stranger spirits.

Cures: In the event of sickness, a number of responses may occur. As noted, the patient becomes excessively downcast and despairing; he or she withdraws from all activity, and a man will normally remove his pig's teeth and other decorations and avoid the proximity of sacra. Specific minor cures may also be tried. Water is thrown on the patient to remove the sickness. For pains of any kind, stinging nettles are used to rub the painful areas or milk-exuding plants are rubbed on afflicted spots. Spice bark is chewed and blown over the sick person, accompanied by a combined whistling/blowing gesture that is used in ordinary conversation as an injunction to vanish. Ulcers and other chronic infections are 'transferred' onto taro. (The identity between man and taro is implicit in many contexts; in this case, so as not to damage the real taro, it is symbolically represented by a wild, inedible taro (*asīk*).) Pus from the sore is introduced under the skin of the taro, whereupon it is replanted, and the infection may switch to it. Alternatively, seeds or seedlings of the very prolific *barem-deim* tree may be used — you smear the pus on the seedlings, throw them into the river and quickly hide behind a tree trunk. Your troubles may then float away with the infected plant. Sickness in men — both boils and toothaches, and throat complaints — may also be cured by cutting and bleeding from the affected area. The theory behind this, apparently unknown to many Baktaman who practise the method, is that men who have been polluted by menstrual blood may develop such complaints, which will be relieved by letting out the unclean blood.

If none of these attempts help, however, the drastic remedy for sickness is a pig sacrifice. This combines an appeal to the ancestors with the mobilization of an *Olip* mountain spirit through a shaman. The rite is led by the shaman, who prepares all the necesary equipment; the sick person must provide the pig. The ritual procedure is as follows. The patient sits preferably off the ground, e.g. on a bark sheet.

139

A post, alternatively a section of *maŋmōŋ* tree, is planted in the ground, preferably while the patient's toe touches it. A small sapling, complete with roots, of the *tanom eisneŋ* or *isoŋ eisneŋ* tree is then incised with three or five lines around the trunk, using the jaw of a water lizard (*sām*). These circles are coloured with red ochre; a line of red ochre is painted on the patient's forehead. Red *eisŋam* berries are laid in a hole beside the post, and the sapling is planted on top after being rotated twice around the patient. The sacrificial pig is tied by the foreleg with a rope that is fastened to pole and sapling and then passes on for the patient to hold. *Kasok* branches (the cordylene used in *Yolam* sacrifices, but of a green rather than red variety) are rotated around the post and tree. The shaman takes his bow, twangs the string facing first left then right, and shoots the pig. While the pig shrieks and blood gushes forth, the red line on the patient's forehead is repainted with pig's blood, the *kasok* branch is dipped in the blood, spells are addressed to the *Olip* spirit and prayers to the patient's clan ancestors are whispered, and then the patient is slapped with the bloody branch on head, shoulders, and back while the shaman whispers his spell and shouts *Ba-ba-ba-ba*. After this, the *kasok* branch is planted and as it grows (which it normally does readily) the patient is supposed to get well. The pig is finally singed and distributed; a part of the fat is given to the ancestor in the men's house or *Katiam*.

The place of the *Olip* spirit in this healing rite is best explained by its supposed relation to the person I have called the shaman. There are 3–4 such shamans active among the Baktaman today, all of them fairly young men; but several older men who are now the cult leaders seem to have acted as shamans in their youth. The two roles, however, are unconnected in any organizational sense; and the curing rite, though it incorporates an appeal to clan ancestors, has no relation to the temple cults. If there is a tendency to combine the roles in a life cycle as I think, this must only reflect the general interests and inclinations of the persons.

A man becomes a shaman by the personal event of becoming possessed by an *Olip*. It is not a recurrent possession or trance, and may be an entirely unique experience: reportedly, the person's body starts shaking, he loses consciousness and then springs up and shouts meaningless words. Clearly, the man's own spirit has been driven out of him by the *Olip*. If he recovers, it means that the two spirits have become congenial and allied, and that he therefore has a friend in the *Olip*. This must also be a singularly powerful spirit: whereas other spirits attack and fight a person's *finik* in a drawn-out battle, the *Olip* over-

140

whelms his *finik* entirely. It is this spiritual ally that is brought in by the shaman's curing rite: the *Olip* can see the spirit that is causing the sickness, and can surely drive it away. This is perhaps even more explicit in the other, smaller performance sometimes done by a shaman: the patient is placed in the centre of a circle of dancers; they sing about sickness and getting well, tell the spirit to go away; then when the shaman gets the word from his *Olip* they attack the foreign spirit with burning sticks, sometimes searching it out and pursuing it further as it flees.

Idioms: These smaller and larger cures and preventive devices seem to apply a variety of rather ad hoc idioms. One common premise for most is that a spirit agency is causing the complaint; only the pregnancy taboos, the rubbing with nettles, and the tapping of polluted blood (doubtfully also the transfer of the sickness to wild taro or other plant hosts) do not entail this premise. Otherwise, we see a number of spirit counter-agents: *Olip*, ancestral spirits, dead dogs, cassowaries, and lizards. The *sām* water lizard is especially interesting: it is particularly emphasized through its minor but necessary place in the pig sacrifice, but also in the children's amulet. Its other symbolic contexts (drumskin, taboo as food for all males) are not particularly illuminating to explain its meaning; rather it must be its natural behaviour that holds the key: it is the only significant mediator between land and the spirit-removing water. More mechanical devices are also used to combat the spirit causes of sickness: gates, strong spice smells, water, fire, rotation of objects to 'tie' the spirit, etc. In the pig sacrifice, the rope connecting the patient and sacrificial animal is significant; it also passes around the young sapling, which is alleged to be an effective spirit-repelling agent. But I am not confident about what is entailed by this: a scapegoat killing, an identification of pig and man before a part-for-whole killing (which is also a possible interpretation of the mutilation of the infant to prevent its death), or something more in the nature of a lightning-rod to guide the course of the spirit to the enticing pork. Informants showed no interest in intellectualizing this problem.

Diagnoses and evaluations: Whatever consistency these conceptualizations have should also be revealed in how different cures relate to different conditions of sickness through a process of diagnosis, i.e. what circumstances surrounding the sickness determine the interpretation or classification imposed on it, and how do such features trigger a specific response?

141

Only one truly diagnostic routine is known, and I only know one case where it was used. The old man Fiŋerok, with a debilitating acute dysentery, had moved into the women's house with his old wife, sick with a fever; their daughter had a late miscarriage or still-birth in a garden house and returned to the home sick. These three together in desperation made a pig sacrifice; a week later when no improvement had resulted they called in a man to divine the cause. He poured water into a leaf to serve as a mirror; over the water he passed an ancestral bone back and forth as he looked at the reflection of Fiŋerok in the water. This way you are supposed to be able to see the face of the spirit that is causing the sickness — in this case the diviner saw nothing and declared it not a spirit, but 'just sickness' which would pass over by itself. In fact Fiŋerok died about two weeks later.

Otherwise during the long idle hours in the men's house there is much conversation about current sicknesses in a manner that might suggest diagnosis: one man suggests an inadvertent breach of taboo as the cause while another argues the plausibility of sorcery. Kimebnok alone was capable of providing three explanations for his skin trouble: it first broke out long ago when he ate half a loaf of sago with trading partners (i.e. it was caused by male sorcery); it would be cured by transfer to a wild taro and rubbing with milk-exuding plants (i.e. it was 'just sickness'); it was caused by the ancestral spirit scratching him at night. In one case, a man very strongly advanced the theory of female sorcery to explain his condition, to the point of almost coming out with a specific accusation. There is no cure for female sorcery other than retraction by the sorceress herself — yet next day he slaughtered his only pig in a curing sacrifice. The point about such conversations and affirmations is that they are all more or less plausible in terms of the various explanations used for sickness, but there is no attempt to measure their varying plausibility and implications against each other; each man says his piece and no conclusion is drawn. Nor is there any evaluation after the event: in the above-noted case of Fiŋerok, the conclusion from the divining was never mentioned when he died, or later; no one said 'I told you so' or 'you were wrong.' If the sickness disappears, so does the problem; if the patient dies, the problem dies with him and no conclusion is drawn from the experience.

Characteristically, diagnoses were expressed, and agreed upon, only in two classes of cases. The one is composed of the chronic conditions of physical deformity and mental illness. One very deformed hunchback is agreed to have become so a considerable time after birth, due to female sorcery. One case of deformity (described as an absence of heels on both feet), recently deceased at the time of my fieldwork, and one living mentally deficient and disturbed are both known to have been caused by parental breaches of pregnancy taboos.

The other class of cases is composed of those where collective action followed from an accusation of sorcery, either in the form of an execution, as in the case mentioned above, p. 132, or in the form of revenge warfare, where the sorcerer belongs to another community. In these cases, public opinion is committed to the interpretation of the precipitating event that justifies their reaction, and thus the diagnosis becomes authoritative. In all other cases, there is no agreed hypothesis that has been tested and no recorded output that has vindicated or falsified the explanation. And in the two classes of exceptions I have noted, it is only in a very literal sense that one can say that a diagnosis has been proved — only in so far as a sorcerer has been killed in revenge, or a deformity bears mute witness to its cause. With such limited procedures for testing and systematizing, one can understand some of the reasons why questions of sickness and cure remain such a remarkably poorly developed field of knowledge among the Baktaman, both compared to other sectors of their knowledge and to other cultures with a comparable technology.

CHAPTER 16

Killing, warfare, and cannibalism

Some Baktaman understandings of the nature of man are expressed in their concepts of spirits, sorcery, and disease. Others, more directly relevant to collective decisions and action, are connected with peace and war, and the social obligations of community. In treating these topics, it is worth while to focus on the time immediately before pacification, that is more than 4 years before my field study, to see the full expression of Baktaman institutions, and the concrete events that have most directly expressed and influenced Baktaman views.

It is difficult to interpret with any confidence the full meaning of acts one has not directly observed; and the fact that these acts are so strongly involved with violence and cannibalism increases the difficulties. When we attempt to understand the human significance of such behaviour, we are tempted towards two extremes. Either we measure them against humanistic ideals, and dramatize their distance from our world; or we see them in the perspective of contemporary and recent Western warfare and inhumanity and minimize the relevance of such behaviour, as we tend to do for our own case. Either extreme is entirely unsatisfactory. Though we have only our own experience from which to generalize when we try to understand the situation of others, we must try to correct for the peculiar features of our institutions. Most peculiar in this connection is the disparity in our culture between, on the one hand, ethical religions, humanistic sensibilities, and a society based on the insistent premises of justice and security and, on the other hand, the known existence of crime, perversity, and war. One of the prerequisites for such a disparity is that the codifiers of our Theory of Man largely live and almost exclusively act on the polite side of this dichotomy; while persons who pass across it are subject to elaborate rites of brutalization or rehabilitation (according to the direction of their movement) before they are capable of adequate interaction. The small-scale and less complex life situation of the Baktaman does not allow such an elaborate schism; and we should be aware that *all* the different acts and values are much more part of a single world, to be practised by the same actors towards the same alters. With this in mind, we may try to connect the actual acts and practices of the Baktaman and their neighbours, the resulting life situation as seen by the actors, and the codifications of knowledge and values that are embraced.

Life before pacification was very profoundly affected by the continual threat and frequent perpetration of violence between people. A gross measure of this is provided by the demographic material (cf. Appendix II): of the 54 deaths that have taken place from infancy until pacification in the sibling groups of the present adult generation, 18 were killed in warfare. This is a reasonable indication that in the pre-contact times, one person in every three died a violent death. Every live man carries the scars and marks of battle, especially from arrow-wounds; every person seems to have experienced pursuit and frantic flight, etc.

This was also a world where attacker and victim were known to each other as social persons. If a man is asked how many people he has killed, the answer takes the form of an enumerating identification of victims, with explanatory comments (the brother of so-and-so, the husband of the woman you met at so-and-so place) for my benefit, leading to a number as its conclusion only: every victim is seen as a social alter. And the Seltaman contingent that joined the Baktaman at the 6th degree initiation included the sole survivor from the massacre in which Nulapeŋ participated, the man who once escaped with Ngaromnok's arrow stuck in his buttocks, and the man who killed Kimebnok's brother and on another occasion crushed Taneŋ's parietal bone and left him for dead, among numerous others.

Some kinds of relations, on the other hand, preclude or limit violence. Within the primary community of Baktaman there is peace; killing is not only banned but solemnly declared to be inconceivable: if it should happen by mistake in a brawl they would all join in a resuscitating dance and thus revive the accidental victim (cf. p. 124). Ambiguous cases are the 10–15% of the Baktaman who were born elsewhere and have married or migrated in, as will be seen; also excepted are sorcerers, who may be lynched (cf. p. 132). The clan is similarly a group in which there is internal peace; since all clans are dispersed over some two to half a dozen communities, this means that fellow clansmen will be on opposing sides when communities fight. In that case they must not kill each other, or see the other's blood shed — you turn your head away when your fellow villagers kill a clansman. Affines, on the other hand — Wi Br or Si Hu — you may see killed but you must not kill them yourself. Kaineŋ, the leader of the Kerabip men's house is in the position of having killed his wife's junior brother; but this was before she ran away from the Seltaman and married him, so he is not at fault. Finally, a trading partner (*naγanum*) is your friend and in the words of an informant 'you may kill him but you are sorry and cry afterwards'; you may, however, under no circumstances eat a trading partner.

Only men who have passed 3rd degree initiation attack in war, whereas younger boys may be involved in defence. Victims, on the other hand, may be of any sex and age; much of the warfare involved surprise and ambush and large-scale battles were few; where warriors met prepared there was much mobility and manoeuvre in attempts to concentrate many against a few isolated enemy or circumvent the enemy men and strike against the unprotected women. Ideals of chivalry were certainly not developed and bravery, though approved in companions, was not an important component in victory. Thus one of the most sung victory songs of the Baktaman celebrates the time when a group of warriors led by Fiŋāteŋ and Bogōreŋ surprised a Seltaman woman, the daughter of Tamibnok, and her child collecting crayfish in a small stream, and killed them:

Tuak-tēm	*karōriyā*	*yaqéy*	/	*kabop-tēm*	*karōriyā*	/
Crayfish-hole	she digs	oh help		Crayfish-hole	she digs	

nātim	*Tamiō-ō*	*yaqéy*	/	*kàbop-tēm*	*karōriyā*	/
Father	Tamibnok	help!		Crayfish-hole	she digs	

fiჳ-karèbiō	*kamen-tēm*	*āyōyē*	/	*yiryōr*
Red-head-of-penis	penis-gourd	! !		you jump

sālō	*ē*	/	*Fiჳāteŋ*	*kàmen-tēm,*	*Bogōrēჳ*	*kamen-tēm*	/
you sleep			Fingateng's	penis-gourd	Bogoreng's	penis-gourd	

bitiჳ-bitēჳ	*sālō*	*āyōyē*	/	*yiryōr*	*sālō*	*yāyōyē*
jerkily	you sleep	! !		you jump	you sleep	! !

i.e. 'She digs the crayfish-hole — "Oh help!" She digs the crayfish-hole — "Oh father Tamibnok, help!" She digs the cray-fish hole. Red headed penis in penis-gourd! She leaps high, she falls dead! Potent Fingateng, potent Bogoreng! In one jerk, she falls dead, in

146

one leap, she falls dead!' Admittedly, it is probably the quality of the verse — here perhaps at its best in alliteration, imagery, and indirect evocation — rather than the military finesse of the event that makes this a favourite song; but clearly it is not regarded as compromising in any way.

Even when surprised in ambush women do not defend themselves; they merely try to escape. I know only one deviant case, told with glee about a now deceased Baktaman: In an attack on a small Seltaman garden hamlet, he pursued a woman trying to escape, and caught her. Rather than killing her, he decided to bring her home and marry her, and so drove her off towards Baktaman territory. Walking behind her, he soon decided not to wait, and forced her down on the ground. As he proceeded to copulate, she complained that the adze in her net bag was hurting her back, and as a gentleman he got off to let her remove the adze — whereupon she swung it at him, cracked his skull and ran away, while he had to return empty handed with a bleeding head.

As is apparent from this, an alternative to killing is abduction in the case of women and children. This does not often happen; usually when women and children are captured, though one person may wish to marry a woman the others have nothing to gain from this, and so she is killed. Likewise, women sometimes run away from their village if their marital situation is intolerable or (more frequently cited) there is a famine; they may get killed where they go or someone may decide to marry them. Without the support of kin, however, such persons are in an insecure position. Thus, for example, Dugieŋ, the deceased father of a now 25-year-old Baktaman, once surprised a Seltaman family in a lonely garden house. He killed the man and abducted the woman and married her, and took the step-son into his charge. But one night as he stood by the fire in the woman-house talking to his wife, the little boy woke up and started crying, saying Dugieŋ's legs silhouetted against the light had reminded him so of his real father. Dugieŋ was annoyed and killed the boy, but let the mother live in a marriage that was stable till his death in a battle with Kasanmin village. On the other hand, the one-time wife of Kayimkayak became hungry and dissatisfied and absconded from Seltaman. She was picked up and married to an Awonklamin man, who later was killed in battle by the Seltaman. At this the Awonklamin became so angry that they killed her and ate her.

It is difficult to penetrate behind the acts to their meanings in these and similar cases: what they reflect of attitudes and conceptualizations

147

of Hu-Wi or (foster) Fa-Ch relations, and interpersonal relations in general. Some evidence of this does, however, emerge from another case in which I was fortuitously slightly involved: the fate of a brother and sister, FaSiCh of my assistant Nulapeŋ, who had been abducted from their native community of Abolgobip and incorporated into the Seltaman. The story is briefly as follows, compressed from the 20-year-old boy's account: 'His Fa, Mo, FajrBr, Br, Si, and self as a baby were in a garden on the fringes of Abolgobip land. The Seltaman attacked, killed the Fa and besieged the house; then by deceit — promising him free passage to fetch water — they killed the FaBr and took the rest prisoner. They were marched off; crossing the Luap river the Seltaman decided to kill the brother too. On arrival in Seltaman village, there was disagreement whether to eat or keep the remaining prisoners. Two trading partners of the killed men took them in, one marrying the Mo, the other looking after, and later marrying the Si and serving as foster Fa of the boy. He was so small at this time, he does not remember anything, but his Mo told him about it. Several times later, in times of war, there were moves to kill the boy, but his foster father prevented it. When he grew bigger, he often thought he would like to kill someone for killing his Fa, but didn't know how, and didn't know the way to Abolgobip (the Seltaman only let him learn to know the northern part of their territory). Now, he has given up such thoughts — indeed, he was too afraid to ever really do it. He does not know the Abolgobip dialect and feels at home among the Seltaman. But he has heard that his remaining FaBr in Abolgobip pines for him; and every time his uncle cries for him, he feels it in his chest and falls ill.'

Digomsok, a Seltaman now settled in Baktaman, was only 10 years old when the boy was abducted and did not take part in the raid, but had just previously been given hospitality by the boy's father. So when the boy grew, Digomsok was good to him; he helped him through when he was being initiated.

What the nature of the relationship had become between these captives and their Seltaman hosts was in part revealed by the intervention of Nulapeŋ. Arguing from the edict of pacification, he insisted that the brother and sister be offered the option of returning to Abolgobip. A decision on this involved both their judgement of the real danger of Seltaman sanctions, and their evaluation of their present, enforced life with their father's killers compared to a free but unknown life in Abolgobip. Their indecision lasted for several months; the boy seemed to favour going 'home' while the sister was passive and I

148

think very frightened. She finally decided to go but immediately reversed her decision when the Saltaman refused to let her take her infant child with her, claiming it as theirs. The boy long insisted that he would never go without his sister, the only person in the world with whom he felt truly identified; when I left, he was however, planning a visit to Abolgobip. By cultural codifications, their identity seems to be defined by their Abolgobip birth, and basically they accepted this premise. What held them back seemed not to be the positive commitments of relationships to various Seltaman, including marriage, but fear.

The original causes of war are, at least in retrospect, generally accusations of male sorcery, even in those cases where the acknowledged consequence has been territorial expansion. Such sorcery may be compensated by a gift of pig; if this is not given, revenge is required. For people killed in war, on the other hand, no compensation is given; and there is no clear concept of exact talion, but a general see-saw of revenge and counter-revenge. This often leads to escalation: from plain killing, to killing and throwing the corpse in the river, thus destroying its soul, to cannibalism, to destruction of temples and sacra.

Thus, in Ngaromnok's childhood c. 25 years ago the Seltaman and Baktaman were friendly for a while. Then an old Baktaman man died; his relatives accused the Seltaman of sorcery but they denied it and would not compensate. The Baktaman armed themselves, came to a Seltaman garden house but found only an old and well-liked woman there; she talked them out of doing anything. When the Seltaman warriors heard about this, they became angry, and ambushed and killed a Baktaman. For this double injury, the Baktaman attacked, killed five, and ate them. From this point on, the fighting see-sawed back and forth. After a long run of defeats, the Baktaman became very frustrated and incensed. A Seltaman widow was married to a young Baktaman (the present leader of the men's house in Kamsurbaŋ hamlet). The Baktaman turned on her, killed her and ate her, though she had a young daughter by her Baktaman husband. He protested and would not take part in the meal, but her many other neighbours and companions of several years apparently did. When I expressed my surprise at this tale, a group of informants explained, as a mitigating circumstance, that the woman was quite old.

After this and other Baktaman successes, the Seltaman mounted an all-out attack on the main village and destroyed the Baktaman *Amowkam* temple.

Various phases of warfare are associated with ritual which presumably codifies significant aspects of collectivities and the nature of their joint action. The *Yolam*, and particularly the *Yolam* leader, are central for this purpose.

In preparation for premeditated attack, a *Wonsā* ritual with a blessing of the fighting arrows (cf. pp. 70 f.) is highly desirable; the marsupials *kayāŋ*, *kutēr*, and *sōb* (all of them with 'white', buff fur) are regarded as the best for such arrows. It is also best if one dries sacrificial marsupials over the holy fires and then burns the *whole* animal in sacrifice on departure. The prayers to the ancestor, addressed especially to the long bone shrine on the fire post, specifically request him to bring the enemy close so they will be easy to strike and kill with the arrows. Pork fat is sacrificed and rubbed on the ancestral long bones and mandible, which are then put in the quill netbag and carried off to war. The skull on the other hand stays in the *Yolam*, and the old men remain with it, tending fires and praying.

From this point until after the battle, four taboos are observed: you do not drink water, lest your arrows become powerless, and you do not eat marsupial, or bananas, or have intercourse, lest your smell should attract the arrows of the enemy. If more than a prowl and ambush is planned, the fighting shield is carried to battle. Normally the warriors establish a convenient base camp and sleep there before attacking; in this brush shelter the cult leader will again pray to the ancestral sacra he has brought with him. Unless unforeseen events intervene, he remains with the sacra during the fighting, and the warriors return to the base camp at its completion and tell him of their results.

If they have succeeded in killing one or more of the enemy, the result is announced on the return at a distance from the village. This announcement takes the form of a conventional song which is sung on the farthest ridge within earshot of the village; the song is supposed to be cryptic and only understood by persons who have passed 3rd degree initiation, and is taboo for others. The text in the case when a woman has been killed is:

I waneŋ-ō,	*waneŋ-ō* /	*Kowngi*
Oh woman,	woman	(place name in the mountains).

waneŋ-ō /	*waneŋ*	*gowri-ō* /	*i waneŋ-ō,*	*waneŋ-ō*
woman	woman	I-have-cut	Oh woman,	woman.

150

In the case of a man having been killed, the text is:

Towē,	*towē*	*Kerabip*	*towē*	*korgoŋ*	*dayorī*
Over there, over there from		Kerabip,		slit throat	he has died

naremarō	*tarbeko ī*		*woγō*	*abipō*	*ī-ō*
having killed we come			oh water	oh village	oh.

As messages, these songs have the simple signalling effect of mobilizing the villagers for the rite of cleansing the killer; it is interesting to note that the theme of cleansing is only cryptically suggested by the word 'water' in the second song — which in characteristic Baktaman fashion is not the actual cleansing agent used in the rite.

The men who have killed have the spirit or spirits of the dead clinging to them, and will be harmed unless they are rid of them. So as they enter the village, they pass between two lines of women carrying branches of the *bin* tree and are whipped by them, especially on the shoulders and back where the spirit tends to ride. The population then dances and drums to celebrate the victory all night; in the morning a pig is slaughtered, and the killer stands with his back up against the rising smoke from the cooking pig, again to drive away the dead spirit. Conquered property of the dead is similarly cleansed in this smoke. Arrows that have wounded or killed a man cannot be used again, but a stone adze so used can be cleansed by rubbing it with the leaves from the victory feast.

The loss of a man in battle leads to mourning. If, however, more enemy have been killed than one's own losses, the major part of the community celebrate victory and only the close relatives of the dead mourn. If one's own losses are greater than the enemy's, one sacrifices a pig at the end of mourning and, ideally, goes off promptly for revenge.

Informants are definite that there was no periodicity in fighting; periods of peace or truce were broken at any time by deceit or attack. No ritual phase of your own or of the enemy was a bar to fighting; thus in the massacre in which Nulapeŋ participated, two of the victims were wearing 4th degree initiation pandanus wigs; and killing an enemy is *always* good for your own taro, no matter what phase of taboo you may occupy. A much admired ruse used by the Aogobmins to the S.E. once was to invite visitors to a major initiation and turn it into a cannibal feast by slaughtering all the Baktaman and Seltaman vistors. Indeed, when the Baktaman invited guests to participate in 6th degree initiation in 1968, rumours spread among

151

Kasanmin and Kwermin that this was the plan then, and that my presence absolved the Baktaman from the restrictions of pacification; so all the Kwermin and some of the Kasanmin wisely refrained from coming.

As noted, cannibalism is an escalation of the war against the enemy, and is done in anger and lust for revenge. It has a public and a secret aspect. Overtly, it is a public, secular feast. The enemy killed are cut up and carried home after the battle, or captives are marched home and then killed. As with pig, only 7th degree initiates can slaughter and cook; and a pig is always cooked together with the human flesh. There are no taboos on human flesh for any category of man, woman or child; but despite the assertion of informants I do not feel certain that rules may not obtain to particular cuts, as in the case of pork. The long bones, however, must not be split for marrow, or your own bones will go bad. In telling about cannibalism, male informants mentioned the fact that female breasts and genitalia are eaten with an emphasis which suggested to my, perhaps oversensitive, ear a trace of sexual aggressiveness. In view of the disgust attached to the eating of dog's penis in 3rd degree initiation I would not think that the male organ is eaten.

The secret aspect involves sacramental eating of human flesh and pork in the *Yolam;* this is known only to 7th degree initiates. It is an exclusive ritual of the *Yolam* as a war temple: the ancestor gives you victims in response to prayers for them, and so he should receive part of the meat. A half leg of pig and an equivalent piece of human flesh are steam-cooked with the sacred cooking stones; the seniors eat it with prayers of thanks and offerings of scraps to the holy fire. Such sacraments are also supposed to be exceptionally good for the taro.

There is an apparent callousness in these practices, and in the way informants speak about them; but it is also highly relevant that many people turn out in fact to be unable to eat human flesh. Children often to their surprise and disappointment vomit when they first try eating it, and even some of the greatest warriors among the Baktaman admit somewhat shamefacedly that they are still unable to eat it, or more non-committally, do not like it. This is so despite a definite codification that such meat is ritually harmless and nutritionally 'good for you;' it is only obliquely recognized in the emphasis that human flesh always be cooked together with pork, so that all participants regardless of personal weakness and sensitivity can participate in the feasting.

The same discrepancy between private significance and cultural codification of cannibalism is suggested by a dream and its interpretation. A young man one morning reported he had dreamed that his (deceased) mother died, that he cut out her genitalia and buried them, and then cooked and ate the rest of her body. He and his listeners read this as a sign that somebody might have slaughtered a pig in a neighbouring hamlet; there did not seem to be a cultural basis for any interpretation acknowledging a special significance for the cannibalism theme.

It is important to recognize that Baktaman ideology can in no sense be characterized as warfare-oriented, despite the prominence of these activities in their pre-contact life. There is no special importance attached to bravery and none to a respect for fair play in warfare; no trophies are collected (except the enemy's fighting shields, which are adopted if conquered); no foreign heads are used for any ritual purpose; no tally of killings is kept as a sign of repute. The spirit of a man who dies in battle does not go to an especially privileged Valhalla — on the contrary, he becomes an ever restless tree spirit and his skull cannot be used in the temple. There are strong suggestions in the way informants recount wars that there is at the time of battle a considerable atmosphere of fierceness, anger, and excitement; but fear seems the more prevalent emotion associated with violence. This attitude to warfare is also very clearly revealed by the response to the mere declaration of pacification on first contact: no aggressive acts between communities have subsequently taken place. Even when telling about successful raids informants are more prone to praise the present peace than express nostalgia for the pre-contact insecurity, in contrast to their positive attitude to other pre-contact features, such as health and taro size.

Thus, the assertion of violence does not seem to be positively sanctioned. Why then its prevalence in pre-contact times? I feel that some features of the above material suggest an answer which is also consistent with conclusions in the previous three chapters. Baktaman conceptualizations of alter as human being — and indeed their knowledge of themselves — do not go very deep; their tact and attentiveness are based on practice and intuitive understanding, but are not supported by generalized propositions about man as a social and moral person. The ritual codifications connected with warfare concentrate on efficacy in killing and protection against harm to self, as for a hunting expedition, and certainly say nothing about the tragedy of premature death for the victims; and this may be true of such rituals everywhere. But the Baktaman seem to lack alternative places to turn for a more moral view. It seems undeniable that when a sizeable proportion

153

of the population cannot stomach human flesh at all, they have sensibilities which their cultural codifications give them no aids in conceptualizing and, thereby, understanding and deepening. Some of their relations do contain injunctions against violence and they seem very largely observed: the Baktaman are not just generally vicious, and where they have moral rules to hold on to, they do. I would even go so far as to suggest that many of them may feel, subjectively, these obligatory relations in a more humane way than their culture codifies them. Thus, the explicit sanction against killing a clansman is that seeing his blood is dangerous for you; whereas my understanding from some of the case stories I have been told is that their subjective feeling is much more like compassion. But there is nothing in their cultural codifications to help them articulate this attitude, much less to hold it up as a generalized moral imperative in interpersonal relations. As a result, where injunctions of this kind are *not* specified, men are easily moved and can act in a mood of dominant, unrestrained anger. Thus the warriors who went off to kill, and found a lonely Seltaman woman looking for crayfish (p. 146) were doubtless very angry over the acts that had been perpetrated against the Baktaman. As I know them, I also suspect that they were very afraid, and greatly relieved that they found only a defenceless and convenient woman on whom they could vent their wrath and wreak their legitimate vengeance. In a later chapter we shall return to the problem this view poses, of how such inadequate conceptualizations persist in a culture.

PART IV

Codes in Baktaman ritual

CHAPTER 17

Structure in non-verbal codes

In most of the preceding text I have sought to relate symbolic acts to their context in messages, designs, and situations. Thus we have been able, somewhat in the manner of a participant, to build a growing understanding of the meanings of idioms on our understanding of the contents and intent of the messages, and vice versa. In this part of the text, on the other hand, I shall focus on the communicative vehicle itself, to see what structures and patterns can be identified which are responsible for carrying and communicating these meanings. The view-point will thus be analytic, and will seek to identify the specific features which make this ritual behaviour capable of containing information.

I should like as far as possible to do this without prejudging the nature of the communicative devices. Obviously, there is no escape from working within the limitations of the idioms that I have been able to understand; but I want to leave it as open as possible for empirical discovery how they relate to each other and which systematic relations between them may entail (aspects of) their meaning. In chapter 1 I spoke provisionally of 'codes' and communication in major 'media'; we should now look carefully to see what the empirical description has brought out. Specifically, I do *not* want to assume the existence of a single, unified ritual code in which these messages are uniformly cast; and I do *not* want to assume that whatever different symbolic systems there may be are of similar basic structure and can all be designated as 'codes' in a single, strict sense. Finally, I want to be sensitive to the apparent fact that different parts of the audience to some of the messages hold apparently highly disparate keys for decoding the messages they receive. These caveats particularly constrain me from lightly applying terminology from linguistic or other rigorous schemata as frameworks or metaphors for my analysis.

Let us look first at some of the clearer idioms and how they may cluster in sub-systems. Cassowary feathers are used as a sign of 7th degree initiate status (cf. pp. 53 f., 233). They appear on the net bags worn by seniors, and in their head-dresses in conjunction with forehead bands of white fur or shell. Thus they belong in a series of signals of initiation status, the complete set of which may be represented as follows:

Degree:	1st	3rd	4th	7th
In nose	0	pig's tusk, quills of cassowary	white horn-bill feather (temporary)	cassowary feather, white fur, shell band
On head	0	0	«	«
On back	cuckoo-dove feather	eagle feather	black horn-bill feather	cassowary feather, bird-of-paradise plumes

The actual object 'cassowary feather' seems to be an idiom and to have an invariant meaning of 7th degree as indicated; but there is no basis for the simplistic assumption that all significant objects have a similarly invariant value. Thus 'soil' also has meaning in a number of contexts. As something to live in it is polluting, cf. the impurity of animals living below the ground or creeping on it, and elevation above ground is an idiom of purity. Dirtying yourself with soil is an idiom of grief; but applying it in decorative patterns on stomach and chest is a festive sign in women and children. Soil used to mould hearths for the fire is neither clean nor unclean; soil gives growth to taro and must not be polluted by semen from incest; white soil is hung in bags over the pigs' sleeping corner to bless them. Idioms are thus frequently a specific operation on things or with things, rather than the thing itself.

Such operations can be more difficult to isolate than the objects themselves; they are more inextricably a part of a larger message. Thus 'Kimebnok rubbing the ancestral long bones in the *Yolam* with pork fat, while mumbling inaudible formulae before an assembled congregation' may serve as an example. If 'rubbing . . . . . . with . . . . . .' is an idiom, we may trace it in other messages:

Rubbing	ancestral bones	with	pork fat	(white)
			pigment	(red)
			leaves	(red)
«	senior men	»	pork fat	(white)
			leaves	(red)
			dew	(rarely only)
			nettles	
			water	
«	1st degree novices	»	pork fat	(white)
			pigment	(red)
			dew	
			nettles	
«	pigs	»	white soil	

But it will remain problematical whether the stroking (of painful or damaged body parts) with stinging nettles is 'the same operation' as the others, or indeed whether the operation Kimebnok is doing is not 'smearing' and thus different from most of those mentioned. Native verbal convention is no sure guide, specifically because of the tortuous complexity of Faiwol verb patterns and the purposeful deception and secrecy incorporated in their terminology, and generally because we have no reason to presume the existence of one-to-one relations between verbal and non-verbal idioms. If we work from the understood intent in some of these constellations and inductively try it in the others, however, it seems highly plausible that the basic meaning of the operation can be identified as 'furthering increase (growth, strength)', excluding the case of seniors washing and rubbing themselves with water. If so, we *have* isolated an idiom in this class of events.

The precision of this does not seem to be increased by asking what else Kimebnok may do with the bones; pray to them, sacrifice to them, hide them, burn them. The two former seem to mean the same as rubbing (p. 69), the next is highly ambiguous (pp. 118, 120), the last not allowed. Rather, we increase our understanding by observing how the pork fat has a secret name and comes from a secretly slaughtered pig — but also how rubbing with water is specifically forbidden and 'opposite' as an operation (p. 52).

In the list of rubbing operations, I have added a colour coding which reveals a structure of underlying identities and contrasts. Thus the substances with which one rubs are white or red or colourless dew, and they are applied as follows:

	White		Red		Dew
	soil	pork fat	pigment	leaves	
Bones		X	X	X	
Seniors		X		X	X
Novices		X	X		X
Pigs	X				

In the way they are applied they thus generate a complete set of identities and distinctions between ancestors, novices, seniors, and pigs. What might the discovery of this pattern be an answer to? It hardly reveals the source of Baktaman distinctions between man, boy, pig, etc., nor does it seem to define the meanings of the idioms. I would be more inclined to see it as an artefact of the senior man's eagerness to bless the growing boys and further their growth by all possible means, while retaining most knowledge and privilege for themselves.

Implicit in some of the reasoning I have pursued immediately above is a simple use of contrast which seems to lead nowhere when attempted. Even in constructing the key for initiation signals, which clearly do have some kind of contrastive structure, we do not arrive at the meaning of cassowary feathers by replacing them, but by observing their associations. Nor can we say from the associations of the cassowary feather that it *signifies* 7th degree status, since we could not disprove a claim that it means rather *Katiam* residence (in contrast to the other residential alternatives), the right to slaughter pigs, advanced age, or other features associated with a complex of connotations around 'cassowary feather' but *not*, contrastively, around 'cuckoo-dove feather'.

Thus, though any person with competence in Baktaman culture would immediately identify initiation rank from the various feathers a group of dancers wear, I see no indication that these contrasts are in any sense the source of the feather's meaning. Nor can the meaning of cassowary feathers be derived from, though it is clearly consistent with, the features 'black' and 'feather'. Intuitively I would rather favour an argument that — unless feathers and decorations were emphatically codified as women's things — the cassowary feather is bound to be chosen as most suitable as an emblem of senior men: this enormous (it is the second largest animal known to the Baktaman), swift, elusive black jungle 'ostrich', bipedal and also in other ways unique in a fauna of animals that hide rather than run, which eats the sacred, phallic pandanus — what better image could one find? The

160

aura of connotations surrounding a cassowary feather, which makes it a good emblem for 7th degree status, seems entirely independent of any contrastive coding of other feather emblems. Similar considerations of suitability have been suggested for these other emblems as well (cf. pp. 53 f.), and can be advanced for the pig's tusks and bird-of-paradise feathers included in the set.

In other words, it seems that the meanings of the idiom derive not from contrast with the meanings of other idioms in a subsystem of 'signals of initiation status'. Rather, each idiom is employed because of its inherent aptness as a metaphor or analogue. As such, each idiom draws on a wide field of connotations, peculiar to itself and different for each idiom in the sub-set. In other words, though the emblems are used contrastively, a number of dimensions and aspects of their meanings are in no sense contrastive. It would therefore not be useful to organize the search for sources of meaning in terms of such contrasts.

When in the following I try to isolate some of the more tightly codified, clearly connected sets of symbols I therefore wish to do so without presupposing that the sources of their meanings lie in the structures I thereby depict, and without employing analytical procedures that would assume this. I shall also explore some of the looser allegories that serve to organize the conceptualizations of sectors of life and the codification of idioms. Chapter 1 sorted these idioms provisionally into objects and acts, dividing the former into public (such as emblems) and secret (e.g. sacra), and the acts into positive (rites) and forbidden (taboo). Since the operation of forbidding creates the distinction of public vs. secret, and provides a framework for much codification, it is important to clarify it first.

11

CHAPTER 18

Taboo

The Baktaman concept of *eïm* (in central Faiwol dialect *awím*) embraces prohibitions and limitations on the behaviour of persons. But the physical objects that are hedged with such prohibitions are also *eïm;* what I have referred to in the text as 'holy' or 'sacred' is described by them as *eïm;* and a man associated with the sacred, e.g. a cult leader, is himself *Kinum-eïm* (*eïm* man). The sanctions behind *eïm* prohibitions and limitations are of a supernatural or magical character; where they are specified they tend to be great and terrifying — wasting sickness, skin disease, destruction of the taro, etc.; they may also be supplemented by human sanctions, such as the supposed killing of unauthorized persons who so much as look into the *Katiam*. In this syndrome of features the concept of *eïm* seems to fall within the bounds of our anthropological concept of taboo. A distinctive feature of the Baktaman system of taboos is the prominence of prohibitions that are specific to a category of person or locality, while very few of the taboos have general application.

Thus, if we contrast those Baktaman taboos that are universal with those that are status-specific, subdividing each category with respect to duration as permanent vs. temporary, it is readily apparent that only few are truly universal and permanent, viz: the prohibitions against eating the *eiraram* marsupial, the domestic variety of rat, a nearly legless lizard and certain snakes, and things grown on the village premises. The few other things not eaten by Baktaman are not forbidden in this sense, but merely (rightly or wrongly) not thought potentially edible; the taboo foods by contrast are clearly explicitly forbidden.

The universal, collective taboos that are of a temporary nature are even fewer: garden work is forbidden subsequent to any birth or death in the Baktaman population, or a visit by anyone to the ossuary

162

cave. And all animal foods are forbidden to all Baktaman during preparation for the *Wonsā* ritual (pp. 68 ff.).

The vast majority of foods, acts, etc., are permitted for some people while forbidden to others. Such status-specific taboos of permanent character prohibit all incumbents of a status at all times from engaging in an act which is permissible to others; they may variously limit him in marrying, killing, eating, touching, seeing, or knowing (cf. the Table of food taboos, pp. 165 f.). Temporary status-specific taboos obtain for certain actors after an event (e.g. after having eaten wild pig, participated in a rite, etc.), or during an event (initiation) or a condition (menstruation, wearing red pandanus-paint, etc.), or while being in a place (temple, garden). The statuses encumbered with such constraints are, to varying degrees, all the formal statuses in the social organization: child/adult, sex, initiation grade, clanship, affinity, position as cult leader, trading partner; only close cognatic kinship statuses are relatively free of such signalling.

This association of statuses with taboos has some important correlates in the signalling of the definition of social situations among the Baktaman. We should remember that social persons everywhere are an aggregate of statuses — of alternative, organized capacities to interact in certain ways. In many other social systems, 'social situations' may be defined by actors, whereby their interaction is focused and constrained by only *one* of these capacities, i.e. they can signal that other than this one status is temporarily irrelevant. If statuses are conceptualized by actors as rights and privileges, such signalling is simple: the rights and privileges of other statuses are temporarily laid aside, made latent, by the very choice of not activating them. If, on the other hand, statuses are conceptualized and identified prominently by taboo, how can one signal that they are laid aside, are to be considered irrelevant during a particular encounter? The discontinuation of the negative act of observing a taboo can only be signalled by the positive act of breaking the taboo: capacities cannot be publicly laid aside except by being renounced. In such a system, the only way the definition of situations can be manipulated is by the addition of other, temporary or situational taboos: actors may assume temporary ritual statuses or locate themselves in spaces where certain options and limitations obtain. Thus the wife who remains in the village 'defines a situation' where the husband's sexual rights cannot be activated; the husband who eats wild male pig forestalls any demand on his labour in the gardens for a week's time; two men who meet in the *Katiam* define a situation that allows certain otherwise taboo matters to be discussed. In all other respects, taboo imposes severe constraints on the possibilities of switching in the definition of situations.

The characteristic feature of Baktaman social organization noted before (pp. 25 ff.) — the relatively unchanging social capacity of an actor from one encounter to the next, his stable identity as a whole person in most of his interaction — is consistent with this association of statuses with taboos.

Our interests in this analysis, however, go beyond the immediate social implications of a codification of statuses by taboos; we are also interested in understanding the reasons behind the pattern of taboo acts and objects. The taboos themselves may be grouped under certain headings. Some concern information: knowing, seeing, and revealing. We have seen the importance of secrecy in Baktaman ritual and in sacralizing objects and acts; taboos constitute the constraints on information flow that create this secrecy.

Other taboos seem to be concerned with preventing the act of combining certain things: pork fat and water, 1st degree novices and fire, the fire-stones for cooking cassowary with those for cooking marsupials, pigs, and man.

In relation to affines, the taboos enjoin name avoidance — most strict for WiFa and WiBr and reciprocals, but also for all members of the clan — as well as physical avoidance. When a man greets WiFa, WiMo, WiBr they shake hands by means of a stick only, and you must not sit down, much less sleep, on or by the sleeping place of WiFa or WiMo.[1]

The regulation of movement in space involves a variety of idioms and capacities: women are debarred from men's houses and temples, men are debarred from women's houses at night, and from menstrual huts; all are temporarily debarred from the whole village during 7th degree initiation. Persons who have eaten the meat of wild pig, cassowary, marsupial, snake, or fish may not enter a growing garden; after eating snake or fish a man must likewise not touch the central housepost of the *Yolam*, or the sacra within. Various temporary states during initiation likewise restrict movement in special ways, as noted in the description.

The most pervasive taboos concern eating and drinking. Extensive regulations of this during initiation have been noted; and some of the post-initiation taboos are of long duration. Permanent constraints are placed on the sharing of single items of food (a bunch of bananas; a

[1] The rule has relevance vis-à-vis this latter person only in the case of garden houses and forest camps.

single taro, sweet potato, etc.; a single game animal such as a bird, cuscus, etc., but *not* a whole pig or a man): initiated and uninitiated must not share in one such item, but each have their separate one; and a pandanus must not be shared by men of highly discrepant initiation rank. Some eating taboos are even more involute: having eaten the meat of a wild pig caught by a dog, you must not eat breadfruit for a while, lest the white milk sap of the breadfruit by way of your teeth → the pork → the dog's teeth make the dog weak like a suckling puppy.

The major food taboos, and the statuses to which they pertain, are summarized as below. The Table raises the question of why these foods are tabooed, and why the taboos are associated with statuses in the particular pattern exhibited. In isolating an underlying pattern in this, we may hope to learn about the fundamental bases for conceptualizations in terms of taboo.

Clearly, we are not dealing with a system for the monopolization of privilege: men are subject to far more dietary restrictions than

	Ch	W		M		
		123	4	5	6 7	(init. grade)
Pig: self-tended			· · · · — — — — — — —				(optional for Wi)
self-owned			— — — — — — —				
dorsal cuts			— — — — —				
ventral cuts			— — — — — — —				
wild female		— — — — — —					
wild male		— — — — — — — — —					
Dog		— — — — ?					
Nuk: categories 1		— — — — — — — — — —					
2		— — — — — — — — —					
3			— — — — — — —				
4			— — — — — · · · · · ·				(outside temple)
5		— — — — —					
6			—				
7		· · · ·					(pregnancy)
flying fox		— — — — — — — —					
fruit bat		— — — — — —					
Birds: Brush turkey		—					
Brush turkey			— — — — — · · · · · ·				(outside temple)
eggs			— — — — — · · · · · ·				(outside temple)
Cassowary		— — — — — —					
Swallow		— — —, — — — — —					
4 black/red birds		— — — — — —					

(continued next page)

165

	Ch	W		M			
		123	4	5	6 7	(init. grade)	

Lizards:
  legless lizard ————————————
  ground lizards ——————————
  water lizards, tree lizards ————————
Snakes:
  1 ground snake ——————————————
  2 black tree snake (?) ——————————
  3 *woktuŋ* water snake ···· ——————— (pregnancy)
  4 ————————
  5 *dī* snake (after initiation or Wi pregnant)

Ground frogs ——————————————
Tree frogs ——————————
Tadpoles ···· ———————— (by pers. incl.)
Fish ················· (after initiation)
Crayfish ——————————
Praying mantis ——————————
Grasshoppers ——————————
Breadfruit worms ——————
White larvae ——————
Burrowing grubs ——————
Honey ————————————
Village-grown plants ——————————————
Pandanus ················ ⎤
Pitpit ················ ⎬ (after initiation)
Leaf cabbage ················ ⎦
Certain bananas ················ (at warfare)

women and children. Senior men do enjoy the exclusive right to eat wild pig, cassowary, and honey (this latter is a weak taboo occasionally broken by the women), but this is almost balanced by the prohibitions against many marsupials, reptiles, and invertebrates. Men in the prime of life carry the greatest load of prohibitions, children the smallest.

An interpretation in terms of social and ritual value following Radcliffe-Brown (1952) has its attractions. There is no doubt that many of the species tabooed are of importance, and it is plausible that people's understanding of their importance is affected by the ritual injunctions, as in the case of wild pig (see below, pp. 201 ff.) or first fruits regulation of the taro (cf. p. 91). The collective taboos following death and childbirth in the community certainly function in this way. The Baktaman use the enforced inactivity in part as an occasion when their population size and the crisis of their survival as a people are in fact discussed. However, too many animal species are involved in food taboos for this kind of insight to serve as a very discriminating one; and the distributions of taboos on statuses, particularly the disparity between junior and senior men, are not accounted for.

In terms of ritual importance it is quite clear from the material that we are dealing with codifications that rank men in accordance with initiation step, and uninitiated women and children below the initiated, with the only slight ambiguity that arises from the woman's natural fertility and taro-giving role. I have also suggested the presence of a dominant codification of purity/pollution associated with the above/below ground dichotomy, and its elaboration as a scale of levels of elevation from the ground (cf. also Bulmer 1967). We may look for congruity between these two ranking hierachies. In general, animals that crawl on the ground are dirty, living off the ground is good, etc.; there is a tendency for less important members of the community, such as children and women, to be allowed more dirty foods, whereas the purity of men is protected. But the correspondence is only rough and does not account for the most interesting cases such as wild pig, the varieties of marsupials, brush turkey and cassowary, etc., or their allocation between men of different degrees of initiation.

Without entirely abandoning this image of physical levels of purity, Leach's stimulating reworking (Leach 1967) of taboo and categories may be exploited: instead of expressing a homogenized scale of pollution/purity, taboo may be employed as a means to create categorical discontinuties by banning or sacralizing the intermediate forms. Legless lizards and flightless birds in the list of taboo foods invite such considerations; but Leach's demonstration of how major categorizations of space and habitat are reflected in taboos (ibid, pp. 42 ff.) is particularly challenging.

The major categorical division of space for the Baktaman is beyond doubt the tripartite schema of garden-village-forest. The taboos immediately associated with each reveal a clear pattern: Entry into the *garden* is taboo to a person who has recently eaten the meat of wild pig, cassowary, marsupial, snake, or fish; if a birth, death, or visit to the ossuary has taken place; if you are menstruating; or if you are a 1st degree novice. The *village* is tabooed to menstruating women and to participants in rites during certain phases of separation;

intercourse and gardening activity are also tabooed there. Finally, the *forest* is entirely free from special taboos; anything that is allowed anywhere is allowed there, even objects and acts that normally belong inside temples.

Relatively few animal categories bridge these divisions in any obvious way. Only dog and pig are domesticated. Dogs are like men in that they sleep in the village and hunt in the forest, and they are eaten by men and not by women. Pigs sleep in the village, forage in the forest, and eat garden produce entirely like people; like people they are also eaten, but whereas people of own groups (ɔ: village, clan, trade partnership) are not eaten, only men observe the constraint of not eating pigs of their own household (owned or tended). Domestic rats, on the other hand, are wild animals misplaced in the village; they are vermin and taboo to all. Wild pigs are ambiguous in numerous ways: the consorts of domestic pigs, residents of the forest and raiders of the gardens — but they are allowed to (senior) men and taboo to juniors and women instead. Gardens being a rather limited habitat in a vast expanse of forest, relatively few other species can be characterized as particularly involved in both zones.

The divisions water/land and particularly below ground/above ground/in the air are more productive. Only water lizards, water-snakes, and in a different sense tadpoles-frogs bridge the water/land distinction; all are taboo to men but only ground frogs are taboo to all. And the water lizard, though regarded as particularly powerful and used for curing, is not treated differently from tree lizards as far as eating goes. The most frequently noted mediation which is given significance by the Baktaman is that of burrowing, especially from tree or air and into the ground. We have seen this theme in the creation myth (cf. pp. 83 f.) — yet, as noted, the cuscus of this myth is *not* taboo. And even clear parallels do not provide bases for generalization: thus swallows fly in the air and sleep under ground, and are taboo to all men; but the species of insectivorous bats that similarly fly in the air and sleep in caves are edible by all, while fruit bats which sleep in trees are taboo until 6th degree initiation.

Baktaman taboo seems to some degree amenable to several of these schemata but not adequately handled by any of them; particularly the association of numerous taboos with only some statuses is troublesome. Nor can we recognize the typical features of totemism in this: the social categories that are contrasted by taboos are unequal statuses and not homologous descent groups, and the taboos do not seem to generate any system of symmetrical, contrastive emblems.

In one specific sense, we see Radcliffe-Brown's view of taboo directly vindicated in the Baktaman material: the act of tabooing information, epitomized in the secret marsupial hunt (pp. 81 f.) creates the secrecy whereby sacred occasions and objects acquire their ritual and acknowledged social value. This seems to stand as a basic premise of Baktaman religious thought; but the multiplicity of specific applications of taboo is not derivable from this generalization, or from any of the other perspectives attempted in the previous pages, despite their partial fit. But these should have brought us to a point where we can recognize the fundamental character of Baktaman taboos as injunctions against the *association* or *combination* of things, states, and persons. Invariably, the taboo classifies two such ideas and substances as distinct and inimical in their essence: water and pork fat; cooking-stones for cassowary/pandanus and cooking-stones for pig/marsupial/man; pandanus juice on the skin and pandanus juice in the stomach; woman and sacred information; all but the cleanest of lizards and male vigour; 1st degree novices and fire; any particular status and its tabooed foods.

If so much is clear, difficulties seem to arise as one attempts to put these particular dichotomizations together in a larger scheme. Let us inspect some major dichotomies established by Baktaman taboos (below). Wild male pig is inimical to the *Yolam* temple and to children, but that does not mean that temple and children can be

Some major dichotomizations of Baktaman taboo:

Male wild pig	*Yolam* taro garden young men women children cassowary	Fish	*Yolam* taro garden infants pregnant mothers	Water	Pork growing boys perishable sacred powers
	Garden	wild pig marsupial cassowary snake fish death birth menstruation 1st degree novices drums		Village	food production intercourse menstruation 1st degree novices

associated; *Yolam* contrasts both to wild male pig and to fish, but that does not relate these two in either harmony or special relevance of any kind to each other, etc. In other words, the assertion that two ideas or substances are inimical and distinct from a third substance does not entail any statement about their relationship to each other. Taboo, although in every case of its particular application a binary idiom par excellence, is *not* used to construct a dualistic universe. Rather, I think the image that best assists our comprehension of the system is one of a chemistry of essences, or perhaps more aptly an alchemy of harmonic and inimicable principles. Taboo is used to differentiate and separate objects and acts that are supposed to affect each other adversely. We may think of it as purity and pollution, but if so in the chemical sense whereby any basic substance may be purified and the presence of any and every other substance in the mixture is then an impurity or pollution.

The Baktaman clearly express the idea that things hedged by taboo are 'strong'; taboo both protects this strength and protects potential victims *from* the strength. A system of taboos thus entails an analysis of the structure of reality in terms of implicit concepts of power and damage. It can thus be used to construct a model of the world of much greater complexity than one of dualism. There are dirtier animals and cleaner animals, and men in their higher state of ritual purity must be more careful to avoid dirty foods (such as lizards and crayfish) than women, who have not done anything to concentrate in them such ritual power. But all taboo foods are not simply dirty: light-coloured and long-furred marsupials embody power of sexuality and growth which is too strong for 1st degree novices in their present precarious phase, and so they are taboo to them — but not to adult men and women, or to small children. Likewise, certain red-and-black birds embody knowledge to which lower-degree initiates have part of the key, but which is appropriate after 6th degree only; and so taboo keeps the two apart, but need not constrain women, who know nothing, or fully initiated men, who know enough. Finally, we may note how aspects of fertility and strength are differentiated as between the *Yolam* and the *Katiam* through contrastive taboos (on drums, wild pig, types of sacra, etc.). What is generated this way is both a conceptual distinction and clarification, and an actual store of concentrated power of a certain kind. This is also consistent with the pragmatic view of taboo taken by the Baktaman that other systems are entirely acceptable and practicable in other contexts — to retain the chemical image, there are alternative processes for purification and synthesis, each with their advantages and disadvantages, and possibilities for improvement.

Taboo is thus both the basic means of creating sacrality and power, and a means of distinguishing and defining basic constituents of the world, and their various properties. If we read this code merely as a system for dichotomizing the world in a binary mode we see only a shadow of its meaning; if we recognize its use in a criss-crossing structure of dichotomies we may see how it allows the Baktaman to construct and clarify a more complex classification of reality.

CHAPTER 19

Colours

In the tricolour of red (*qais'fɨr*), black (*mitik*) and white (*buyun(in)/ dalān*) we see a code, or set of symbols, of obvious importance to the Baktaman. Some meanings associated with these colours emerged from the analysis of initiation rituals: red is clearly an idiom for descent and the ancestors, black indicates male solidarity and seniority, and white stands for food, prosperity and plenty. But it is instructive to explore this code more carefully, since it is easily identifiable and isolable, and widely applied. It can provide us with a paradigm of analysis, both of levels or components of symbolism and degrees of audience reception; and we may explore the possible sources of the various meanings.

As with the other symbols, we cannot derive the meanings of colours from simple contrast (cf. chapter 17). If we exchange the black head-dress of seniors with red feathers, as in 4th degree initiation (p. 74), they still signal 7th degree initiation rank, but are appropriate to the *Mafom* context only. But white feather head-dress would just not make sense, nor would a black forehead band. And in our exploration and analysis of meaning we are limited by the particular constellations within which the colours happen to occur and will not pose hypothetical, verbal conundrums (cf. pp. 157 ff.).

This still gives us ample material, as colour symbolism seems to permeate much of Baktaman life; but we need a methodology in the place of that of minimal contrast with which to check our interpretations. For one thing, we need to check just when colour *is* significant. Thus, in the forests around Baktaman there grows a very striking small shrub with green bifoliate leaves and a waxy, conspicuous flower cluster. The stems of this cluster are a strong, deep red. On these stems glistening black berries develop, which suddenly turn a clear white when they ripen. It should be unnecessary to itemize the numerous ways in which this plant embodies Baktaman colour symbolism — essentially, it expresses all the major interrelations and mediates the oppositions of the tricolour scheme; and my fascination with the shrub increased as my understanding of this scheme developed. The Baktaman, however, are totally uninterested in this plant, but seek out the less spectacularly orange-red *eisŋam* berries for their healing rites (p. 140), and contrive contrasting red-and-white symbols by combining fur and feathers, or by painting. The lesson is very simple. The *post hoc* explanation of the use of certain plants and animals as symbols in ritual, on the basis of some feature in them, such as colour, which strikes us as fitting, is methodologically inadequate and anthropologically banal at best. Even when such conjectures are elicited from informants they remain *post hoc* and of doubtful weight.

I have two methodological suggestions. Firstly, the *contrived* appearance of a feature in a context gives a much greater indication of significance than its prominent but inescapable presence. Thus when seniors melt pork fat with red pandanus juice and red *berber* bark juice to the accompaniment of war-cries, pour the mixture on red ochre and smear the novices all over with the resultant paint to the chant 'I paint you red!' (p. 74), then the significance of the colour is more unquestionable than when the novices turn red from being tortured with stinging nettles (p. 65). Lack of attention to this difference can only lead to false simplicity — and over-systematization — in our attempts to interpret meaning.

Secondly, symbols achieve their symbolic value or content through this contrivance, through the design and activity of persons, rather than by virtue of their natural qualities. A ubiquitous association may well be unnoteworthy or banal — the obvious need not be said, even thought it may well appear frequently in ritual messages as a signal or idiom to express something less obvious. Thus the Cross, rather than tears, has been developed as the focal Christian symbol for suffering, just as marsupial fur, rather than foliage or sexual fluids, seems to provide the focal Baktaman symbol for fertility and growth. With the aid of these simple guidelines, let us investigate Baktaman colour symbolism.

The various contrived occurrences of colour described in the previous chapters are summarized in the Tables, overleaf, showing public and secret contexts respectively. The heightened 'truth' value of the secret statements should be remembered. Is it possible to identify a core meaning, or a range of meanings, for each of these colours?

Red seems the most clearly and variously manipulated of colours, particularly in its secret ritual uses. From the variety of message con-

173

texts in which it figures we can read its core meaning. This is facilitated particularly by the separation/association rules implied by the Baktaman elaboration of taboo; but the procedure seems to provide the most generally applicable step in discovering meaning. The associations shown in the RED column of ritual uses reads almost as a dic-

Public uses of colour:

	On persons		
	Body	Neck	Head
Women	0	WHITE tusk necklace WHITE incisor necklace WHITE Job's tear necklace	0
Men	RED body paint (1st and 4th degree novices, pp. 51, 74)	WHITE tusk necklace WHITE incisor necklace WHITE tusk in nose BLACK quill in nose	WHITE shell on forehead WHITE fur on forehead WHITE feather on head (4th d., novice) RED feathers on head (4th d., seniors)

On objects:
>   RED paint on: ends of new bow
>   pig- and bird arrows
>   *Yolam* post (p. 113)
>   Spirit gate (p. 139)

>   RED, BLACK and WHITE paint on:
>   Marsupial- and man-arrows
>   shields
>   drums
>   *Amowk* temple façade.

In ceremonies:
>   WHITE earth rubbed on pigs
>   RED paint in curing ceremonies (p. 140)

In supernatural beliefs:
>   RED and BLACK skin of dead *sabkar* (p. 127)
>   RED cliff residence of *Olip* spirits (p. 129)
>   RED blood on female sorcerer's adze (p. 132)

174

Secret ritual uses of colour:

Degree	RED	BLACK	WHITE
1st	Body paint of pigment and pork fat	Salt at aggregation rite	(Taboo marsupials)
2nd	Ancestral bones painted	0	0
3rd	Stripe on skull	Dog intestine Taboo string Stones for beating	0
4th	Body paint of pigment, pandanus, *berber*, pork fat	0	0
5th	0	0	0
6th	Stripe on skull	0	Tying with shell bands Stripe on skull
7th	Stripe on skull	0	0

tionary definition: red belongs with growth and increase (ɔ: pork fat), ancestors, and maleness (pandanus). The particular relevance of maleness can be specified further: whereas the 'female' part of the wig in the 4th degree initiation is *not* painted red, women do have their foreheads painted and subsequently anointed with the blood from the pig sacrificed to the ancestors, at the curing ceremonies. Thus 'red' is separated from 'female' as a symbol of male sexuality in the 4th degree initiation (and e.g. on bows and arrows); but in its meaning of patrilineal descent women partake in it. Some interpretations of red in other contexts are also supported by the clarification of this range of meanings: the red cordylene plants outside the *Yolam*, and their unique use in the *eiraram* sacrifice, are of crucial significance in signalling ancestral presence; likewise, the redness of the *dubkon* leaves is doubtless also significant (p. 69).

None of this material equips us particularly to answer the question of the *source* of this significance for the colour red — why it has been chosen to symbolize such a set of ideas. An identification of red paint and blood has been made in the curing ceremony; blood seems in verbal contexts to be identified as the life essence; and it is specifically the blood of a clansman that one must not see shed in war (p. 146). But the theory of procreation makes the mother's (menstrual) blood the source of prenatal nourishment; and in general the associations

175

do not seem sufficiently necessary and compelling to validate an interpretation that makes 'blood' the basic referent of red, and the meanings derivative from this.

White emerges with an equally clear meaning as red for those who command the deepest secrets of Baktaman ritual and myth. It is too strong to be associated with 1st degree status, it is taro/food/plenty in the creation myth (p. 83 f.), it is the force that gives taro in the white stripe on the ancestor's forehead (p. 92). It joins the sacred marsupial and the male bow in 6th degree initiation (p. 86); it is the transformed substance of the ancestor, including its refraction in the shape of *eiraram* (p. 186 f., and Myth 2, Appendix III). Senior men who know the secrets and perform the cult may wear it on *their* forehead. So white stands in its most abstracted sense for a cosmic force of growth and prosperity, deriving from the ancestors; just as red symbolizes their effect on descendants so white symbolizes their effect on the world. On a more concrete level, white is taro, in a world where people thrive only as their taro thrives; but its presence is also apparent in other food forms, in the white of cooked pork fat and in (mother's) milk. It gives health and vigour directly, as expressed in rubbing with fat, rubbing pigs with white earth and the use of milk-like sap for curing (p. 139); it also embodies our dependence on the ancestors (cf. the breadfruit-taboo to protect hunting dogs from the weakness of such dependence, p. 165), and may carry the seeds of an attitude of humility towards the world, where red stands for aggressiveness and pride (cf. war-song, p. 146).

Again, as in the case of red, I cannot show that these meanings of necessity derive from the inherent properties of the colour white; rather, I have assumed it to be a true symbol, the meanings of which can only be understood from its contextual occurrence in this particular Baktaman code system. Surely, the Baktaman could have chosen another concrete symbol to represent this cluster of ideas, and yet successfully have communicated about it; they might have settled for *green* as their metaphor, and spun a story of association over young shoots, and foliage, and green sap — or red, and seen the fresh meat that men supply continuously to women and children as the epitome of nurturing. In pursuing the imagery of white they have likewise had to ignore the occurrence of this colour in numerous prominent contexts: the white fogs and clouds that shroud their world much of the time, the raucous cockatoos that make themselves conspicuous in the trees, the bursts of white flowers that occasionally relieve their gloomy forests. To trace the colour symbol to any particular source

176

would here, as in other historically undocumented cultures, be mere conjecture; what *can* be demonstrated is the way in which the choice of white as a vehicle for this concept facilitates a Baktaman codification of connection between staple foods, nurturing, and an abstracted power of growth, all within the context of an ancestral cult.

Black is the most difficult of the tricolour to decode. In secret ritual use it is prominent only in 3rd degree with the explicit association of male solidarity and perhaps strength (pp. 64, 67); emblematically, it clearly signals status as fully initiated senior. The rejection of white salt in favour of black at certain sacramental meals (p. 57) demonstrates the special suitability of the association of blackness and the extraordinary potency of salt. Yet these pointers do not add up to an unequivocal concept. Failing in my attempt to understand the sense of black from these contrived contexts, I fell back in the field on a search for a *source* of its basic meaning. Since black colour occurs so relatively rarely in the natural environment, this seemed a possible course. Speculating on this one day at noon, as I lay in the men's house, I suddenly focused on the colour of the familiar ceiling on which my eyes were resting — shiny black from years of smoke and tar from the fires. This indeed is the source of black in the physical sense that the pigment for black paint is scraped or soaked off the inside thatch of the men's house ceiling. It also epitomizes male solidarity and group identity: the black insides of houses encapsulate the major sodalities of men's house groups and temple congregations. Though also, to less extent, characteristic of women's houses, it provides an outstandingly suitable symbol of male unity and commitment. This is confirmed by Kimebnok's use of the explicit verbal idiom of 'blackening the *Yolam* ceiling' (p. 118) for the cult activity following the rethatching of the *Yolam* at 6th degree initiation. What we have done is thus not to find the 'source' of the meaning of black, but to modify our *a priori* distinction between the contrived and the spontaneous in agreement with the Baktaman view that the blackness of men's houses and temples is highly symbolic and significant, and a desired result of cult activity. In conclusion, it would seem that black is made the vehicle of a conceptualization of corporate solidarity, strength, and reliability, expressed by male groups in their joint cult of the ancestors.

The Baktaman tricolour, fully displayed on arrows, shields, drums, and the *Amowk* temple façade, thus embodies a not inconsiderable part of Baktaman thought about self, ancestors, and the world. But these objects do not *explicate* the full refinements of conceptualization, and actually very few Baktaman bring the necessary knowledge to

177

their reading of the colours on a shield so that they can decode the full message. What then might be the message received by most spectators?

Assuming that senior men do not break taboos and inform women of male secrets (and in view of how they lie and deceive junior novices this seems a fair assumption) the *women* will have only the public contexts summarized in the Table (p. 174) from which to develop their understanding of a colour code. From this, RED clearly emerges as the sacred colour. Apart from the occasion when ancestors and *Olip* spirits are called to cure a sick woman, red is clearly a male colour, explicitly associated with virility and sexuality. It is a quality in which a woman can take vicarious pride, as when she congratulates and is congratulated on a son's or brother's 4th degree initiation (p. 74). It would seem to be strong and secret, and not particularly associated with ancestors for her.

WHITE occurs in such a clear and consistent context of wealth objects that its connotation as 'valuable' must be the dominant one. This is adequately consistent with rubbing pigs to make them valuable, and may serve as a gloss for the value of taro and milk, though there is no verbal or unequivocal non-verbal expression known to me that would indicate such an abstraction.

BLACK is emblematic of senior male status, probably epitomized in the bisexual, secular dances when fathers and later husbands wield the black drum and carry their cassowary feather ornaments. Participation in the pride of this status may also be had when these cassowary items are deposited, as they frequently are, with the wife for safe-keeping, and hang in the inner corner of her house by her sleeping-place. This female view of black as a symbol of male exclusiveness and privilege comes close to the inside male view of black as loyalty and fraternity between males.

To the extent that little boys have any codification of colour symbolism at all, it would correspond to that of their mothers — at any rate, it is plausible that this would be the major component of the connotations which these colours might have for them. Step by step such connotations will be modified through the initiations, as discussed especially after 3rd and 4th degree initiations (pp. 66 f., 77 ff.). It is notable that these modifications, though profound, are very much in harmony with the initial meanings; they represent an increase in both applicability and precision, but not a denial of previous qualities. Thus RED remains strong and secret, associated with virility and sexuality. What is added and profoundly modifies this is the perspective of descent, of man's tie with the ancestors and his assertion of his aggressiveness and virility by virtue and with the support of the powers of patrilineal identity. WHITE continues to be wealth and value, but now linked to a mystic premise that these are blessings from the ancestors and created by ancestral cult, while the concept of value itself is abstracted to encompass staple food, nurturing, all that one receives in a relationship of dependence. Finally, BLACK becomes not just senior male status, but a symbol for the essential prerequisites of that status, such as loyalty, solidarity, and corporate activity in the jungle, in warfare, and in ancestral cult.

The major keys to these deeper understandings are first given in 2nd degree for red, 3rd degree for black, and not till 6th degree for white. But it must be remembered that the major conceptualizations, of which colour symbolism is only one vehicle, are built through a diversity of multi-code messages and surely do not emerge in as discontinuous and stepwise a fashion as this summary might suggest.

CHAPTER 20

Natural species as vehicles for communication

Natural species, particularly certain birds, mammals, and, among plants, the pandanus, figure prominently in a number of Baktaman rites. Clearly, they provide symbols for the expression of Baktaman understandings, both with regard to nature and society. How and why do these natural species become communicative devices — in what sense do they constitute a code and how are the meanings of the elements, or symbols, determined? Drawing on contemporary anthropological analyses of such materials, we may turn initially to two main possible sources of meaning. On the one hand, each separate species may have characteristic features and qualities which make it an apt metaphor for an idea or abstract thought (cf. e.g. Turner 1961). On the other hand, the relations between species in a taxonomic structure may be regarded as isomorphic with the relations between other categories or conceptions, and thus may provide a vehicle for their expression (cf. e.g. Levi-Strauss 1963).

For an examination of the role of these alternative sources of meaning, the taxonomic class of *nuk*, comprising roughly 'furred animals', offers a convenient field. The Baktaman recognize no less than 37 distinct kinds of *nuk*, of varying ritual significance. Besides the elaborate system of food taboos *nuk* are also differentiated in their uses in sacramental meals, and in the special association of some of them with taro, fire, childbirth, etc.

The category *nuk* embraces nearly all mammals known to the Baktaman, i.e. all except man, pig, dog, and bats — and thus includes all varieties of marsupials and rodents. My list of 37 kinds is derived from a range of habitats from sago swamps as low as 500 m altitude to cloud forests above 2000 m. I have not been able to do a systematic ethno-zoological study of this fauna but have had the opportunity to observe the commoner species while hunting and eating them together with the Baktaman. Thus all my identifications must remain tentative and some will doubtless prove to be quite wrong; the material is reliable with regard to Baktaman categories, not their suggested zoological equivalences. Yet, the material is adequate to show certain features of the system.

The zoological status of these 37 folk taxa seems quite firm; though there was considerable variation between persons as to their command of folk zoology there was never doubt about the identification of a dead intact specimen as a member of only one taxon, and such attribution was consistent as between persons and over time. However, some of the taxa distinguished may be colour variants only, and may be even male vs. female of sexually dimorphic species — though sex distinctions in most taxa are usually expressed by suffixes.

As in practically all Baktaman classifications, there are no explicit intermediate taxa. There was, however, ready willingness to group them in categories according to habitat, colour, or use, when discussing them. Spontaneous explanations would also be given: '*Kayār* — you know, the long-nosed *nuk* that lives in tall grass.'

Some taxa have alternative names, and some — but not all — of the ritually most important ones have secret names that are used in certain ritual contexts (cf. Table, p. 183). These names are simply alternative labels for the same categories; the only exception is the bandicoot *kayūk* which is also known as *sanōk*, the proper term for domestic rat. Baktaman distinguish these two senses of the word *sanōk* and will if necessary specify for precision which sense they are intending.

The Chart overleaf groups the 37 kinds of *nuk* by probable zoological category, and by major habitat (on the ground vs. in the trees). Every one of these kinds has symbolic association with one or more social categories of Baktaman, and one or more fields of their daily activity.

The most comprehensive mode of association between *nuk* and human categories is by secular food taboos, as indicated on the chart. Only two species are categorically forbidden to all Baktaman: *sanōk* (*Rattus sp.*), and *eiraram* (marsupial mouse = *Phascolosorex sp?*). Most people regard these two with equal revulsion; they are unwilling to touch them and repelled by the idea of eating them; only men who have passed 5th degree initiation (cf. p. 81) — in 1968, 52 persons of the total 183 — have the view that they are forbidden for opposite reasons: rats because they are unclean, marsupial mice because they are the prerogative of the *Yolam* ancestor (cf. p. 69).

A group of forms composed of gliders, all ground-dwelling rodents

Chart: The kinds of *nuk* (ɔ: furry mammals)

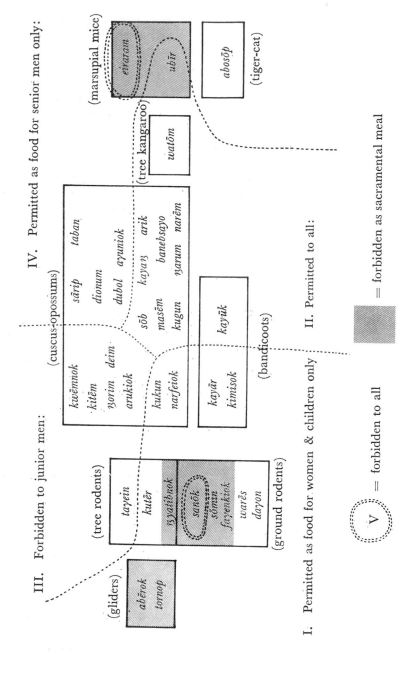

III.   Forbidden to junior men:

IV.   Permitted as food for senior men only:

(tree rodents)

| *taɣein* |
| *kutēr* |
| *ʒɣatibnok* |
| *sarōk* |
| *sōmn* |
| *fiɣenkiok* |
| *warēs* |
| *daɣon* |

(ground rodents)

(gliders)

| *abērok* |
| *tornop* |

(cuscus-opossums)

kwēmnok	*sārip*	*taban*
kitēm	*dionum*	
ʒɣorim *deim*	*dubol*	*aɣuniok*
arukiok	*sōb*	*kaɣaʒ* *arik*
kukun	*masēm*	*banebsaɣo*
narfeiok	*kugun*	*ʒɣarum* *narēm*

| *kayār* | *kayūk* |
| *kimisok* | |

(bandicoots)

(tree kangaroo)

| *watōm* |

(marsupial mice)

| *eivaran* |
| *ubir* |

| *abosōp* |

(tiger-cat)

I.   Permitted as food for women & children only:

II.   Permitted to all:

V = forbidden to all

= forbidden as sacramental meal

182

Marsupials with secret names, and alternative names

Profane names	Secret name	Probable indentification
Eiraram/babianim . . .	*Burusyayai*.	Marsupial mouse
Kayaŋ	*Wirmitin*	Brush-tailed opossum
Kwēmnok	*Awārek*	*Pseudocheirus sp.?* (large ring-tailed opossum)
Sōb	*Eitemkāyak*	*Phalanger sp.?*
Kitēm/tifōl		*Pseudocheirus sp.?* (smaller ring-tailed opossum)
Kayūk/sanōk		Bandicoot

Associated with pregnancy taboo:
Kayār   (bandicoot)

Taboo to both parents after a birth:
Deim   (light coloured long-tailed medium-sized cuscus)
Arik   (light and mottled, long-tailed, medium-sized cuscus)
Sārip   (white, spotted, large, flat-faced cuscus)
Watom   (tree kangaroo, *Dendrolagus sp.*)

Especially used for pre-battle ritual:
Kayaŋ   (brush-tailed opossum)
Kutēr   (tree rat)
Sōb   (*Phalanger sp.*)

Especially used for taro ritual:
Kitēm   (smaller ring-tailed opossum)

Associated with origin myth:
Kwēmnok   (large ring-tailed opossum)

Forbidden except as ancestral sacrifices:
Eiraram   (marsupial mouse)

Associated with fire-making:
Ubir   (pandanus-dwelling marsupial mouse)

and most tree-dwelling ones, most bandicoots, *kugun* (a small opossum) and *narfeiok* (striped phalanger?) are regarded as somewhat impure and so allowed as food for women and small children only; in the case of *narfeiok* the prohibition is also relaxed for old men.

Eight of the twenty kinds of cuscus-opossum (*Phalangeridae*) are allowed as food for all persons, as are tree kangaroos, one of the

183

bandicoots, and *ubir* — a marsupial mouse very similar to the forbidden *eiraram*. A special category is composed of forms forbidden to
lower grade initiates, but allowed to all others; these include *tayein*
(an arboreal mouse) because of its smell, and five of the cuscus-
opossum group because of their light colour or long fur — all features
harmful to male growth. Finally, six forms are allowed to senior
initiates only: the fierce tiger-cat (*Satanellus sp.*) and five cuscus-
opossums, all of them large and white-buff or orange-red in colour.

Some special food taboos are also observed, depending on the person's condition, cf. the Table: one of the bandicoots is forbidden to
pregnant mothers, while three cuscuses and the tree kangaroo are
forbidden to both parents after the birth of a child, lest the animal
spirits attack and kill the baby.

One may thus see social categories expressed in categorical food
taboos, but the system has considerable complexity and lacks the didac-
tic clarity of totemism. Thus the contrastive character of the animal
symbols is unclear — they are not dichotomized emblems as in totemism (cf. e.g. Radcliffe-Brown 1962), but themselves compound
categories of species. Furthermore, the social categories with which
they are isomorphic are not descent groups in which membership
status is permanent, but — in the case of men — the changing membership groups of age and initiation grade. Indeed, the knowledge of the
total system of taboos is very imperfectly distributed in the population,
so that many persons are in doubt about the permissions and prohibitions that pertain to themselves and ignorant or misinformed
about those pertaining to other categories than their own. This is
hardly surprising. The chart, p. 182, indicates by roman numerals the
five main subclasses of *nuk* that are generated by secular food taboos.
These classes, however, are unnamed and remain only implicit taxa;
nor are they distinguished by the eating/avoidance behaviour of any
one status category. Note, as in the accompanying diagram, the dichotomies that persons must learn to make with changing status through life:

Social status:	woman; child	1st degree initiate	middle grades	senior grades
Permitted	I, II, III	II	II, III	II, III, IV
Forbidden	IV, V	I, III, IV, V	I. IV, V	I, V

Women and small children operate only with two classes: I + II +
III vs. IV + V. First degree novices add the distinction of II vs.
I + III; in middle initiation grades only does the distinction I vs. III

184

become relevant, while only senior initiates have run through the permutations of food taboos that generate the full set of implicit taxa. No wonder then that only these senior men have an adequate knowledge of the whole system of dietary restrictions.

Though social categories and natural taxa thus in a sense prove to be isomorphic, the natural taxa can hardly be experienced by a groping Baktaman mind as 'good to think' (cf. Lèvi-Strauss 1964 p. 89) but rather as a highly mysterious vehicle for thought.

By the time a man is initiated to 5th degree, however, a new dimension of meaning and complexity is added to *nuk* symbolism. Through participation in the secret hunt to provide ritual offerings in the temples, he learns that many 'forbidden' animals, even in category I, are indeed edible and suitable for sacramental commensality. On a deeper level of mystical truth, a new tripartite division of *nuk* thus emerges, as indicated by stippling on the chart: a) gliders and four of the rodents, which are ritually unclean and cannot be used in cult; b) most species of *nuk*, which, when secretly hunted, become ritually pure foods appropriate for sacramental meals; and c) the *eiraram* marsupial mouse which is food for the ancestor only (I return to the other species, *ubir*, shortly).

Within the main category b), however, the different species are in no sense equivalent (cf. Table p. 183). The most important special significances relate certain species to warfare, and others to taro fertility. In connection with premeditated attack and warfare a preparatory *Wonsā* rite is held (cf. p. 150) in which *kayaŋ* (brush-tailed opossum), *sōb* (*Phalanger sp.*) or *kutēr* (tree rat) are preferred. The idiom here is simple and explicit: all three species are observed by the Baktaman to be particularly fierce and brave when attacked, and so are especially suited for warfare. In the case of taro ritual, as we have seen (p. 94) *kitēm* (a small ring-tailed opossum) is explicitly preferred, though *kwēmnok* (large ring-tailed opossum) figures in the central creation myth (Myth 1, pp. 83 f.). Both species are similar in having long, rich fur — a feature which is symbolically important (cf. p. 90), but which they share with several other species of the *Phalangeridae*.

The criteria by which Baktaman understand *kitēm* to be particularly powerful in taro ritual are thus not immediately apparent. To obtain a better basis for recognizing them, however, we need to consider the implications of secrecy in Baktaman epistemology (cf. chapter 24) and the effects of this on the use and substitution of symbols. In a number of features of ritual performance it seems undeniable that officiators must be seeking to create an oracular or cryptic effect: the transmission of messages is linked with strong meta-messages of wisdom unrevealed and the incompleteness of the recipients' understanding and knowledge. Such secrecy may be seen to *create* the truth value of information. It is also justified by the theory of the danger, noted in the discussion of taboo (p. 170), that premature revelations are *harmful* to the recipient, who should be protected from them — as in the case of growing males and the marsupials of category III. Purposive deception is also practised, as noted in connection with initiations. From these considerations, I venture to suggest as a general principle applicable in a number of cases, that central symbols will tend to be replaced by other, more cryptic, symbols. In the particular case under discussion, I will argue that *kitēm* is directly substituting for *kwēmnok* with a number of recognizable effects on the messages communicated. *Kwēmnok* is the animal in the creation myth; it has the secret name 'Ancestor'; its life is patterned as the inverse of man and his taro, in that it sleeps under ground and feeds in the trees; its strong front paws lock at death in the grasping gesture of 'holding back the taro' which accompanies the telling of the origin myth, etc.; yet the otherwise similar *kitēm* is celebrated in the rites, e.g. in 6th degree initiation. Note the way in which the *kitēm* appears in this rite: after first being identified with 'white' and 'valuable' for the novices (p. 86), it is then exposed to a larger audience with only its hairless, scaly tail showing (pp. 86, 87), until finally it is used in the secret fur-burning climax (p. 90). By showing the naked tail, the fur becomes secret and significant, and to the initiates who know, the naked tail symbolizes fur which by a second burning in the gardens becomes or 'is' taro. But if further knowledge, e.g. of the myth, suggests to the most senior men that *kitēm* is *not* the true referent of the rite, if it really symbolizes *kwēmnok*, then *kwēmnok* likewise becomes or 'is' Ancestor, as its secret name suggests. The meaning, by being veiled through this substitution, becomes richer and truth comes closer to the few who know; the deeper mystery can be apprehended by virtue of the secrecy and symbolism that protects it. Under cover of this multiple secrecy, *kwēmnok* may also be allowed to permeate more of everyday life with its hidden connotation: all except the particularly vulnerable young novices may eat it, fathers may fix its curled tail as a life-long decoration in the ear-lobes of their children, etc.

A recognition of this principle of substitution helps increase our understanding also of the symbolic significance of the closely similar marsupial mice *eiraram* and *ubir*. It is the latter form which lives in the sacred pandanus trees; it raises its litter in a nest of shredded pandanus leaves indistinguishable from everyday tinder; it is secretly invoked in fire-making. The ritual value and significance of fire are attested in numerous ways: it is taboo to 1st degree novices; it is used in the torture of 3rd degree novices; it is implicitly equated with ancestral skulls and female genitalia in sorcery; and most pervasively, it is the vehicle of communication — through burning and smoke — between the tangible world and the supernatural. Yet it is not *ubir*, but *eiraram*, which is equated with the substance of the ancestor in Myth 2 and identified with him in the *Wonsā* rite. *Ubir*, on the other hand, is allowed as profane food to all Baktaman, though *not* allowed, as far as I could ascertain, in secret sacramental meals. If *eiraram* is seen as the symbolic substitute of *ubir*, and thus a symbolic representation of the power of fire and fertility, its otherwise inexplicable selection as the supreme sacrificial animal becomes understandable. But the imagery involved here is far from clear to me.

There is thus little doubt that the various kinds of *nuk* serve the Baktaman as concrete vehicles for abstract thought; but the concepts and thoughts they embody concern qualities and processes of purity/ pollution, aggressiveness, and, most important, fertility and growth — and not primarily social groups, as would be the case in totemic cult.

The same can be said about the ritually important birds. We have seen how a set of bird species provides emblems for distinctive initiation grades (cf. p. 53 f.). This set is significant, not so much because it is isomorphic with the set of initiation statuses, as because each particular bird species expresses a quality or property particularly apposite to the initiation grade it symbolizes.

Two bird species only stand out as highly significant for cult purposes: the cassowary (p. 110) and the brush turkey (p. 115). These are clearly selected for properties which make them apt symbols in allegories of fertility, agriculture, etc. The brush turkey (and other species of *Megapodes*) provides particularly striking imagery, as will be summarized later.

But the most pervasive imagery — intertwined with that of the cassowary — is developed around the pandanus or screw-palm. The ethnobotany of this group would be a demanding anthropological topic, and is still to be done. A variety of species are recognized by the Baktaman under the higher-order taxon *eim* = pandanus. As in the case of marsupials, our understanding of pandanus symbolism will be facilitated if we recognize the principle of substitution of one species for another similar species in the central mysteries.

The most valued pandanus among the Baktaman is clearly the one that develops a scarlet red fruit or cob, up to 3 feet in length and with a pleasant, tangy flavour. Such red pandanus trees are carefully claimed and harvested, and their fruits cooked and eaten. Cooking is hedged by taboos and conventions: the fruit is carefully hollowed out with special gouges made of cassowary femurs; they are cooked with cooking-stones used for cassowary, not those used for pig and marsupial; and any one fruit is shared only between men of identical or very close initiation rank, not freely between men and not at all between the sexes. The association with the cassowary is an empirical as well as a ritual one: cassowaries seek out pandanus fruits, particularly of the smaller *mund-eim* variety, as eagerly as man seeks the big pandanus, and are caught in snares at the base of such trees. The red pandanus is thus clearly associated with cassowary, and thus with fully initiated male status.

I have occasionally alluded to the phallus-like shape of these pandanus fruits. This similarity in shape is clearly a premise for Baktaman symbolism. Thus, the penis gourd that covers the male organ of every man is attached by means of a small circular band (*eimfarēt*) at its base. This band is plaited, in complex design, by each man for himself, and made of fibres from pandanus leaves. Indeed, these fibres are drawn specifically from the leaves that cover the developing pandanus fruit; thus the identification penis = red pandanus fruit is quite explicit. This imagery is also extended, in that a similar circular band, of the same fibres, occurs in only one other context: on all arrows, to attach the arrowhead to the shaft. The identity of arrow and male organ is thus expressed through the medium of the red pandanus.

The red colour of the fruit is also celebrated in song, and its sacred character utilized and made explicit in rite, viz.: its use in colouring the 4th degree novices. The association of pandanus with fertility is made most explicit during that initiation through the complex use of pandanus leaves in the artificial wig worn by participants (cf. pp. 72 ff.). The associations with sexuality, with hair as a symbol of fertility and growth, and with puberty and male maturity, are unequivocally indicated in these rites, and entirely consistent with the other connotations of pandanus. Characteristically, however, the red pandanus is replaced in this rite by another species of pandanus, called *ein* or *sēr*, as far as the visible and identifiable leaf material is concerned — while the red pandanus is used in the sacred ointment, the components of which are known only to senior initiates.

188

Thus again, the principle of symbolic substitution is used to augment the secrecy and mystery of the rite.

The further association of pandanus with fire, both technically and ritually, was indicated in connection with the brief discussion of fire-making and *ubir* marsupial, above (pp. 32, 186 f.).

Finally, pandanus is ritually associated with sacra and the ancestors in the consistent use of pandanus leaves to wrap sacra and contain ancestral shrines. This is true in both *Yolam* and *Katiam*, in men's houses where any such shrines occur, in the construction of sacred gates, and in *Amowk* rituals in the gardens.

I suspect that further material would have revealed even further permutations of pandanus symbolism; but these major facets should suffice to show the pervasiveness of connotations and imagery developed around this plant. By a number of contrivances, Baktaman associate it with the cassowary, 7th degree initiation, penis, arrow, sacred red colour, hair, fertility, fire, and the ancestors. As in the case of the other natural species, of mammals and birds, pandanus is used in these various contexts as a concrete symbol for qualities and processes given ritual attention in their mysteries.

A variety of natural species thus serve the Baktaman as communicative devices, in that they are systematically vested with certain meanings. It is hardly meaningful, however, to speak of sets of such species as 'codes'. They are not reciprocally arranged in structures which are isomorphic with social arrangements or other features of reality; rather, they enter individually into larger ritual contexts or messages, each of them as a separate, more or less dense symbol carrying an aura of connotations. It is also relevant to our analysis that the participants and audiences in the rites in which such symbols occur come to the occasions with very different knowledge and premisses, and thus must derive dissimilar, and in part rather reduced, understandings from the events. Indeed, the messages are often made increasingly cryptic in the service of mystery by the veiling of insight behind layers of symbol substitution.

Among the sources of meaning that invest these species with significant connotations we may frequently recognize some of their natural features: remarkable shapes, observed habits, etc. Other natural features obtain significance only in terms of some arbitrary or highly derivative Baktaman premisses, such as fur = growth and fertility, or white = taro and plenty. But even given these principles, the relevance and meaning of such symbols cannot, to my understanding, be derived deductively from their natural features. A highly

189

significant, and often dominant, source of meaning seems to be the very operations which the Baktaman perform on these symbols in their rites: through such contrivances associations and identifications are created which constitute a tradition of knowledge and understanding in which the symbolic values of these concrete objects are largely generated. It is through our attention to these operations, and the allegories which they may exploit and develop, that we may deepen our understanding of Baktaman communication.

CHAPTER 21

Sacrifice and commensality

The focal operation in every Baktaman ritual is a sacrifice. Its crucial importance is most directly illustrated by the injunction, explicitly stated by Kimebnok and others, that one must never under any circumstances enter a temple in which the fires have gone cold without presenting the ancestors with a substantial food offering. Through such a sacrifice, and only through it, does one establish communication with the ancestors; only by the goodwill that the offering creates can one elicit the benefits which these ancestors control; finally, only such an offering can provide the food for sacramental commensality between congregation and ancestors.

The classical anthropological question which has been asked of such material has been whether sacrifice 'is' gift exchange with the deity, expiation, communion, or a host of other things (cf. Evans-Pritchard 1956, pp. 272 ff. for a summary of such alternatives). Our interest here is rather to look in detail for evidence of the conceptions and knowledge which are communicated between officiators and participants through the acts of sacrifice which Baktaman perform in their rites. The meaning of sacrifice must be what it teaches participants about reality. It follows from this that we are not so much interested in exploring the verbal concepts associated with the act as the actual understandings contained in the non-verbal messages structured as sacrifices, Likewise, the category of actions which I propose to view under a single perspective as 'Baktaman sacrifices' is not primarily established and justified by the existence of a single Faiwol gloss, as much as by the non-verbal conceptual unity which I can descriptively establish for the operation.

The ritual operation of presenting an animal or a part of an animal to the ancestors, and then immolating it or sharing it with them, takes a variety of forms. These have been described in context in previous chapters; they may be summarized under the following headings.

Curing ceremonies (pp. 139—141) are the most common form of blood sacrifices, in which a domestic pig is ritually killed, the sick person is anointed with its blood, spells are said and prayers directed to the ancestors, and finally the meat of the victim is distributed to the community while some pieces are discreetly taken as offerings to the clan ancestors.

Initiations (cf. e.g. 6th degree, pp. 84—90) also always involve blood sacrifices of pig, except that of 5th degree. Some of these pigs are slaughtered publicly, some secretly; both pork fat and meat are presented to the ancestors and shared among various circles of the congregation. The presentation of fat and meat to the ancestors is accompanied by prayers.

Eiraram (cf. pp. 68–70) is sacrificed to the *Yolam* ancestor whenever it is killed in a secret hunt. The whole animal is cooked in sacred leaves, presented to the ancestor, and later burned. Both presentation and burning are accompanied by prayers.

Special rituals also occur (e.g in 6th degree initiation, cf. pp. 84 ff., 90 ff.; in warfare, cf. p. 150) when other marsupials, killed in secret hunt, are offered *in toto* to the ancestors. For this purpose, the whole animal is dried over the sacred fire and then burned, either in small pieces or all at once. These offerings are also accompanied by prayers. In the climax of 6th degree initiation, the *kitēm* marsupial in question is beaten with a stick, presumably symbolizing killing, before the ancestral bones while prayers are said (p. 89).

Marsupial sacraments (cf. e.g. p. 80) are the normal sequel to secret hunts; in these, the animals killed are consumed in a joint meal in the *Katiam* or *Yolam*. All parts of the animal are either eaten by the ritually competent congregation or burned as offerings to the ancestors — the latter thus receive all the bones and other inedible parts, as well as scraps of meat. Each participant gives his offerings separately to the ancestral bones and the fire, accompanying them with prayers. This is the most frequently recurring form of offering.

Human sacrifice (cf. pp. 116, 152) took place in conjunction with cannibalism, when cuts of human flesh were brought into the *Yolam* and shared between senior initiates and the ancestors. The presentation of bits of this flesh, and its burning, were accompanied by prayers for success in war, and taro fertility.

All wild pigs and cassowaries felled also automatically should lead to sacrifices: as in the case of secretly hunted marsupials, all bones

192

and scraps should properly be given to the clan ancestors in the *Katiam*. Some hunters are very meticulous about this and carry quantities of bones from distant hunting camps home to the *Katiam* to burn for the ancestors, while others are quite careless. Such bone offerings are accompanied by prayers for hunting luck.

Minor sacrifices of pork fat may also be arranged, both in the temples (e.g. pp. 88, 89) or in the forest (e.g. in fishing, p. 41). In the latter case, a separate fire is lighted and a small ancestral bone, such as are carried in tiny net pouches around the neck, is constituted as an impromptu shrine; prayers are directed to this ancestor and the fat burned on the fire.

The most outstanding common feature of all these forms is the invariable association of sacrifice and prayer: no prayer is ever said except in conjunction with an offering, and no offering is ever un-accompanied by prayer. A number of other features are also stereotypically present: the ancestors' share of a sacrifice is invari-ably delivered to a concrete relic; and its burning, rather than kill-ing, the significant act of immolation. In nearly all cases, sacrifice implies a sacramental meal, hedged with taboos so that the *whole* victim is consumed by congregation (who eat) and ancestors (for whom it is burned) and by them alone. The only exceptions are those particular sacrifices which *only* the ancestors consume, and the flesh of man and domestic pig, where each cut, rather than the whole indi-vidual, is regarded as the relevant unit for ritual purposes.

If Baktaman regard sacrifice as *the* means to communicate with the ancestors, what ideas do they have about the character and mechan-ism of this communicative medium? Do they conceptualize this question, and do they answer it with Evans-Pritchard that they are giving a part of themselves to the deity (op.cit. p. 279), with Robertson-Smith that they are partaking in the substance of the deity (Robertson-Smith 1927), or with Mauss that the victim is an intermediary (Hubert and Mauss 1964)? Let us investigate what the detailed operations imply of identifications between man, victim, and the ancestors.

In the case of pig sacrifices, the identification and substitution of pig for man seems explicit and basic to the operation. This is most insistently expressed in the curing ceremony: the red ochre line on the patient's forehead is repainted with the victim's blood, which is also spattered on his head and shoulders; contact is main-tained between man and beast through the rope which the patient holds; finally, the flesh of the sacrifice is distributed to all those people who, according to sorcery belief, may be yearning for the flesh of the man. In the case of pig sacrifices at initiation, the requirement that some of the pigs must be of one's own stock (e.g. 6th grade) suggests the same idea, especially seen in connection with Baktaman notions of the special relation between owner and pig expressed in their rules against consuming one's own animals.

In the case of marsupial offerings, on the other hand, there is no evidence supporting such identification of man and victim. On the contrary, the possession of an offering depends on luck in hunting and thus, at least in part, on the goodwill of the ancestors. Once when a group of men were out on a secret hunt for marsupial sacrament, they broke off their hunt prematurely and returned to the village because they saw no game and realized that something was wrong. Indeed, the infant son of one of the group had died in the interval, creating or implying a ritual state in which the ancestors 'would not release the game'. On another occasion, the lack of success was attributed to the cult leader's inadequate attentiveness to the ancestral skull while the hunt was in progress (p. 120).

Marsupials are thus in the Baktaman view controlled by the ancestors, though they are not as explicit as some New Guinea people, who identify marsupials specifically as 'the ancestors' pigs' (Rappaport 1967:40). None the less, the identity of substance between marsupial and ancestor is strongly implied, as in the secret name 'Ancestor' for the *kwēmnok* cuscus, and the identification in Myth 2 of the *eiraram* marsupial mouse and the ancestor's tooth.

We thus see two rather divergent identifications of the victim in sacrifice: as a substitute for man in the case of pig sacrifice, as partaking in the substance of the ancestors in the case of marsupials. Do these discrepant identifications entail a clear contrast between the two operations that are here subsumed under the common label of 'sacrifice'?

One might argue that the contrast is in part an artefact of the difference between domestic and wild animals: pigs, after all, live in the village and are controlled by their owners whereas wild animals can only be hunted — so the slaughter of the former has an aspect of surrendering part of oneself which the killing of wild animals cannot have. But such an argument might also be read to indicate that the contrast is indeed fundamental, and parallels the Domestic : Wild :: Culture : Nature dichotomizations claimed for pig and marsupial symbolism in areas of the Highlands (cf. Strathern 1968).

To my understanding, however, there is little to indicate that

Domestic vs. Wild, or indeed Culture vs. Nature, are basic constituting dichotomies in Baktaman cognition. The Baktaman division of space is fundamentally tripartite into village, garden, and forest (cf. pp. 20, 167), and as between the three, Man and Culture are not clearly anchored in any one. Foods of a variety of kinds are harvested both in forest and garden, whereas plants grown in the village cannot be consumed. Menstrual pollution is destructive to village and garden, but harmless in the forest; while men who are in a special ritual state, e.g. from eating cassowary, may move freely in village and forest, but may not enter the gardens. Persons may reside in any of the three zones; but their refuge when threatened by disease, or when death draws near, is by preference the forest. Nor indeed are pigs so clearly identified as 'domestic' and 'cultural': they forage and move freely in the forest, more than one in three were caught as wild piglets, and all of them were fathered by wild boars.

My understanding of the relationship of the Faiwolmin to their natural environment was affected before the beginning of proper fieldwork by an incident which residence and participation with the Baktaman only served to extend and confirm. Accompanying an annual patrol, I saw the Patrol Officer recruit volunteers from a group only once previously contacted to accompany him to Olsobip Patrol Station, to cement relations with the group. From their point of view, this would be a journey that took them far beyond the limits of the known world. The 3–4 men who dared to go stood in readiness in the grey of dawn as the patrol prepared itself for departure. They carried *no* luggage with them on this momentous journey through forests and over mountains and rivers into the unknown, no tools and — with their understanding and trust in pacification — no weapons; they had, however, removed all body ornaments so as not to provoke spirits by self-pride. In this condition, they had full confidence in their ability to cope with the physical environment, and in due course return to their home unaided. 'Culture' does not provide a distinctive set of objects with which one manipulates 'Nature' — one is prepared to be one with an environment in which all places, species, and processes are understood as being basically of one unitary kind, agreeable to man.

I therefore fail to see evidence of a pattern that would make of pigs vs. marsupials an expression of a fundamental dichotomy of domestic vs. wild, and thus appropriate victims in conceptually contrasting operations in relation to ancestors. Indeed, since I have argued that the essential act of immolation in Baktaman sacrifice is the burning of the food offering, rather than the taking of life, the two variants of the operation are even more alike in their essentials. In this perspective, seeing the victim as part of man or as part of the deity are merely two alternative renderings of the basic feature of Baktaman sacrifice, which is to make the *presence* of ancestors in a relationship to man concrete through the consummation of a concrete interaction — viz.: that something passes between them.

That this primitive (in the sense of radical, non-derivative) concept of sacrifice should appear with varying interpretative superstructures is hardly surprising; the very existence of them as contradictory depends on the codification of a distinction which need not have been clarified in this particular tradition of knowledge. Indeed, Baktaman make a variety of statements of different content about sacrifice without apparently regarding them as contradictory; rather, they would seem to be partial and supplementary within an undifferentiated, embracing viewpoint. Thus, when Ngaromnok scoffed at the idea of being an ancestor because there can be no joy in receiving only bones and smoke (cf. p. 111), he clearly felt he was being blasphemous, but also that he was arguing within a true framework of premises. Likewise, Kimebnok could without difficulty sometimes entertain the view that the ancestor was being ungrateful and blameworthy in not doing *his* part (cf. p. 120) — thus adopting a simple exchange model for the relationship consummated through sacrifice. Yet at other times he was clearly moved by the awesome experience of ancestral presence, and the mystery of communion and fertility which the sacrificial rites generated. These are not contradictory views because they have not yet been conceptually differentiated; Baktaman rituals cannot be understood unless they are seen as attempts to grapple with elusive conceptions, rather than as completed and tidy cognitive schemata.

The communion of commensality seems to constitute an integral aspect of Baktaman sacrifice, in that it is almost invariably part of it, and in that it provides imagery for the same basic idea of ancestral presence as contained in prayer and immolation. To recognize the true import of this imagery, it is essential to construct a correct context for connotations of the constituent acts.

The basic act of sharing food among the Baktaman occurs in an everyday context of institutions and conventions which renders it rather different from what we might otherwise assume. The household in the sense of the maritally based unit of coordinated production is *not* a commensal unit, and the everyday commensal group is *not* a

196

kinship group. We have noted the variety of dietary restrictions and opportunities which tends to make every individual's daily menu separate and unique (cf. pp. 165 f.), also the residential dispersal of the household/elementary family unit (p. 20). Add to this the rather haphazard and individual character of cooking and eating that follows from technology. There is no *table* around which to practise commensality, nor is there any pot in which to prepare a joint meal. The focus of eating is a continually functioning fire, in which tubers of various sizes are individually baked. The two degrees of fellowship in this operation are (i) the joint fire and (ii) the ready-baked item of food. The developmental prototype of sharing in a person's experience will be primarily the mother breaking off a piece of her ready-baked taro to give to her child, and secondly the group of kin and non-kin persons of similar ritual status who share one fire. For males — who are the ones who codify the idioms of ritual — this is followed by other similarly constituted membership groups based on personal selection within a category of ritual equals (e.g. young boys, men's house groups, hunting parties, gardening mates).

Codified ideas about sorcery provide an immensely significant addition to these sources of connotations. I have noted the power for evil which a person attains if he can obtain a fragment of food from another person's unfinished meal (cf. p. 131). The obverse of this is seen in the meticulous care which persons expend on keeping track of crumbs, finishing up a portion, burning peelings and scraps, etc.

In this situation, then, the sharing of food becomes a powerful idiom for equality and trust. Those who eat together are of one sort, ritually; and those who share food literally place their life and fate in each others' hands. There is no imagery here evoking the holy family or quasi-kinship identity; there is a strong and clear imagery expressing unity and mutual trust between members of a sodality.

The variants of commensality practised in the various sacrificial rites express different aspects of such a unity. (i) When an item of food is shared between man and ancestor — as when a part of one's sanctified piece of meat or pork fat is detached, presented to the ancestral relics, and then thrown on the fire while the rest is eaten, then the unity of Ancestor and Man is made tangible and confirmed in the strongest terms. Characteristically, all but the most experienced senior men are reluctant to perform this sacred act; they seem to experience it as presumptuous and perhaps even sacrilegious, and need encouragement and reassurance from seniors that this indeed is the right thing to do. (ii) Equally strong in its affirmation, and more readily accepted for its meaning, is the sharing with fellow members of the congregation. As noted in some of the descriptions (cf. e.g. p. 88), this takes the double form of allocation of shares to each participant and the secondary dyadic exchanges of small pieces of each man's share with all or most others, as an extra, individual affirmation of fellowship. (iii) The giving of shares of pig to the whole community — at big rituals or at curing ceremonies — affirms the widest circle of fellowship. Such raw meat can be shared between persons who are ritually debarred from commensality, yet belong together in real community. As noted (pp. 152 ff.), a cannibal feast has a ritual intensity so that the cooked flesh may be shared freely within the whole community; at the same time, the idiom of simultaneous feasting is so important that pig must also be slaughtered to provide those too sensitive to eat human flesh with equivalent meat. (iv) Finally, the exclusive sacrifice, consumed by the ancestor alone (p. 69) belongs at the other end of this continuum and has perhaps its developmental prototype in the childhood experience of gathering or hunting wild foods taboo to oneself, but allowed to senior men. The occasions when the father receives and consumes food which the child has provided, are clearly occasions for great mutual pride, and a kind of vicarious commensality and fellowship. They therefore provide an apt alternative metaphor for the ancestor-man relationship.

The Baktaman rite of sacrifice thus comprises several phases, including sanctification (by secrecy), presentation, prayer, immolation, and commensality. It also appears, through a detailed description, to be multivalent in its symbolic significance: it is part of a reciprocal transaction, it is a surrender of oneself to the deity, it is a partaking in the substance of the deity. My argument is that these are not alternative, but undifferentiated or very diffusely conceived aspects of the meaning of the rite. This meaning can most adequately be understood in what it achieves for the congregation during its occurrence: it conjures the ancestor forth in a concrete presence by consummating an interaction with him. Thus this positive rite, like the negative rites of taboo, may be seen not merely as expression, but also simultaneously as *production*, of the mysteries and processes which are celebrated in Baktaman religion.

CHAPTER 22

On the variety of metaphors in Baktaman rites

A wide variety of other symbols also recur in the rites described in chapters 3–16. Our question at this stage of analysis concerns their sources of meaning, and the kinds of information they carry in appropriate communicative contexts. Our analysis in the immediately preceding chapters has made it increasingly clear that the symbolic value of the elements depends to a large extent on their uses as metaphors. Thus, for example, the unity of mutual trust is like sharing a meal — such commensality is a metaphor which simultaneously explains, affirms, and creates the condition of mutual trust. Likewise, the consummation of a sacrifice is a metaphor for the presence of intangible ancestral alters; and the male organ is like the mysteriously potent red pandanus fruit, like an ancestral relic wrapped in its pandanus leaf, like an arrow. Through metaphor something familiar or distinctive is used as a model or analogy for something less familiar or less obvious, something less clearly conceptualized but now illuminated by the analogy. Often its use as metaphor will act back on the more familiar element and also clarify it by subsuming it under the more generalized model implicit in the analogy; but the essence of metaphor is the use of the familiar to grasp the elusive and unrecognized, rather than the mere ordering of phenomena by homology.

We may now focus on three rather different sets of symbols to show these relations, and explore the variation of idioms that coalesce in Baktaman ritual: (i) dew, fat, fur, and hair, (ii) the wild pig, and (iii) male and female. As emphasized in the preceding analysis of commensality, it is important to construct an empirically correct life context for the objects and activities involved, to understand the premises and connotations they embody as metaphors.

The first set, composed of *dew, fat, fur,* and *hair*, constitutes a relatively unelaborated but pervasive group of symbols associated with growth and increase. The ritual operations in which they appear will be remembered: Dew is rubbed on the body by 1st degree initiates every morning, and by men intermittently through life. Fat is likewise rubbed on the face and body. Fur is identified with taro growth and burned in temple and garden. Hair is identified with pandanus and vitality, and the ancestor's hair with vegetation in general and taro growth in particular.

Our understanding of just why these objects are ascribed these particular meanings is aided by an awareness of certain Baktaman premises. a) Growth in boys, pigs, and taro is basically one and the same process. This is indicated e.g. in their invariable association in prayer: whenever men sacrifice these three aspects of growth and welfare are mentioned together, and they are all felt to result from the ancestral favour which this one operation creates. b) There is a close identity between man and taro — when one thrives so does the other. We have seen this implied in curing magic, and in sorcery; it is also a major theme in the sanctions behind taboo; and it is experienced, of course, in the pragmatic connection between taro plenty and human welfare. c) Health is associated with the tight skin whereas weakness, hunger and other undesirable states are indicated by 'loose' skin, i.e. wrinkles and shrivelling. This again is equally true of man and of taro.

But these premises provide the Baktaman with very little insight into growth and increase. They focus on certain *correlates* of growth, but give no leverage to understand the *process*. It would seem that the Baktaman are in fact rather ill equipped to conceptualize such a process. They lack a calendar and other ways of handling the continuity of time; they have no scale of weights or in fact linear measures by which they can specify cumulative results. If I am right in stating that even their personally remembered past appears to them as kaleidoscopic (cf. pp. 21 ff.), there are few familiar prototypes in their experience which can be used as metaphors for the process. So in their ritual expression of the process which they celebrate and desire, the Baktaman seem to be groping for something only diffusely understood, and the metaphors used are such as can provide a minimal cognitive grasp of it: Dew accumulates on leaves. Fat grows inside the pig and makes its skin hard and tight. Hair grows out where it is cut off. Fur covers the body, like vegetation covers the ground. All these are images that can evoke the idea of increase; and rubbing with them, extending them as with a wig, or burning them and transferring them by smoke as with the fur of sacrifices, are all operations which serve as concrete symbols for the process. At the same time, these symbols are not emotionally very evocative; they are fairly neutral vehicles for thought, and not very deep thought at that. And even their symbol value has in part to be contrived: by repeated dew rubbing, by ritual fur burning, etc.

Wild pig, on the other hand, is a very different kind of symbol. It is an animal of consuming interest to the Baktaman. Endless conversations about it are pursued in the men's houses. Much activity — fencing, burning, visiting gardens, spying, hunting — is directed towards it. Enormous excitement is generated when one comes close to the village — as great among those who cannot eat it as among those who can. Elaborate traps are built, and tended, to catch it. It is a frequent subject of dreams. Thunder is often explained as a signal that a pig has died.

In all this interest, several themes are prominent. Wild pigs ravage the gardens — i.e. wild pig is seen as the great despoiler, with which man is continually at war. Hunting, or even meeting them is dangerous — i.e. wild pig is fierce and terrifying. Domestic sows depend on them for impregnation — i.e. wild pig is potent and masculine. Wild pork is delicious — i.e. its meat has high value.

We have noted the ways in which wild pig appears in ritual. Wild sows and piglets may only be eaten by men after 4th degree initiation, wild boar only after 7th. All wild pork is highly prized as food, and gifts of wild pork are very highly valued. Through the special taboos on entering gardens after eating such meat, however, it is opposed conceptually to garden fertility. Yet it is used in sacrifice in the temples without the sanctifying requirements of the secret hunt — except that wild boar is banned from the *Yolam*. But even this has its special exception: one wild boar mandible has been incorporated among the *Yolam* sacra.

In contrast to the previously discussed set of symbols, the wild pig thus carries a powerful and ambivalent load of affective and cognitive connotations, even regardless of its ritual uses. The conceptual muddle of the Baktaman with regard to wild pig is illustrated by the sudden decision of Aŋabieŋ, a relatively experienced, adult man in initiation set (b), to distribute shares of a wild female pig caught in his trap to all the women of the community. Kimebnok and other seniors intervened in great shock to protect the taro, all parties were very angry, and the man in question ran away to the forest for a long period in fear and chagrin over the reaction to his initiative.

The problem for the Baktaman would seem to be to make this

clearly important and multivalent natural symbol understandable and consistent in terms of ascribed ritual significance. In attempting this, they have focused primarily on one aspect: the destructive force despoiling the gardens. Yet the other aspects cannot be entirely expurgated, and assert themselves in the feeling of the fitness of offering wild pig as sacrifice in *Katiam* and *Amowkam*, and making exceptions to incorporate one wild boar symbol in the paraphernalia of the *Yolam* war temple. Reality seems to be more complex than symbolic schemata, and to insinuate itself into the understandings and feelings which empirical objects elicit in the participants in ritual. As a consequence, the wild pig becomes a rather ambiguous metaphor, neither clearly illuminating nor fully illuminated through its place in Baktaman ritual.

A third set of idioms in Baktaman ritual employs aspects of the differences between *male and female*. Sex roles and physical sexuality are obviously both familiar and pervasive in the life of every Baktaman; we also assume that they have strong affective connotations. As such, they should provide a rich potential source of images and metaphors for things less familiar. Particularly, one might expect human sexuality to provide a key metaphor for horticultural fertility and growth, since a connection is recognized by the Baktaman between intercourse, conception, and the growth of the foetus. This seems to be the case in many other parts of New Guinea: in the Highlands, the sex dichotomy is widely reported to be constituent of a dualistic world view (e.g. Meggitt 1964: 204ff.), partly associated with stark sexual antagonism; in the Southern Lowlands, fertility rites utilize gross sexual idioms (van Baal 1966: 807ff., Landtman 1927, Serpenti 1965); peoples of the Sepik area likewise give sex dichotomization and sexual imagery a prominent place in their ritual life (e.g. Tuzia 1972). By contrast, as should have emerged clearly from the preceding descriptions, such imagery is *not* particularly elaborate or basic in Baktaman rites, at least not at the overt level. To explore the connection between instituted ritual idioms and their sources of meaning in everyday life, it might be illuminating to examine more closely the place and precision of male/female imagery and compare this to the previously discussed idioms of dew and wild boar. One reservation about this comparison, however, should be made at the start: Whereas idioms like dew, or wild boar, are objects external to the self and thus usable as metaphors so long as persons have information about them, sex roles and sexuality are part of the self and can only be used as a model for other phenomena to the extent that persons have achieved some degree of self-awareness through analysis, and some social self-consciousness through distance from their own social behaviour. In this sense, male and female may to the actor constitute problems to understand rather than aids to understanding.

Again, we must start by summarizing the specific empirical character of male and female roles in Baktaman life, to provide the relevant premises and connotations which they might embody as metaphors. Quite clearly, the segregation of male and female is a fundamental premiss for the Baktaman both in daily life and in ritual: in the former through residential segregation and the companionship sought during everyday tasks, in the latter through a categorical conceptual bipartition of the congregation.

As noted previously, however, this does not imply that the division of labour between the sexes is categorical and strict. Most tasks may be performed by either sex. However, women predominate in cultivation and food preparation, whereas felling trees and fencing are exclusively male tasks. Burning is often a joint operation, but with the man in charge of the fire. In hunting and collecting, men predominate though both sexes are active; hunting with bow and arrow, however, is a strict male prerogative. The generalized pattern, and conventional expectation, is thus that the wife provides her spouse with cooked taro, while the husband gives her game.

Warfare is also a male prerogative, in which women are expected to be the passive victims. The only exception to such passivity noted is the anecdote of the Seltaman woman who resisted being ravished (p. 147). In domestic quarrels, on the other hand, the wife is often violent and beats her husband with firewood or other objects. Men do not feel dishonoured by such treatment, and freely complain of the resulting pains and bruises to arouse public sympathy.

The sexual act takes place in forest or garden, never in the village. Baktaman have heard of a custom practised further west, of husband and wife sleeping together at night; they have pornographic joy in accusing their Seltaman neighbours of this in the dance song:

Taiok-dīm, Wāγas-dīm		*Taiok-dīm kunum-ō,*	*Waγas-dīm*
(place-names in Seltaman)		Taiok-mountain men,	Oh,
kunum-ō		*mirirīp nōγē*	*mirirīp-*
Waγas-mountain men oh.		night-time	night-
kar	*senenamar-ō*		
copulate	copulate with me (female speaking)		

Taiok-dīm kunum-ō,   *Waүas-dīm kunum-ō /*   *ām-tei*
Taiok-mountain men,   Waүas-mountain men   in the house

sanenamar-ō,   *mirirīp noүēi,*   *mirirīp ē-i*
you copulate with me   night-time oh,   at night oh.

Both sexes freely express mutual desire and a positive evaluation of intercourse. In the following dance song, the girl is pining to grow up so she can have a man:

Mugō   woүán-sik   tabéb burū /   kunum-sō
Breasts   quickly   grow large,   man-together

waneꞁ-sō   weꞁ-weꞁ /   kābum   kanuүō /
woman together   converse   go into   the forest

bu-koꞁ-koꞁ   bayeir   mugō   ē-i / bu-koꞁ-kōꞁ
(bird mimicry)   spirit   breasts

ei-ei; sabkār   mugō ei; bu-koꞁ-koꞁ ei-ei
          ghost   breast

A Baktaman recently composed the following song at his wedding dance:

Baktaman   boꞁmit   kerēre /   mōrēp-teyo
Baktaman   (species of tree)   stand erect;   I desire you

kerērbi   ye-e / kerērbi   dayru
you make it erect   you make it erect spread-legs

rēp teyo   yē-ē ā ē / kerērbi mōrēp-teyo yē-ē
I desire you

Such mutual attraction also leads to jealousy between spouses: a wife throws tantrums if she suspects infidelity or is faced with the possibility of a co-wife; a husband is reluctant to relinquish marital rights if a wife deserts him, and seeks revenge on the rival if the wife has intercourse with another — an act always interpreted as rape, with the woman as an entirely passive party. Excessive sexual indulgence, on the other hand, is regarded as damaging and weakening for the man and gives him 'loose' skin. A certain fear of menstrual pollution is also felt.

How are these practices and attitudes reflected in the forms of ritual: do they provide metaphors and are they themselves the theme of ritual activity?

Overt sexual imagery is quite limited. For some purposes *Katiam*

204

and *Yolam* are referred to as big sister — little sister, but the reversal of their relative importance implied by this suggests that we are dealing with a standardized deception rather than a 'real' truth, and casts doubt on the significance of the sex ascription. To explain the ban against wild male boar in the *Yolam*, on the other hand, seniors would point out that *Yolam*, like boar, is male and the two thus in conflict, whereas *Katiam* and *Amowkam* are female and so compatible with the maleness of boar. The imagery around phallus/pandanus/arrow has been indicated (pp. 188 f.) but is not matched by female images. The idiom of novices crawling between the legs of seniors seems *not* to be symbolic of rebirth (p. 65). The only image of sexual complementarity in the major rites is found in the over/under male/female symbolism of the wig braids in 4th degree (p. 74). In female sorcery, on the other hand, sexual imagery is more pronounced. The sorceress uses male paraphernalia for her aggressive purposes (p. 132), and the magical operations equate vagina = fireplace = the inside of the ancestral skull.

As a substantive theme of the rites, the male-female dichotomy is constantly emphasized as a premiss. Secrecy is expressed as a prohibition to tell 'the women' though in fact children and men of insufficient initiation grade are equally debarred from knowledge — somehow, women conceptually epitomize the excluded category. But beyond this, the theme receives very little elaboration. The myth that provides a rationale for the exclusion and a version of the relationship of male and female principles (Myth 3) is known by very few and seemed improbable and irrelevant to the audience. Menstruation is not tied in with wider imagery and the menstrual hut itself was claimed to be a recent institutionalization of courtesy to women — previously, each person had improvised private arrangements of temporary forest shelters or used old garden houses while the polluting flow lasted. In the major rites, the place of women is peripherally acknowledged as a significant audience, as providers of pigs (e.g. 6th degree), and as providers of taro (1st, 3rd, 4th, 7th); but this seems merely to affirm what is already known, rather than to contribute insight into the phenomena of sexuality and interdependence.

Explicit sexual metaphors are thus not prominently or widely employed. But as our analysis of the major rites proceeds, we shall see a deep homology emerging between the man-ancestor relationship and the male-female relationship. Just as the male role is to provide the woman with game (birds and mammals) while receiving garden produce (taro) from her, so also man gives meat sacrifices to the ancestor and receives the blessing of taro fertility in return. This is not a homology that I ever heard verbalized. But some idea that the control of (vegetable) fertility which men obtain from the ancestors is comparable (and superior) to what women have in physical fertility and taro production is part of the basic understanding of fully initiated Baktaman. However, I do not feel that it would be correct to see the male-female relationship as the *source* of the metaphor of sacrifice in transactions with the ancestors, or female productivity and fertility as the familiar analogue for the force of growth and fertility that flows from the ancestors. Rather, a diffuse, intuitive grasp of their homology emerges as an understanding from the multiplicity of metaphors contained in Baktaman rites.

A comparison of the three sets of idioms discussed in this chapter — dew, etc., wild boar, and sex roles — shows that all of them serve as metaphors: they provide images or models which assist in the conceptualization of a property or quality in some other phenomenon. In the case of dew, fat, fur, and hair we see a physical characteristic of the concrete symbol isolated, and given occult significance, in a ritual operation, and then used as a means to comprehend the mystery of growth. In the case of the wild boar, one of its aspects — its behaviour in despoiling gardens — is linked to a model of forces promoting and threatening fertility. However, it would seem that other aspects of this concrete symbol remain immanent in it and are experienced by Baktaman as undeniably significant; so its precision as a metaphor is confounded. Finally, in the case of male and female we can see various concrete aspects of these familiar roles sketchily and unsystematically used in particular metaphors, while most of their expressive potential remains unexploited. Further, the male/female dichotomy itself is generalized as the epitomy of in-group versus out-group, and thus provides the paradigm for secrecy. Finally, at a deep and vaguely articulated level the conceptualization of male and female may provide an analogue for the conceptualization of reciprocity between man and ancestors, and the nature of the ancestors' prestations.

Methodologically, the three sets of idioms should serve to illustrate the futility of reasoning *from* the apparent properties of a concrete symbol *to* its codified meaning as an idiom; whereas we do see how one can trace, from a codified meaning, the sources of this meaning. Thus, we can identify *post hoc* the aspect of a concrete symbol that makes it an apt metaphor for a particular idea, and thereby empathize with the world view which such codifications entail.

206

CHAPTER 23

On the interpretation
of ritual idioms

The discussion of the preceding chapters has shown that the idioms of Baktaman ritual are best understood as metaphors: the relations, processes, and properties which are the subject of rites are largely represented by symbols which serve as concrete analogues to that which they symbolize. Baktaman ritual messages are, in other words, cast in analogic rather than digital codes (cf. Bateson 1972). Indeed, it is increasingly recognized in anthropological literature that this is a fundamental and general characteristic of ritual (cf. e.g. Turner 1973:353). But the implications of this general insight for method and theory in the analysis of rites are less widely recognized and understood.

The basic nature of an analogic code provides certain opportunities for the interpretation of its idioms. A metaphor is not an entirely arbitrary symbol; there is an inherent connection between form and meaning. The two questions (i) What does a certain idiom mean? and (ii) Why is that particular idiom selected as a vehicle for that particular concept?, are therefore both sensible and connected questions, as they would not be in a digital code such as a computer program or, largely, a language. Our understanding of the meaning of dew rubbing is thus aided by our observation of how dew occurs; and our understanding of the conceptualization of solidarity and trust helps us recognize why commensality is utilized for its expression.

On the other hand, this immanent coupling between form and meaning in the particular idiom also imposes a number of constraints on analysis. The most burdensome, in terms of the developed theory for the analysis of (digital) codes which permeates anthropological thinking on ritual,[1] is the weakening or perhaps elimination of contrast as a source of meaning. Where symbols are arbitrary, as in a

[1] cf. Leach 1968 ('Ritual', in *The International Encyclopedia of the Social Sciences*).

digital code, their meaning can only derive from the place which each symbol occupies, in terms of inclusion and contrast, within the code as a whole and only within it. Much analysis of language has proceeded from this premiss. What e.g. 'MAN' means is explicated by showing how it contrasts in the relevant pairs man: beast, man: woman, man: child, man: god. (cf. Frake 1961:119). And the transformations that can be made on the conceptual vehicle itself — e.g. as between the written and the vocal realization of 'MAN' — are such as do not affect its meaning because it retains its contrastive features. No transformation links any particular realization with that which it signifies — it remains an entirely arbitrary vehicle for what it conceptualizes.[1]

Compare this to conceptualizations and transformations in an analogic code. If we symbolize man with $\overset{\circ}{\wedge}$, the vehicle for conceptualization is a transformation of that which it conceptualizes or symbolizes — it is not arbitrary. Its meaning depends on an understanding of this transformation from object to symbol, and the experience from reality which it evokes when reversed. Meaning arises independently of any total code and not from the symbol's systematic place among a limited set of alternatives within such a code. As shown in chapter 17, this does not prevent such symbols from being *used* contrastively (e.g. the features signalling initiation rank); but it does seem to preclude a procedure which presupposes the logical closure of a digital code and which derives meaning from such contrastive occurrence.

Other, partly related, considerations constrain the procedures we may use in interpreting ritual idioms. Most directly from the above, it seems to follow that we cannot order our material on ritual analytically in anything like semantic domains: idioms do not derive their meanings from inclusion in contrastive sub-sets, any more than from contrast on lower levels. Their association in messages, and empirical co-occurrence, would seem to be the only sound criteria by which to order idioms. Chapters such as those on taboo and colour explore classes of idioms, not domains of meaning.

A characteristic feature of much ritual is that it is collective — i.e. it is an aggregate of the simultaneous activity of several actors — and that many of its idioms have continual existence, such as sacred objects. This has striking implications. Thus, there can be no mono-

---

[1] I do not imply that this represents a fully satisfactory analysis of language, merely that it exemplifies legitimate understandings of a purely digital code.

logue; a person must assert whatever his message is through acts fully embedded in a flow of interaction and simultaneous expression. Under these circumstances it does not seem plausible to expect the meaning of messages to depend on very tight structures and particularly not on syntactic sequences: the realization of any particular feature at a particular moment is too contingent. Where clear efforts are made to realize certain sequences — as Kimebnok does, e.g. in his management of 6th degree initiation — these are often of dramatic rather than syntactic nature, i.e. they enhance the force of the message but are not inherent in its meaning and could in principle be reversed. Only certain very gross and simple sequences seem to have a syntactic character, e.g. the major phases of sacrifice, which *must* be realized as a string of events.

The multiplicity of actors, and of sacred and other objects, also entails a loose structure of messages in the sense that a multiplicity of uncoded elements will inevitably be present. Sometimes these pose major problems of stage management (e.g. pp. 70 f.); but a welter of them are simply ignored. Novices and unperceptive participants may be confused by this and miss much of the imagery — yet that which they do perceive does not depend on a tight total structure for meaning and so can reach them and make sense to them. For this reason, a ritual message can be interpreted simultaneously by different participants using different keys for decoding (e.g., the differing keys to colour symbolism pp. 178 ff.) and focusing on different elements (e.g., the parties to 1st degree initiation, pp. 56 f.), ignoring the rest as irrelevant or incomprehensible. Complex messages cast in analogic code are specifically suited for such multiple interpretations; while the events and objects among which their crucial symbols are embedded cannot be dismissed analytically as 'noise.'

A further characteristic feature of rites is that, as far as participants are concerned, they *do* something as well as *say* something (cf. Richards 1956:112 ff.). This feature was particularly emphasized in the discussion of taboo and sacrifice, but is equally true of whole rites such as the various initiations: they produce and affirm, and do not merely assert. An implication of this is that ritual messages, besides being embedded in social interaction, are also embedded in a means-to-end context. An analysis which ignores this and analyses ritual events *merely* as communicative events constructs spurious problems and invites the use of inappropriate concepts. Thus, for example, a concept of redundancy has questionable validity if the instrumental aspect of ritual is recognized — it is as if in felling a tree the first stroke of the axe is considered to contain the message and the rest were redundant. It makes more sense to recognize a complex theory of fertility in the innumerable modulations of Baktaman ritual. For example in 6th degree initiation taro grows 'because' the *Katiam* and *Yolam* fires have been kept burning, collective taboos have been observed, secret marsupials have been obtained, the novices see the white stripe on the ancestor's forehead, a Baktaman pig is sacrificed, prayers for taro are offered, etc., etc. Just as the welter of stimuli generated in a rite cannot be dichotomized as message vs. noise because of the looseness of structure and multiplicity of keys, so also the repetition of messages cannot be dismissed as redundancy, because of its possible place in an actor theory of instrumentality.

The perspective that rites *do* something also places Baktaman practices of secrecy and deception in a somewhat different light. To have persons — such as novices and women — participate in limited roles in a (mystical) productive enterprise which they do not understand is rather different from merely speaking to them in a secret language which they cannot interpret. It is the *concerns* of Baktaman ritual — taro, growth, pigs — that integrate even the most passive and excluded categories, such as women, into the cult and make of the whole population one unified congregation with a common purpose, despite the instrumental necessity of unequal responsibility, secrecy, and exclusion.

Despite this embeddedness of the elements of ritual in a means-to-end context, it has proved most useful to see the relationship which obtains between the ritual elements and that which they represent as one of metaphor. In identifying these idioms as metaphors, I wish to draw attention to two connected features: (i) A metaphor is an expression that uses the more familiar and evident as a model to grasp and clarify the less evident and elusive. Even where everyday phenomena are described by unaccustomed metaphor, as often in poetry, we may argue that this is so, since aspects of quality and significance are thereby revealed which were previously unrecognized. (ii) Metaphor uses imagery from one domain or level of experience to illuminate relationships, objects, and processes in a different domain or at a different level. It follows from this that the domain of thought or experience which is being explicated by metaphor is that which metaphor is used to illuminate, not that from which the idioms of metaphor are fetched. There is thus no justification for an assumption (such as seems implicit in much structural anthropology, and as I myself unthinkingly initially intended to make

210

in connection with parts of this material) that ritual will provide a systematic ordering of the substantive domains from which its concrete symbols are drawn; on the contrary, it is the themes of the rituals, not their sources of metaphor, that are explicated and ordered in the rites. There is then no longer anything puzzling in the fact that some sexual imagery occurs in Baktaman rites but no systematic picture of male versus female is elaborated (cf. pp. 202 ff.) — we are merely seeing how familiar models are brought in as aids to the understanding of problematic topics. Likewise, we failed in our search for structural patterns in the ritual uses of marsupials, because these animals are not the theme of the rites, although their meat is a vehicle for communion and their fur is a symbol of growth.

To some extent, however, the metaphors which form the conceptual tools of ritual are also fashioned in the rites themselves. Imagery is not only fetched from various domains of the mundane world; the contrivances of ritual practice create and elaborate associations which provide material for metaphor. A simple example is the way ancestral sacra, 1st degree novices, and 4th degree novices are painted with red colour — this provides a field of experience which invests the colour red with new metaphorical content. Likewise, the various contrivances of taboo have cognitive and affective consequences. In the case of most marsupials, for example, I do not find it particularly illuminating to search for the characteristics that make them taboo. Rather, we should observe how the practice of taboo moulds subjective experience: people make marsupials taboo thereby to understand life better — for example, so as to be able to use them to communicate with the ancestors in sacrifice.

It is also by this additional basis for metaphor that a number of inherently independent idioms are joined together and fashioned into an analogic code; and the kind of structure that characterizes such a code should be understood in its interlinking of metaphors. Through ritual operations, bases of metaphor are modified and added, the multiple connotations of concrete symbols are harmonized, there is an increase both in the precision and the multiplicity of the metaphoric content of each idiom, and it is related to other idioms in a single key — using that term as much in its musical as in its communicational sense. Clearly, the Baktaman are not equally successful in this for all their idioms. It is instructive to compare their efforts in clarifying the symbolic value of wild boar — where they have done poorly (pp. 201 f.) — with that of pandanus. In the latter case, a clear and complex harmony of connotations has been achieved (cf. pp. 188 f.), relating the symbol closely also with many others in a — loosely structured — analogic code.

Having established some fundamental characteristics of an analogic code, it is time for me to face squarely the problem of meaning — what in my terms does an idiom 'mean' and how are such meanings established by the anthropologist. My simple intention has been to discover what people understand from an idiom in its appropriate contexts, and to call this its meaning. Such meaning I have sought to establish by a back-and-forth reasoning connecting idiom and message content. In cases where I felt I had a plausible, contextual understanding of a ritual message I reasoned deductively to what the idiom must mean to give this message. In other cases I reasoned inductively from a hypothesis of what an idiom means, and tested the entailed message content against my general understanding of Baktaman knowledge and values on this topic. I also assumed that initiation rites would be organized to allow a progressive understanding of idioms and development of sacred knowledge, and tested my interpretations against this.

Such analysis, though it is based on arguments of consistency, does not imply any assumption of uni-valence in idioms. Nor does it imply an assumption of intergration in culture. It is essential to avoid the elaborate exercises in logical consistency so readily pursued by anthropologists in their exegeses, even when their intentions are explicitly otherwise (cf., e.g., Turner 1969b, p. 9 vs. pp 49 ff.). Any consistency claimed must be tested and built up piecemeal. Finally, I have emphasized the inappropriateness of deducing directly from a concrete symbol's objective properties and apparent suitability to its actual meaning (e.g. pp. 172 f.), and conversely emphasized the indicative value of contrivance for meaning.

This position differs fundamentally both in its assumptions and procedures from that of contemporary structuralist anthropology of the Lévi-Strauss tradition (cf. Lévi-Strauss 1962). The most productive idea of this tradition — that a folk taxonomy provides a paradigm for native thought and thus offers the key to the meaning of the elements of myth and rite — has recently been compellingly restated by Mary Douglas: 'By focusing on how anomalous beings may be treated in different systems of classification, we make a frontal attack on the question of how thought, words and the real world are related' (Douglas 1973:29). In some of the preceding text, especially in the discussions of taboo (pp. 166 ff.) and marsupials (pp. 184 ff.), I have attempted to proceed eclectically and use also such viewpoints on the analysis of Baktaman material. Negative results in these attempts are neither methodological nor logically very compelling; but they are consistent with some more general theorectical considerations. One may be justifiably unhappy about a method where structures or patterns must be constructed merely with a view to make all the pieces fit and without opportunity for falsification at any stage. The naive question of how much of these thoughts have actually been thought by the actors concerned can be raised (cf. Douglas 1966: 91) but not resolved in such a structuralist framework. Furthermore, as noted above, digital assumptions on which the structural argument rests seem unjustified in the analysis of analogic codification. The self-evident is *not* being explicated in metaphor; and if one wishes to focus on the sources of metaphor it seems essential to distinguish at least the two strata of mundane connotations and ritual contrivance, and not design a single and uniform structure to fit an unsystematic assemblage of data from both strata. Such a procedure merely reintroduces a simplistic assumption of total logico-deductive integration in culture as between pragmatic aspects of folk taxonomy, ritual codes, and native speculative philosophy. Let us rather use material on ritual activity for listening with receptivity to statements made about the subject-matter of these rites, thereby learning what knowledge and attitudes the actors are communicating. This position forces us to see ritual events in their social, interactional context, and the information they contain in the context of cultural knowledge and its transmission. To effectuate this, it is essential to distinguish the message contained in any particular ritual statement from its implicit premises, and the structure of the communicative vehicle from the structure of thought.[1]

The perspective explicated in this chapter also makes us capable of handling the implicit problem posed by the ubiquity of certain concrete symbols (e.g. water, fat, feathers, pandanus, cuscus, cassowary) in a number of different New Guinea cultures. A comparative analysis would be a vast undertaking; but we may refer briefly to the example of the cassowary, as analysed by Bulmer (1967) for the Karam, a people some 300 miles east of the Baktaman. Bulmer's

---

[1] cf. Chomsky 1968:23 ff., and his critique of Lévi-Strauss pp. 65–66. A penetrating critical review of corresponding problems in ethnosemantics is given in Keesing 1972, e.g. p. 314: 'New developments in semantics, on both the anthropological and linguistic sides of the disciplinary border, increasingly cast doubt . . . that the labeled lexical categories of a language reveal directly the cognitively salient pieces into which a people segment their world of experience.'

discussion is characteristically careful and shows the various connotations and associations of cassowary in Karam culture, without
implying any necessity attached to these relations; he develops a
concept of 'special taxonomic status' as a descriptive summary of
features of culture and cosmology at large (ibid. p. 19). A structuralist
construction on this material (Douglas 1973:32–34) makes logical
necessity out of such relations where I would see a more freely creative
elaboration and harmonization of connotation in a particular tradition. The structuralist view asserts dogmatically 'the imprinting
upon nature of the rules and categories which are dominant in social
life' (ibid. p. 32) where I would see the familiar, whatever its character,
utilized as metaphor. And to understand how cassowary — variously
classified and variably associated in terms of its relations to environment and man — has a special place in rite and cosmology among
Karam, Baktaman and many other New Guinea peoples, the structuralist would have to construct innumerable such tight models and
then generalize by abstraction from them, where what I think we see
are the results of cultural creativity, in a number of different traditions,
over a few simple metaphorical possibilities. How such creativity asserts
itself, and is channelled by the special qualities of a culture and a
society at a particular time, are the themes of the last, fifth, part of
this study.

PART V

The sociology of Baktaman knowledge

CHAPTER 24

The epistemology of secrecy

We have seen how the knowledge contained in Baktaman ritual is hedged by taboo and secrecy, indeed how the importance and validity of the rites are directly linked in the actors' understanding with the observation of secrecy. A similar practice seems to characterize the management of all information, also in profane matters, where secretiveness and deception permeate much intercourse. Observing these practices during fieldwork soon led me to the provisional formulation of a thesis that the value of information seemed to be regarded as inversely proportional to how many share it. From this it would follow that if you seek to *create* highly valued information, i.e. basic sacred truths, you must arrange worship so that few persons gain access to these truths. But there is also a paradox in the premises: if the value of information is greater, the fewer persons have it, its value is greatest when it stops being information at all ɔ: when only one person has it and he does not transmit it.[1]

In connection with 5th degree initiation (pp. 81 ff.), when novices participate for the first time in the secret marsupial hunt, we reached a somewhat different formulation: secrecy sanctifies; by virtue of it animals which are normally unclean achieve new properties which make them suitable as offerings. Thus deceit and exclusion seem to

---

[1] The patrol officer in a neighbouring area, intrigued by my explanations of the functions of secrecy and frustrated in his efforts to interest the influential leaders of his area in local democracy, decided to apply this insight. His attempts to inform the population about their rights to elect representatives to government bodies had resulted only in the nomination of unimportant, junior men for such offices. To convince the seniors of the importance of such nominations, he made a great show of secretiveness in telling only the select few. He was then suddenly entirely successful in convincing these seniors about the value of the information and the importance of nomination; but they in turn guarded the information so closely as to preclude nomination procedures and general ballotting.

create the preconditions for deeper truth, i.e. knowledge with greater power. The analysis of taboo (pp. 170 f.) provides us with a paradigm of this: the proper handling of knowledge — its limitation, protection from association with contrary substances, its refinement and concentration — may be seen as increasing its potency. Obversely, knowledge may be dangerous (to uninitiated, taro, growth) and must be controlled and contained.

These various formulations have sought to extract the epistemological premises of the Baktaman practice ot secrecy. To clarify such ideas we should look systematically at Baktaman knowledge from this point of view. I shall focus my discussion in successive stages on

(a) the synchronic structure of knowledge
(b) the learning process of the individual, and the meta-learning it entails as to what is knowledge.
(c) the dynamics of this tradition of knowledge in communication and transmission, particularly what are the conditions of credibility and confirmation, and what are the epistemological consequences of the processes subsumed under the label of 'secrecy'.

Synchronic structure: I have previously used the image of Chinese boxes to characterize the structure of Baktaman knowledge: it is constructed with multiple levels, and each level is organized so as to obscure the next level. There is every indication that this depicts the distribution of actual knowledge, and not just pretences about secrecy (cf. e.g. p. 55); and the information made available at one level bears witness, in terms of knowledge at deeper levels, of having been purposefully distorted and garbled on certain points (cf. e.g. p. 61) to preclude independent deduction from one level to the next. Such a complex structure of knowledge cannot be generated logically from a simple profane/sacred distinction; and the different systems of ideas at each level seem to have an appreciable degree of separate order and coherence.

The social organization which sustains this structure is, of course, mainly that of initiation grades. But the actual practice of differentiation and exclusion of persons in ritual activities shows an even greater complexity than the major initiation grades 0–7 would indicate. Thus some initiations are composed of distinct phases with distinctive steps in the acquisition of knowledge (e.g. 1st degree, cf. pp. 51, 56. 57). and smaller exclusive sacrifices and communions stratify the fully initiated 7th graders (cf. e.g. pp. 88 f.).

Note also the absence of an age set system or similar rules implying an identity between levels of knowledge and extant social groups: at any time only some initiation grades are occupied (in spring 1968: 1st, 5th, 6th and 7th). The other levels of the system can then only be retained if conceptualized by the seniors quite abstractly as levels of knowledge and not concretely as social groupings.

For this reason a straightforward Marxian explanation of the structure of knowledge as a direct reflection of social differentiation and privilege is unsatisfactory. Admittedly, secrecy is manipulated in many ways with a view to retaining privilege for the seniors. I have tried to show where this empirically is or is not the case, e.g. in the degree of correlation between ritual status and secular authority (pp. 107 ff.), the relative burdens and advantages that spring from the taboos associated with each grade (p. 165), and in the analysis of a particular case of ritual change (pp. 91 f.). It is clear from this that the complexity of levels of knowledge cannot be explained plausibly by such inconclusive differences in privilege, quite apart from the elaboration of levels beyond the number of social groupings actually represented in the population. To understand this system of knowledge, we must look beyond its synchronic structure at the empirical processes that characterize it.

Secrecy and learning: All advance into this system of knowledge is through the formal initiations. In describing them, I have tried to show how they step by step instill a syndrome of attitudes to knowledge. From that first, frightening early morning when initiations started, and through a series of subsequent stages, the novice develops a fearful awareness of vital, unknowable, and forbidden power behind the secret and cryptic symbols. He realizes the existence of veil behind veil, and how modest and largely incorrect his own understandings have been. He comes to recognize the futility — and danger — of speculation and curiosity about ritual knowledge, how his own ritual acts have meaning only by virtue of the deeper knowledge of the seniors, who provide him with a set of instructions for action and an (unknown) wider context which assures that these acts are not dangerous and destructive. At the same time he comes to know the pervasiveness of secrecy and direct deception on which the structure is built. This learning, especially when combined with the circumspection in everday life that springs from sorcery, cannot but colour social experience profoundly. A Baktaman will experience no social relation which can embody for him a conception of truthfulness and trust: fathers must systematically deceive sons, men deceive women and vice versa, all public life is permeated with the protective tactfulness of sorcery fear. It is true that distrust and deceit undermine social relations in many societies; but under circumstances such as these they have more profound epistemological consequences, for two main reasons. Firstly, they cannot easily be conceptually dichotomized with a truthful ideal, since the secrecy from which they spring is a necessary and 'good' thing: without it the structure of sacred knowledge could not be maintained and the welfare-preserving cult would fail. Furthermore, in contrast to the many populations who participate in the universal religions and similar intellectual traditions, the Baktaman also lack the idea of an all-knowing god in terms of which abstract, absolute truth can be conceptualized. Deified ancestors are, like other people, deceitful, forgetful, and egocentric; though they embody greater power than living man can attain they do not provide a template for truth.

At the road's end, therefore, the senior adept and cult leader is the custodian of knowledge which has the highest authority in terms of the conventions shared by his group, but which he himself has no reason to trust — it is merely 'all our fathers told us before they died' (cf. p. 102). The acknowledged occasional failure in transmission of ritual knowledge, e.g. regarding the location and character of clan sacra (cf. p. 109) can hardly make this a comforting imprimatur and does not lend such knowledge the epistemological status of truth, no matter how powerful and dangerous it may be. The fearfulness and doubt instilled in the course of initiation by the practices of secrecy thus seem to remain till the very end, when only unknowable veils can separate man from the mysteries.

The dynamics of secret tradition: We may now attempt to connect more closely the macro-structure of Baktaman knowledge with the understandings and activities of those who participate in it. Clearly, the conditions of credibility and confirmation in a system structured by taboo and secrecy become quite special. We can usefully contrast them with those of what might be called Socratic traditions, where conviction through dialogue represents the supreme confirmation process. Note the way new information is handled by novices after initiation: it is *not* explored in conversation to pursue its implications, not exploited to discover connections, deeper meanings, and hidden secrets. Rather, it is handled the way little boys in occupied Europe during the war handled the unexploded ammunition they found: treasured for its unknown power, potential danger, secrecy — not with any real intention to use, and not to be experimented with to discover what destruction, or noise, an explosion really makes. So, there is not only an inhibition against speaking about the revelations of Baktaman initiations, but a wariness and vagueness in *thinking* about them — it is their secrecy and exclusiveness, not their potential for enlightment, that give them value. In this sense, the ritual symbols of the Baktaman are *not* 'good to think'. Their credibility and conviction arise from the fact that they are 'good to act', in their proper setting: there they are shaped so as to fit, so as to generate a vaguely conceived significance, confirmed in a mute fellowship of privileged participation. In this connection, the fact of mutual participation in rites across community boundaries — fraught with profound distrust and a risk of real danger — lends further authority to the knowledge which the rites embody.

The absence of a conception of abstract truth means that this 'knowledge' is not conceived by the actors as necessarily represented by the actual understanding of any of the participants. This obviates the apparent paradox formulated at the beginning of this chapter on the nature of valued information. It is more as if the rites sought, with greater or less effect, to make an undifferentiated knowledge/truth/ reality immanent and potent in the situation. The rite's aspect of 'doing something' thus clearly predominates for the actors over its 'saying something'. The doubts and fears of cult leaders are perhaps best understood in this perspective. Thus, among the Seltaman, an *Amowkam* temple has been abandoned because nobody 'dares' lead the cult. In 1968 one wall had fallen in exposing the supremely secret *Amowk* skull to public view. Yet this regrettable condition was some-how clearly preferable to letting some 'sorcerer's apprentice' activate the temple and let loose powers beyond his control. Likewise, when a cult leader is sick he does not appeal to the *Yolam* ancestor for health, but withdraws from his powerful presence until he is well, and has the courage to activate the 'knowledge' that gives health and prosperity.

The epistemological implications of the Baktaman practice of secrecy is thus in a certain sense a pragmatic conception of knowledge: its reality is demonstrated by its potency and power. But the way knowledge alters the world is indirect, through the mobilization of the reality of ancestral power in cult. And so instead of developing a 'theory' of growth and health and fertility the Baktaman develop a 'mystery' of these themes. Secrecy is an essential precondition of this mystery. It dramatizes and inculcates a deep emotional experience of the *partial* nature of our understanding compared to the uncharted fulness of reality. The veils of disguise by which the practice of secrecy structures knowledge in successively deeper layers seem to be the conceptual and didactive mechanism whereby this attitude is main-

221

tained. As noted in connection with marsupial symbols, secrecy can also serve to bring the mysteries subjectively closer by the practice of symbol substitution: protecting the secret of *kwĕmnok* = ancestor by substituting another marsupial for *kwĕmnok* makes the first identity deeper and thereby truer (cf. pp. 94, 186). Finally, the practice of secrecy sustains the ambivalence of fear of ignorance/fear of knowedge, since these conflicting attitudes can remain unresolved through not being formulated as analytic dialogue, in verbal discourse, and thereby persist as a source of awe in the experience of the mysteries.

Through these mechanisms of ritual and secrecy, Baktaman knowledge attains many of its characteristic features: constantly communicated about yet poorly shared and precariously transmitted; creative and complex yet poorly systematized; moving and rich yet puzzled and groping in its thought and imagery. To understand these features more fully, however, we need also to look at other aspects of Baktaman ritual communication.

CHAPTER 25

Ritual, speech, and knowledge

A major property of Baktaman ritual — and indeed of all ritual activities — is its multi-channel character. Different aspects of a ritual performance reach the participant by way of each of his different senses; and the diversity of meaningful features and idioms is very great. Thus, in the single act of presenting a piece of *kitēm* marsupial meat to the ancestral skull, a multitude of different aspects are simultaneously realized. The act is the dramatic climax of a sacrifice and communion in which the ancestor is present. Smoke/smell, itself of intangible spirit substance, conveys the offering to the world of the spirits, as it does in many other ritual and gardening contexts. The fireplace through which the offering is mediated radiates the mysterious heat/power, associated through the *ubir* marsupial with the virility of pandanus. The *kitēm* itself embodies the public food taboos with which it is encumbered; also the mystery of the secret hunt in which it was shot, and the special taboos and secrecy which obtain on such occasions. The smell of the remains of its singed fur evokes the mystery of growth. But it also carries the familiar associations of its natural occurrence in the forest, its habits and habitat. Simultaneously, it is a symbol for *kwēmnok*, who *is* the ancestor. The actor stands in the forbidden temple where the ancestor dwells; in doing so he embodies and realizes an identity built up through a series of initiations, and partakes in an exclusive fellowship of the elect, who are simultaneously engaged in the same phase of the rite. The sharing of an item of meat calls forth the spectre of sorcery dangers — and also the positive affirmation of solidarity and trust. Beast, skull, and temple are cast in symbolic colours. And some of the participants know Myth 3, with its rendering of the first sacrifice in the context of male/female struggle.

How is such a multifaceted event understood by participants, i.e. what is its message content? and how should an anthropologist proceed in his attempt to describe, document, and analyse such ritual behaviour? A major property of rite, and a difficulty in analysis, has already appeared in the above description. There is no obvious way whereby we can ascertain definitely that a particular actor, or any actor, at the moment of presentation of his piece of *kitēm* sensed all or any of this multi-channel syndrome. Ideally, the reader should, like the Baktaman and to some extent myself, go through the initiations, accumulate the other experiences from which connotations spring, and then *do* the sacrifice to 'understand' its import. Instead I have constructed a verbal description and evocation of what I have reason to believe is the crux of the experience. But in translating it into this entirely different medium of language, I have of necessity transformed the material drastically. Most fundamentally, I see no way of retaining its basic constitution: the definitiveness of the act of sacrifice and the ambiguity of its meanings. In putting it into words, I am creating a defininitiveness of meanings while introducing ambiguity as to the reality of the act — was I really there, was it really so, does it still take place? My thesis in this whole study, which I wish to argue most explicitly in the present chapter, is the separateness and integrity of non-verbal forms of communication — yet even as I argue this, I am forced to communicate their character to the reader by translating all the evidence into a linguistic code.

Such a problem of translation does not only arise between verbal and non-verbal codes — we may expect it also to obtain as between different forms of non-verbal expression. It is important not to prejudge such issues in our attempts to analyse ritual. When the Baktaman choose to cast their knowledge in a variety of simultaneous channels and expressions, we should seek to understand its consequences and, if possible, its reasons. A major explanation lies in their clear wish to *act* on the world and not just speak about it. But different vehicles of expression also have different potentials or strengths in what they can express. Just like construction in plane geometry represents a mode of understanding or insight which is difficult to put into words, so also colours, objects, acts and configurations are vehicles for understanding which cannot freely substitute for each other. When the Baktaman choose to use many at once, we should be prepared to find that they also say different things, with different clarity and implications. We should further understand these messages as potentially complementary and connected in a total context, but not as parts of a single code.

The most pressing issues of translation arise, however, as between verbal and non-verbal codes, and concern the place of native explanation and exegesis in the anthropological analysis of rites. Let us be very clear as to the maximal claim that can be made for such verbal explanations. The absurdity of going to Beethoven and asking him to 'explain' his 5th Symphony rather than play it is obvious. Just as no one would engage a symphony orchestra if the same could be said in words, so we can assume that rites say things that cannot be said in other ways. Yet to remain with the musical analogy for a moment: there is such a thing a verbal music theory and criticism; and surely this is both relevant and an aid to the understanding of music? If so, should not the same be true for exegesis in relation to rite? There seem to be two kinds of linguistic material at issue here: native terms for the parts of rites, and native verbal explanations for the contents and meaning of the rites. In the case of individual native terms, we have cited doubts as to the isomorphy between lexemes and the parts of thought (Keesing, op. cit. p. 331) and there is all the more reason to doubt the assumption of identity between lexemes and the meaningful elements of rites. Obviously there *are* a number of such words in any language, and in the preceding description of Baktaman ritual I have noted some of their own words; but these cannot provide or underwrite a *framework* for the analysis of the rites, as explicitly claimed by some of the most influential scholars in this field (e.g. Turner 1969a:15).

What place then can native *explanations* have in providing such a framework? I was extremely conscious of this question during field-work and wished to distinguish categorically between the generalizations and analyses which were part of Baktaman praxis, and those which arose from my investigations. The technical problems of observer effect and influence during long and intensive fieldwork are of course rather special. The relationships that are developed with friends in the field are inevitably based on reciprocity and compatible learning, and through this it is easy, and perhaps common, to launch 'informants' in intellectual careers as analysts of their own society. In this capacity they can naturally provide a number of excellent insights — but these insights can *not* be used as data on the contents of their cultural tradition. And once this process is launched, it becomes impossible for the anthropologist to tell which items are inherent in the tradition he is studying, and which represent the feedback of his own activity. Working as I did with an essentially uncontacted population, it seemed particularly valuable to avoid such adulteration of the material.

My field procedure was consequently to rely very heavily on observation of (1) spontaneous, unelicited word and act. (2) I paid particular attention in this to *Baktaman* questions and explanations to each other — in men's houses, in the fellowship of hunting and working, during initiations and other rites. (3) Only secondarily, and with much reticence, did I ask my own questions, and then only when they seemed cast in a native pattern and received easy and natural response.

Careful observation of this procedure led to the empirical *discovery* that the Baktaman have no exegetical tradition. I am struck by the lack of factual comparative evidence in the anthropological literature on the presence and degree of development of native exegetical tradition and praxis; and without the careful restraint I practised, I might not have recorded its absence. As social relations in the field deepened, it would not have been difficult to obtain native help in my efforts to understand: to *make* them systematize and translate verbally in response to *my* need for system and verbal codification. My strong suspicion is that the bodies of native explanation that we find in anthropological literature are often created as an artefact of the anthropologist's activity.

Indeed, we may note that the concept of exegesis is used sloppily in contemporary anthropological literature (e.g. Turner 1969b, esp. pp.11 ff.). In some cultures, beyond doubt, there *is* a native tradition of exegesis, in the sense that there is a body of knowledge and procedures for verbal explanation and analysis of rites which form part of the competence of ritual specialists. The anthropologist working in such cultures can submit to the discipline of native exegetical praxis and thereby gain access to yet one more mode of expression for religious thought. His problem then is not to pursue this scholarship too far, and add his own 'personal dimension to the interpretation of an alien religious ideology, to raise the generalizations to a higher power than the empirical content of the material warrants' (Firth 1959:139). But the mere fact that specialists and others can provide explanations of greater or less complexity when challenged is no evidence of the existence of such a tradition. It is in the praxis of social interaction which structures debate and instruction, as much as in the substantive themes of the conversation, that an exegetical tradition is found.

The special dangers of working through verbal explanations and exegesis towards an understanding of ritual spring from the basic differences in the constitution of these two forms of communication.

I have argued (ch. 23) that ritual communication is cast in analogic rather than digital codes. These two kinds of codes are differently handled by their users because of the difference in the way they are constituted; we may characterize their structures respectively as 'emergent' and 'paradigmatic'. We have noted how an analogic code is built on metaphors, which each separately derive their meaning from an analogy between symbol and that which it symbolizes. There is often a readily apparent stereotypy in such imagery — the transformations are of a kind and so sets of metaphors may be seen to be of a family. The idioms of dew, fat, fur, and hair (pp. 199–201) are clearly so related, and we may add the rubbing of white earth on the pigs and the rubbing of the skull with red leaves to the same family. Having understood one of these, the others fall more readily into place; but no one of them can be used as a paradigm for the class, and when we find another rubbable or excrescent substance we have no precedent for predicting its metaphorical import. We have indeed now fallen into the pitfall inherent in translation: we have codified possible substances as rubbable and excrescent versus not so, and *look* for paradigms based on this contrast. But in the concrete occur- rence of an object as symbol *all* its properties are immanent and so there is no *a priori* basis for expecting this one aspect, by which we have linguistically codified it, to be predominant and the source of metaphor.

The productivity of language depends on its digital, and conse- quently paradigmatic, features: classes of elements are by definition similar precisely in that the same permutations can be performed on them. Analogic codes do not allow for such permutations — every metaphor is a creative construct, every harmony of connotations and every item of imagery is an emergent addition to the structure of the code.

Let us consider what this entails for the anthropologist's method, again contrasting the two kinds of codes. A linguistic informant brings his paradigms to the act of communication, and applies this competence to produce 'correct' sentences. These sentences form a sample of 'the sayable' and from them the analyst can extract major structural features of the code. Communication in an analogic code, on the other hand, is embedded in the wider context (cf. pp. 208 ff.). The way it can be used, i.e. its structure, springs in part from features of social organization and substantive knowledge. Our material should consequently contain, not what might be sayable in these kinds of metaphors, but what is actually said: what *has* been created and so has emerged as a tradition of imagery and knowledge. The relatively unadulterated material which is the fruit of my rather laborious care in the field was meant to have this character. It contains only questions that arose within the community and the answers that they released, i.e. idioms occur in the context of messages generated by Baktaman praxis and express knowledge which is current in that tradition.

The elicitation of verbal explanations and explications of these rites and other non-verbal messages would only create unnecessary confusion. The translation of non-verbal messages into a verbal code introduces a schematism and productivity into the communication which all too easily carries away both informant and anthropologist. This certainly did not prevent me, while in the field, from wishing that I was dealing with a culture with an exegetical tradition, and that I could find a Baktaman version of the Wise Man of Dogon (cf. Griaule 1965), who would explain it all to me. But in such a situation I might never have come to question the importance of such mytho-poetic systematization for the constitution of rites and knowledge. The striking *absence* of such verbal activity in Baktaman, combined with the complexity and wealth of non-verbal messages, now force this issue upon us. Would Baktaman ritual become different, and would the knowledge which it transmits change, if they were to develop such verbal fields of expression? Or would myth, exegesis, and explanation merely form a verbal web, an inconsequential accretion on non-verbal communicative behaviour which is shaped by other processes and structures?

Such a question seems fruitful, though methodologically hardly capable of solution. But some features of the material provide suggestions. We have seen how a dichotomy of above/below ground seems to be expressed in secular food taboos (p. 167), likewise how male and female are dichotomized in many contexts. Maleness is also associated with bow and arrow and hunting, with the upper cuts of pork; the female is associated with gardening, with the lower cuts of pork, with dirty, ground-living foods; the upper and lower pigtails on the 4th degree wig are called male and female respectively. I think it would have been relatively easy to make certain Baktaman informants schematize this in anthropological fashion as male : female :: above ground : below ground :: superior : inferior :: clean : dirty, etc., though I am fairly positive that no such string of associations has ever been constructed by them to date. I have in fact tried to show how poorly male/female imagery is exploited in Baktaman ritual (cf. pp. 202 ff.).

But I imagine that if the Baktaman *had* constituted forums in which to engage in verbal examination of their rites and beliefs, this is a schema that they might themselves develop.

Is this so because they have already classified their reality according to such a dichotomy — i.e. that the duality is already there as a cultural fact and structures their ritual codes, while all that is lacking is a verbal gloss to make this reluctant anthropologist see it? I can find no persuasive evidence that this is so. Rather, I see a very simple non-verbal metaphor sketchily exploited — perhaps because it generates only a banal insight. Dichotomies and duality become powerful and interesting only within the closed worlds of digital codifications; as analogic imagery they remain trite compared to the complex harmonies of which such codes are capable.

An analogic code must consequently be understood in the context of its praxis; the practice of secrecy (ch. 24) and the absence of exegesis are essential features of this praxis among the Baktaman. It is also important to recognize the implications of the absence of writing, and of any conceptual awareness of the possibility of writing.[1] In such a world, only 'real objects' persist while communication is by definition ephemeral. Thus only those messages which are constantly recreated will be transmitted and persist as part of the tradition; i.e. only those metaphors and idioms that catch on and are re-used become part of the corpus of these codes. *This* is the structure that persists — not exemplified paradigms with an almost infinite productivity of 'the sayable', not even the sum of what 'is said', but only that which 'is received' and will be reactivated.

The events which release or trigger messages which produce shared understandings are thus the major framework for ritual forms — i.e. the structure of the ritual tradition derives from the social praxis, in concrete existential situations, which replicates messages. In this perspective, the empirical patterns of events described in initiation rites and other interactional sequences (Parts II and III) are not merely a description of the context of ritual and my observation of it; they also provide the key to an understanding of the processes which determine the very structure of the ritual codes. We shall explore the cumulative aspect of these processes in a later chapter (ch. 29).

The ephemeral nature of communication also has other, more

[1] cf. Goody 1968, pp. 4–5 and elsewhere, on the effects of limited literacy or familiarity with the existence of literacy; also his suggestion of the relevance of this for understanding the Dogon and similar exegetical traditions.

synchronic correlates. One striking feature is the way in which various parts of the cultural tradition seem to alternate between periods of activation and latency. When one woman needs to collect grass for a new skirt, she interests a few others in the same to make it a joint venture; thereupon others seem to be reminded of this option in their use of time and also make new skirts — not as a reflection of ecologic periodicity, but as a social fad. Similar pulsations were noticeable in housebuilding and other technical enterprises. The same is strikingly true of ritual knowledge. When the decision finally emerged that 6th degree initiation was to take place (p. 84), this may be seen as an event which triggered a large, complex message in the form of the initiation rite. But the composition of this message was in no way unproblematical; it had to be retrieved and reconstituted as a body of knowledge. Kimebnok explained to me that he would have to think hard to remember it correctly; he also spoke with members of the (c) set who had last passed through it, with senior adepts like Kayimkayak and Kwoŋkayam, and on several occasions with visiting Seltaman elders. These conversations led to a debate about change in the rite, but they were mainly concerned with establishing what constituted its substance. I was debarred, as a prospective novice, from participating in these debates and can only rely on Kimebnok's conversation about them after the fact. But in a similar discussion in which I participated during 4th degree initiation, the argument did not hinge on meaning and interpretation, i.e. was not exegetical, but merely factual in its purpose and content.

In other words, the image of 'triggering' a message is too simple in that it suggests the unequivocal availability of the substance of such messages; where activation is infrequent it is rather a question of laborious retrival and reconstitution.

Another correlate of non-literacy is the special importance of concrete symbols as uniquely durable messages. Such concrete objects serve as anchors, not only of abstract thought but of ephemeral communications in general. Persons hold on to the memory of a deceased parent, spouse, sibling, or child by tying and wearing mourning bands and often attaching objects associated with the dead person to them (cf. p. 124). Several women who wore their mothers' taro scrapers (*yom*) in this way, explained that the sound of them 'made them sorrowful'. As concrete representations of emotion, they serve to add reality both to the memory and the feeling. Likewise, a woman makes 1st degree insignia for a boy she feels close to 'to see him better', i.e. to aid them both in experiencing their durable relationship. And

230

the sacred marsupials clearly function in the same way for worshippers, as concrete aids to comprehend and retain the comprehension of ancestors and fertility.

Such concrete symbols, and the many acts and operations associated with them, constitute the aggregate, multiple messages of rites. We are now in a position to test our accumulated insights into the idioms and structures of these rites by trying to comprehend the major meanings of such complex messages, and the knowledge which they celebrate and transmit.

CHAPTER 26

Baktaman ritual
as a fertility mystery

To comprehend the full content of Baktaman ritual — the cognitions and values and moods that it codifies — we must see its idioms in full context. The setting for this is real life rather than any particular occasion of ritual contrivance. Let us therefore start concretely with a mature, knowledgeable man labouring in his garden: how do the knowledge and understandings he has gained through ritual provide him with ways of codifying his identity, the reality around him, and his own activity?

The man himself will be dressed in his one essential item of clothing: his *kamen-tēm* or penis-gourd. This is assumed by all males in good time before puberty and clearly expresses his male identity. The term *-tēm* indicates 'hole'; it is used for the burrow of an animal, for caves, and for the earth ovens in the gardens in which taro is cooked. In poetry the penis-gourd is used as a symbol of virility and (imaginatively) associated with the colour red (cf. p. 146); its plaited base-band of pandanus fibres has been noted, and the identification this entails between penis and arrow. Ritual adds complexity and depth to these associations: the mystical power of things that dwell in caves and burrows; the agnatic and masculine significance of red; the intensity of these aspects in the pandanus, which is also the source of fire; the blessing of arrows in the temple to enhance their power to hit and penetrate.

Besides this one culturally required item of male clothing, men also without exception wear coils of rattan around their waist, with which they kindle fire by the secret agency of the pandanus-dwelling *ubir* marsupial. Around their neck they normally wear a small net bag as an all-purpose pocket, but also a tiny, finger-shaped bag so tightly knotted as to hide its contents entirely; in it they carry a small ancestral relic, hanging over their breastbone and so in front of the seat of their soul. To such sacra they occasionally make minor offerings, whereby they call on the ancestors to intensify the general protective power that normally flows from the relic.

The nasal septum is pierced so that a boar's tusk can be worn in the nose; under its sacralizing arch all food which the man eats will pass, in the same way as was done with sacred food at several initiations. Finally, on the head he may wear a white shell band and a cassowary head-dress, associating him with the white, taro-giving stripe on the ancestral skull, and with the full-fledged 7th grade status of priest, drum-master and pig-slaughterer of which the cassowary is the symbol and in many ways epitome. Alternative head-dresses combine the black cassowary with white from cuscus fur, or the white tail-feather of the male hornbill.

Each of these items is hedged with taboos and so defined as harmonic with some and inimical to other substances and properties; each of them has multiple connotations and associations, both secular and secret. I could elaborate these in a paragraph for each but will rather refer the reader via the index to the preceding text; our attention here should focus more generally on the sum of cues and insignia that tell the man who and what he is, what power he represents and is associated with. Essentially, he is an initiate, in command of such rank and privilege as is known in his society; he has some understanding and control of what might be called the occult; at the same time he has enough knowledge to know that man and the world are a much greater mystery than he can fathom or control, that welfare and existence are precarious and need to be cultivated and protected.

He is indeed engaged in this, in the mundane form of cultivating a taro garden, but again within a framework of codifications that deepen and transform the task. The all-purpose tool he uses is an axe — besides which he always carries his bow and a selection of arrows, given him by trading partners in other communities, anointed with red ochre and white lime, some of the arrows blessed during temple offerings. The axe has a handle fashioned of hardwood — the wood that symbolizes the ancestors, and on which the sacra are hung in the *Yolam*. The blade has for the last c. 15 years normally been a steel axe-blade, traded in through a long chain of partners; but such axes are without any codified ritual meaning or power. Technically superior as they are to traditional stone adzes, they lack the latter's mystical powers, and the result is the present sickness and decline of the Baktaman. Properly, the adze should be made of fine-grained polished dark stone, like the stones that give power to novices at 3rd degree initiation.

The garden is a location defined by contrast and taboo: it is separated from the village, where things that grow cannot be eaten, and it is separated from the forest by taboos that protect it from some of the substances and powers there: wild boar, cassowary, and marsupials. Its capacity for growth and fertility is also protected from human birth and death, from menstrual blood and the precarious vitality of young boys; and the programming of this growth is the senior initiate's prerogative and duty — planting will continue until he performs the first harvest, when all further planting in that garden must stop.

When he looks at the garden area he sees and judges such technical factors as varying qualities of soil, moisture, and drainage, the constellation of trees that will give the desired combination of air and shade, the way the trees should fall to allow easy work with gardening and fencing, the convenient places to locate fires. But his secret knowledge also gives him a vision of the true nature of this reality. Using the imagery of 6th degree initiation he sees the ground as something that lives, like a cuscus body or the head of a man; he sees the life force that grows out as hair, fur, vegetation; he sees the ancestral power holding the taro tuber under ground, and then yielding it up as part of a covenant of descent, cult, and exogamy. At the same time he senses this power of fertility like a heat in the ground; and the revelation of 7th degree initiation showed him the whole garden like a colonnaded temple, with the shade-trees as mighty fire-posts carrying sacra, the ground like the sacred fireplace itself baking the food of the future.

So he goes about his labour with this vision and purpose, aiding, purifying, and protecting this welfare-creating process. He fights the trees and fells them, but lets the hardwood ancestors stand as posts of the sacred temple. He calls secretly on *ubir* and makes fire, he burns the litter and branches and saplings and sees the smoke carry power through the garden, and rise from this mystical fireplace to the pleasure of the ancestors, and form its column high into the air and tell the news to those who can interpret it. With his fire he also fights the wild boar, which ravages only the unprotected garden and is afraid to come where men are working: he uses his virility in the endless battle with this great despoiler — and impregnator of his sows.

What he does is also part of a pattern of co-operation with a woman, who complements his activities in planting and weeding and contributes her part to creation of the white, life-giving taro. She is unaware of the mysteries but heedful of her duties and will finally one day let the labour bear fruit when she returns to the village, staggering under the load of their joint produce. But meanwhile he must harvest the forest in secular hunting and give her game; while in an analogue secret mystery he must give game to the ancestors, keeping the temple fires warm so that power of growth will flow from the earth and make taro.

In a literal, rather pedestrian sense one might say that the source of this cosmic mystery lies in a central contradiction of Baktaman theory and practice: while they largely codify the world by a scale of purity and pollution which sees the sky and air as clean and ground as dirty and polluting, at the same time they produce their subsistence, their daily bread, as a root crop. That this is sensed as a paradox by the Baktaman is apparent in a number of ways, e.g. in the imagery of Myth 1. But beyond doubt the most inspired allegory, which represents a focal rendering of the mystery of agricultural fertility, is that of the brush turkey or megapod. According to authoritative ornithological description, 'these fowl-like birds . . . are notable for burying their eggs in mounds they scratch together . . . Incubation is by the heat generated from decaying vegetation in the mounds . . . The incubation period may extend to sixty-three days or longer. The young hatch down-covered and with wing quills large enough to enable them to fly.' (Rand and Gilliard 1967:92). Actual appearances are even more striking. The area of forest immediately around such megapod nest mounds gives an incongruous impression of artificiality till one notices that indeed, all the leaves, twigs, and debris normally littering the forest floor have been systematically removed to build the mound, leaving an area of forest as tidy and compulsive as a weeded garden. In the collected dirt and trash the birds then bury their white eggs, which slowly mature like taro tubers until they break out as birds, the purest of life forms.

This natural phenomenon the Baktaman convert into a potent vehicle of truth and understanding by elaborate veils of secrecy. Publicly, the brush turkey is declared impure because it scratches in the ground and eats subterranean grubs and snails; so only women and children may eat it or its eggs. Hints of special significance are given in that the most appropriate gift from a 1st degree novice to the woman who makes him his initiation insignia is a brush turkey. The song of the taro festival (p. 115) which women sing also makes cryptic mention of the bird; I gather they find it enigmatic, but all my evidence indicates that women and lower grade initiates firmly believe the bird to be impure. As part of 5th degree initiation, it and its eggs are revealed to be suitable game for the secret hunt, desirable as sacrifices to the ancestors and edible by initiates in secret. Finally, some time after 6th degree initiation, with the right it entails to see the *Yolam* sacra, the initiate will discover that the foot of a brush turkey is included with the ancestor's long bones in the pandanus-leaf shrine of the sacred fire post. Thus this metaphor of agriculture obtains the authoritative imprimatur of secrecy and incorporation in the relics in a way that cannot be a fake, and the mystery can be sensed: the power/blessing/association of the ancestor, by miraculous transformation, makes the impure pure; he lets white taro grow in the dirt yet emerge unpolluted, like the white eggs that emerge as birds and literally fly away into the pure world of the sky.

The Baktaman themselves — lacking any conceptual alternative — are not able to characterize the *theme* of their ritual, and I made no effort to formulate the question to them. Other Faiwolmin will label the activities pursued in the temples as taboo things, and things concerned with the ancestors. The cult activities can certainly be concretely characterized as ancestral cult, considering the skulls and other sacra, the sacrifices, and the prayers. But to classify Baktaman ritual anthropologically as an ancestor cult would be entirely to miss the point and import of the sacred symbols. As I hope the preceding pages have shown, their relevance is overwhelmingly to agriculture, growth, and fertility, and they encode this theme in the manner of a mystery cult. To the extent that the different symbols are related, they contribute modulations, harmonies, and elements to this theme; and the aggregate knowledge and significance they give to the process of taro agriculture are indeed complex and moving.

It is my subjective understanding that without such an interpretative context, taro agriculture is a very dull business. As a technical operation it is unchallenging and monotononous; even the most imaginative person would have great difficulties investing the hours, days, and months of toil with much 'meaning' or finding much inherent excitement in it — except for the occasional crash of falling trees, which seems to have a pan-human exhilarating effect. It is through the vehicles of thought and feeling which ritual provides that this rote can be transformed into something of meaning and value, and to the extent that it makes the work of subsistence more tolerable, Baktaman ritual may be said to have an immensely important function, so long as this is not then regarded as an adequate 'explanation' for the existence of these rites. In what he learns through initiations, a Baktaman is given codifications that can lead him to experience

236

what might otherwise be misery or boredom as activity with meaning and quality so that it may emerge for him as the very epitome of the 'good life'. But it should be noted that this apparatus for interpretation is provided for a minority of Baktaman only. I am unable to conceptualize what gardens and garden labour mean to a Baktaman woman, i.e. I do not know what symbols and understandings she uses to interpret her experience. Nor do I see that lower grade initiates, before passing 6th degree, have obtained sufficient knowledge to enable them to savour much of the meaning which the ritual idioms make possible. In large part because of the very secrecy that makes of their ritual knowledge a vital moving mystery, roughly four fifths of the population will thus at any one time be excluded from understanding, with half of them categorically prevented from ever partaking in the insights that ritual creates. Perhaps many of these are content with a prosaic existence; perhaps the effects of taboo, threat, and deceit are to dampen curiosity. Some women seem to be sensitive to a few of the elements of metaphor and to construct small interpretative messages of their own: several women on one or more occasions hung a taro leaf on the domestic fire-post, in a position analogous to where shrines are placed; many practised private forms of pig-rubbing with white earth and had small 'shrines' above the pigs' sleeping places; one had a private, growth-promoting ritual for taro suckers. I would also imagine that authoritative participation in the mysteries by fathers, uncles, brothers, and, in the case of married women, husbands has ramifying social effects: a tenor of (unspecified) significance or 'meaning' is created in what they do jointly together. But without a doubt, the full impact of the fertility mystery is felt only by senior initiates.

What, then, at a more analytical level, is it this ritual does for the participants? In his brilliant portrayal of two varieties of Islam, Geertz tells us that, 'What sacred symbols do for those to whom they are sacred is to formulate an image of the world's construction and a program for human conduct that are mere reflexes of one another. . . . Such symbols render the world view believable and the ethos justifiable, and they do it by evoking each in support of the other.' (Geertz 1968:97).

Quite clearly, this is the vital role of Baktaman sacred symbols — they make sense of the work of gardening in terms that are congruent with the identity and character of man, and they interpret man's task and values in terms that articulate with this picture of reality. Indeed, they seem to go even further, and to provide the main con-

237

cepts whereby reality is comprehended and constituted, and the main vehicles for thought and emotion through which identity is constructed. The only theory of gardening and growth which the Baktaman know is contained in these metaphors and allegories, and the courage, purpose, stamina, awe, and dependence exercised in gardening activity are codified by concrete symbols such as arrows, pandanus, marsupials, temples, and ancestral skulls.

At the same time these sacred symbols have a multiplicity and complexity, albeit in a loose, analogic structure, so I am repeatedly driven to use the imagery of harmonies, chords, or even symphonies. Note, for example, in the preceding description of the man in his garden the multi-vocality of smoke as a symbol: in the temple it transforms offerings to intangible substance and so transmits them to the ancestor. This mystery it performs, in several modulations, in the gardens as well — at the same time as it communicates information to other men, fights the eternal battle with the wild boar, and clears the ground for planting. It also serves as a sign of the 'heat' of fertility in the ground, as support to the metaphor of garden as sacred temple fire, as the place where the food of the future is being prepared, as the analogue to the directly perceptible heat in the brush turkey's miraculously creative nest mound.[1]

Though Baktaman sacred symbols thus go deeply into the very constitution of reality and man, and not only serve to articulate a world view and an ethos, they are at the same time more limited in scope (cf. Geertz 1968:112) than the above formulation of Geertz might lead us to expect. There is much of reality about which these rites have very little to say, and many concerns of man to which they are very marginal or truly irrelevant. For an adequate view of such sectors of knowledge and their dynamic relations, we need to compare the potentialities and praxis of the different sectors.

---

[1] We may speculate on further elaborations of these basic metaphors that I can see no way to confirm or falsify: Is the heat of fertility also like that of living bodies (of marsupials) upon which fur grows, like the heat of the head on which hair grows, like the heat of puberty? Virility is red as pandanus — is it red as fire, is it heat? It dwells in the hole of the penis gourd, like the hole of the earth ovens where the taro for festivals is cooked. In secrecy, persons are killed by burning their food leavings in the fire; when these can also be placed inside the ancestral skull, or inside a woman's vagina, is this because analogous heat dwells there? Suggestion, and invitations to codification, abound; but I am unable to ascertain whether these conceptualizations and analogues are identifiable parts of a Baktaman corpus of knowledge.

CHAPTER 27

Creative and stagnant sectors of knowledge

The complexity of metaphor and imagery connected with gardening and fertility contrast with the relative simplicity of Baktaman expression in many other fields of knowledge. I have particularly noted the lack of elaboration of any notable body of knowledge concerning sickness and cure (pp. 141 ff.), and I have noted features in Baktaman theories of man and of social relations which appear both simple and crude, and indeed inadequate in view of the tact, sensitivity, and understanding which the Baktaman largely practise (cf. sorcery, pp. 133 ff., and warfare, pp. 152 ff.). Some characteristics of social organization and interaction that go with these features have already been described. I now wish to develop the comparison of such stagnant sectors of knowledge with the more prolific fertility ritual, and thereby test some general propositions about the conditions of creativity. Briefly, I will argue that the dynamism of a sector of knowledge depends both (i) on the potential of the major codifications, i.e. the fertility and capacity for precision and development of the symbolic apparatus by which it is handled, and (ii) on the praxis, i.e. the social organization of statuses and tasks that constitute the acts and channel the communications.

Firstly I need to establish the relative creativity of the agricultural rites — not merely the complexity of their idioms, but their actively innovative character. Some concrete incidents of change, and attempted change, have been given in the preceding text, and additional ones are found in my material. Briefly (details will emerge in the discussion that follows), I know of (i) a change in the form of the 6th degree initiations (pp. 91 f.); (ii) a dispensation allowing the (c) set in 6th grade to beat the drums (p. 119); (iii) the replacement of sacred stones in the *Yolam* (p. 65); (iv) the introduction of the stone slab under the *Yolam* skull; (v) the introduction of a wild boar mandible among the *Yolam* sacra; (vi) the construction of Kaineŋ's ancestral monument (p. 139); and attempted reductions of the taboos on eating (vii) white worms, (viii) wild male pig, and (ix) wild female pig (p. 201).

This may not seem an impressive listing of creativity; but it should be remembered that change takes place unrecorded and largely unacknowledged, and I have no doubt failed to recognize numerous cases. Of those noted, three (i, vi, and ix) took place during the year of my fieldwork, and all of them have taken place within the memory of Ngaromnok, i.e. over the last c. 20 years.

Rather than approach these ripples of change from the outside and classify them as successful vs. unsuccessful, or concerned with positive rites vs. prohibitions, etc., we should focus first of all on their specific topic: the symbol that is being modified, i.e. *where* in a system of knowledge the intellectual work is taking place. I would argue that this is far from random, but concentrates in a few, predictable areas:

Wild pig. This is an important, multivocal, and unclear symbol (cf. pp. 201 ff.) and three of the items are concerned with it. Aŋabieŋ's attempt to break the taboos surrounding wild female pig (ix) and give its meat to the women was innovative but doomed to failure; one may argue that it reflects confusion rather than creative thought, but is no less real for that. The attempt to change the rules regarding wild male pig (viii) are more interesting. Baktaman taboos are particularly restrictive in limiting such meat to 7th grade initiates; all western neighbours allow it from 4th grade. About 10 years ago a group of Baktaman novices, visiting the village of the Wokfiakmin to the S.W. for 4th degree initiations, adopted the local rules and ate wild male pig when they were there. Subsequent to their return to Baktaman, the taro failed; and Baktaman seniors see this as vindication that the taboo is the will of *their* ancestors, though other ancestors are different. Thus a few Seltaman of lower degree who reside with the Baktaman *do* eat and receive shares of male wild pig, while the taboo is maintained even for the now very mature (30–40 yrs) 6th degree (c) set of Baktaman. On the other hand, this association of wild boar with 7th rather than 4th degree initiation does not particularly clarify its connotations as a concrete symbol — there does not seem to be anything particularly apposite about associating the beast with the *Amowkam*, and rather better reason to connect a man's competence to eat it with his ascent to full virility at 4th degree *Mafom* initiation. Thus, though the attempted change was defeated, the symbolic value of male wild pig remains unclear and ambivalent.

240

But the most obvious ambivalence arises in connection with the *Yolam* vs. wild male boar opposition (v). This opposition is central to the Baktaman definition of male boar as primarily an anti-taro and anti-gardening force, an enemy and rival to Baktaman male success and thus inimical to the 'male' *Yolam*. Yet as noted (pp. 201 f.), male boar also clearly embodies virility and aggressiveness, and might be seen as a more impressive analogue to the aggressive marsupials used in warfare rites (p. 150), and thus highly compatible with the *Yolam* as war temple. About 15 years ago, events took a turn in this direction. The (c) set had just been initiated to 3rd degree; and as he emerged from that seclusion Ngaromnok came upon a very large wild boar in the act of copulating with a domestic sow. He shot it and killed it. When shortly later the (c) set, as novice warriors, joined their first raid they carried the mandible of this formidable animal with them in a net bag. The raid was successful, and Buryēp, the cult-master at the time, thereupon incorporated the mandible among the *Yolam* sacra without changing the basic rule banning all other male boar meat or bones from the temple. The various codifications of male boar have still not been brought into harmony, nor its connotations as a concrete symbol clarified; and I would expect this to continue to be a matter to puzzle and concern the Baktaman, i.e. one on which their creativity will focus.

White worms and grubs (vii). As in the case of male wild pig, Baktaman taboos are here more strict than those of their western neighbours. The idea is general that the small white worms in breadfruit, white larvae (*ŋāp*), and the large white grubs in rotting logs (*yerōp*) are bad for first degree novices; but the Baktaman taboo extends till 6th degree. There was recently a major move among young men to change this by adopting the western fashion and many men of the (b) set started eating such grubs, which are regarded as a delicacy; but worms subsequently attacked the taro and the taboo was reinstated.

The symbolic value of these insects for the Baktaman is fundamentally based on their white colour, which makes them a metaphor for taro plenty and thus good, though forbidden to lower initiates who are not yet ready for revelation of the mystery of whiteness. In Myth 2 they are also identified with the body and hair of the ancestor, and together with bats, which are similarly identified, they all become permitted after 6th degree initiation when that revelation takes place. But they are inherently ambiguous: white and burrowing they are like taro under ground and stand for increase; white and elongated they are like the ancestor's white hair and stand for fertility; but internal instead of external like hair they could stand for decrease rather than increase; and elongated and burrowing they are like taro-attacking worms and could stand for destruction rather than fertility. The breadfruit-eating worms are even more amenable to the two latter equations. Again, we may understand a continuing puzzlement and concern to clarify such ambivalent connotations.

Stones in the Yolam. Two items of change concern this; both are conceptually simple and the innovations were accepted. (ii) When the village was moved from Weitembip to Kerabobip (cf. Map p. 23), about 10 years ago, the sacred stones of the *Yolam* (cf. p. 65) were mislaid. In replacement, two black stone adzes were adopted — consistent with, and clarifying, the imagery of their use in striking the elbows of 3rd degree novices and thus making them as strong as trees, hopefully as ancestral hardwood trees. (iv) The ancestral skull in the *Yolam* used to lie on the *gāim* nest (made by the *ŋāp* larvae) directly on the floor of the temple. After participating in a major rite, some guests from Wokfiakmin village criticized this arrangement, pointing out that the *gāim* was clean and should not be placed on the floor, equivalent to the ground (though the temple floor is in fact raised c.4' on pillars). Baktaman seniors were suspicious that this might be an attempt to fool them or damage them; but they discussed it and finally decided it was right; so they fetched a flat rock slab and laid the *gāim* on it.

Changes connected with initiations. The change in 6th degree initiation (i) whereby novices were excluded from one of the main commensal feasts has been described, as have the circumstances surrounding it. In this case Kimebnok was forced by collective senior opinion to adopt a new, western fashion of which he did not really approve. As for the drumming dispensation (ii), it is probably not a change but really a stop-gap to allow set (c) fuller expression as de-facto senior men, until initiation to 7th degree can be arranged. (cf. p. 119). But unless an *Amowkam* temple is reconstituted or that of the Seltaman becomes properly active, the pattern may have to be adopted permanently.

These nine innovations show some suggestive patterns. A majority of them are concerned with the clarification of the multiple connotations of a symbol — some where this is and remains problematical, some where the innovation is merely an additional contribution to harmonic precision. All of them are by their nature joint concerns: they involve the form of collective ritual acts and representations,

242

the social allocation of privilege, and the collective effects (in the form of collective consequences of the breach of a taboo) of individual acts.

Only the one innovation that I have not yet discussed seems different in these respects: the ancestral monument (vi) constructed by Kaineŋ (p. 139). This came about in the following manner: to defend the community against a threatening epidemic, he constructed a conventional spirit gate. But when this was completed, he had materials left over: a gnarled post of hardwood, red paint of ochre and pig's blood. An old village site, where he himself had been born, had been partly cleared as space for his present hamlet of Kerabip; so he took the materials there, erected the post and sacralized it with three lines of the red paint.

This is essentially a case of free elaboration, an imaginative personal expression in a readily understandable idiom, but with an entirely novel combination of symbols. I have heard Kimebnok acknowledge this in conversation, but did not understand him to express any unequivocal evaluation of the monument. Nor was I able to pick up any spontaneous praise or criticism from others. The monument has clearly not been the subject of much explanatory discussion — thus all men below 40 remained unaware that Kerabip was the site of a previous Baktaman settlement, and that Kaineŋ was born there. I have no way of telling whether this creative message has been incorporated into a common Baktaman body of knowledge and representations.

My experience in learning and participating in Baktaman ritual communications is consistent with the view that such free elaborations as Kaineŋ's monument are exceptional and probably inconsequential. The interest in ritualizing and elaborating within this potentially immensely rich symbolism is minimal; my own willingness and need to codify were not shared by others. One of many possible examples may serve to clarify: after 3 days of water taboo during 6th degree initiation the novices break the fast with sugar cane or banana leaf sap. The latter is obtained from immature banana leaves which develop as an extension of the trunk in white, thick sheets, curled in the shape of the trunk cylinder. You lay each such sheet flat, shear off the top skin and thereby expose a multitude of large pores, each almost full of cool, slightly tangy water; and you suck or pour this mild, soothing fluid into your parched mouth. This can clearly be done elegantly or clumsily, without spilling or carelessly — it seemed to me an inviting occasion for expressive ritualization, and as a participating novice I was eager to do it right. But nothing has been made in Baktaman tradition of this link in the ritual sequence; any way will do, the point is simply not to drink running water till the next day. Elaborations, as pointed out above, occur where problems and discrepancies are felt and *require* a resolution, not as intellectual speculation or play. The fear, awe, and reluctance that spring from the ritual's character as a mystery cult may in part be responsible for blocking such interpretative elaboration. But that these forms of understanding none the less have very considerable potentialities for development is suggested by the mulch gardens of some western Highlands people (Brookfield 1971), where the heat generated from rotting vegetable material is used to protect the plants against low night temperatures. Such an agronomical technique is clearly a possible transformation from the Baktaman imagery based on brush turkey symbolism.

The purported criteria by which innovations are evaluated by the Baktaman seem to be pragmatic. An agreement that the taro either suffered or prospered entails an authoritative conclusion that the innovation must be rejected or adopted respectively. Behind this, however, we can see other processes operate. The most clearly identified is public opinion: pressure and criticism from cult leaders elsewhere (cf. the role of Seltaman and Wokfaikmin seniors), rivalry within the community between leaders (cf. Kimebnok vs. Taneŋ), or the articulated desires of lower initiates (cf. the (c) set's desire to use the drums). Behind this, again, we may search for factors such as a need for cognitive consistency, and differentials in power sustaining unequal distributions of privilege. The role of such, and other, factors may best be tested by a comparison with differently codified and less creative sectors of knowledge.

The theme of sickness provides an illuminating contrast. Here is a phenomenon that interests the Baktaman greatly, through which man's fate is significantly determined, and where frequent external events activate the interest and trigger discussion and action. Yet it represents a poorly systematized sector of knowledge and one in which I found no evidence of active creativity. Some of the factors entailed in this were discussed in chapter 15. The multiplicity of explanations of sickness was noted (pp. 142 f.) including spirit attacks of various different kinds, sorcery, effects of breaches of taboo, pollution, and disease. We also noted the patterns of diagnosis (pp. 141 f.), cure (pp. 139 ff.) and the absence of definitive collective conclusions or evaluations (pp. 143). This latter reflects the basic codification of sickness: though often considered a collective *concern*, action to resist it is an individual *task* — even such action as building a spirit gate. There are thus ready fora in which to discuss the topic, but no implications that this should commit participants to any kind of collective action. Thus, though sickness is the subject of far more, and freer, analytical discussion than agriculture and fertility and is also codified in fairly vivid non-verbal idioms with potential for development, it lacks the cumulative and systematizing constraint of collective commitment. The fact that so many different *kinds* of explanations are available, many of them involving different non-material agents, also seems logically to militate against systematization and become self-maintaining: even if rigorous analysis were to be pursued, competing explanations could probably not be falsified.

Baktaman conceptualizations of man and social relations present a somewhat different picture. I have suggested (pp. 134 ff.) that the development of a more differentiated model of man's emotions and psyche is blocked by the blanket use of a sorcery model of motivation. Such constant awareness of sorcery leads to great alertness and tact, but not to exploratory or analytical discourse about the complex constitution of the emotions and motivations of others: speech takes the form of veiled accusations, and non-verbal expression, whether defensive or aggressive, is secret and private.

The discussion of obligations and the construction of social relations is similarly sidetracked by sorcery fears, and linkage with the exogenous events of appearance and disappearance of sickness: sorcery theory systematically connects the performance of social relations with the vicissitudes of health in such a way that the latter trigger and resolve discussions of the former. Only in the case of the special roles of cult leaders do debates of a different kind take place, induced by the activities of rival pretenders (cf. pp. 118 ff.).

Ancestor cult likewise fails to provide the Baktaman with an adequate vehicle for moral discourse and conceptualization. With ancestors codified as capricious old men, and linked to the exogenous variable of gardening success, a systematization of concepts to describe the permanence and complexity of social life (e.g. trust and responsibility) is not easily performed in such idioms. A groping attempt is clearly made to articulate the principles of male solidarity and corporate obligations in certain initiation rites (esp. 3rd degree, p. 64), but the symbols employed show a low level of precision and intensity.

Nor do confrontations between alters in overt conflict provide occasions for the development of any body of shared insights in the community. Such events, e.g. marital disputes, are not adjudicated by others but elicit only uncoordinated and tangential public reaction

245

(cf. p. 108). Collective action occurs only in self-help and vengeance, and in the lynching of sorcerers. In various fields of possible elaboration of representations of man and society, we thus see combinations of codification and praxis that in different ways inhibit the development of this sector of knowledge.

The comparison of fertility ritual with these more stagnant sectors of knowledge thus brings out the special features of the former which provide its conditions of creativity. To recapitulate: sorcery beliefs are cast in potentially very productive codes, but among the Baktaman involve a non-productive praxis of circumspection of speech and private secrecy of non-verbal expression. The codification of sickness in terms, among other alternatives, of a variety of immaterial spirit agents removes this field of knowledge from the discipline of pragmatic falsification; and a praxis where collective action is rarely called for inhibits the development of shared criteria for diagnosis and indeed fora that aim at the production of agreement. The development of an explicit and systematic morality of social relations is hampered by the poverty of productive codifications and concepts, and by a similar lack of joint fora; it is also obfuscated by a linkage with sequences of events — sickness and recovery — which initiate and terminate concerns in a relatively random fashion.

The temple cults, on the other hand, are organized in a unique way. They are linked to exogenous events, so these events *trigger* activity; whereas only to a very small extent do they interrupt or terminate the ritual programs thereby initiated. They constitute fora for the production of collective and shared messages. They repeatedly require and produce the necessity of collective commitment and action. These features would seem to embody the main organizational conditions for creativity. Why this creativity should turn mainly towards the elaboration of a fertility mystery rather than a religion of man and society is a different question. The formal structure of an ancestor cult should be at least as adequate for the latter as for the former. But in their metaphors for growth and fertility the Baktaman have a tradition of vivid imagery with which to work and to which they may add, while their relationship to the ancestor is conceptualized as a dependency relation to a capricious and arbitrary alter, not particularly productive of insights. We thus see that their creativity asserts itself where two independent preconditions are simultaneously fulfilled: the symbolic apparatus has great potential, and the organization of roles and fora is such as to trigger and facilitate collective expression.

CHAPTER 28

The temple syndromes

We have seen that the ritual life of the Baktaman is organized around three different kinds of temples, each serving as the locus for differently codified rites. This is quite an elaborate organization, considering that only 54 men (initiation sets b–f), acting on behalf of a total population of 183, use them for their cult. So far we have largely seen these cult activities under a unified perspective: (a) as sets of symbols for expressing and communicating a tradition of knowledge, and (b) as a sequence of initiation into the secret and occult. I shall now focus on the distinctive constitution of different temples and their rites, to see what significance this pattern of elaboration has.

A complete schema should in fact also include the men's house, since it contains shields and minor sacra and is used for some ritual occasions. The full set of temples, and their connection with the sequence of initiations, may then be represented as follows:

Temple		Initiation grade				
Amowkam			4			7
Katiam	2		4	5		
Yolam		3		5	6	
(Kaweram/men's house	1					)

With the loss of the *Amowkam*, the *Katiam* seems to have taken over some of its functions: as the retreat of seniors during 4th degree initation, as the repository for drums, etc. In its minor sacred functions, and as an alternative repository for shields, the men's house likewise seems to be related to the *Yolam*. The main contrast on which much of the following discussion will focus is therefore that between *Katiam* and *Yolam*, for which my data are most adequate.

The *Katiam* (cf. pp. 60 ff., 109 ff.) is designated by the Baktaman as the Taro House and the Big Sister. Although everything inside its door is equally secret and forbidden to the initiated on penalty of death, it is clearly constituted around some central sacred objects: ancestral relics, trophies of the hunt, and the sacred fire. Besides this it contains drums, pandanus gouges of cassowary long-bones, pig scapula spoons, cassowary breastbone drinking vessels, and a considerable amount of personal hunting equipment and adornment. The relics are identified as *clan* relics; in the main *Katiam* in Feisabip hamlet are the bones of six persons of four different clans, in that of Kamsurbaŋ hamlet only one person of a fifth clan. These persons are not identified as the founding ancestors of their clan and their names are personal names unconnected etymologically with the clan names; yet they are clearly conceptualized as 'ancestors' for all local members of a clan. The sacra themselves include mandibles, collar-bones, and fingerbones, *not* skulls or long-bones.

The hunting trophies are cassowary pelvises, wild pig mandibles, and a few skulls. Both male and female wild pig are found; in the Feisabip temple these are carefully identified and kept separate, while in the Kamsurbaŋ temple they are mixed. These should properly be from *all* cassowary and wild pig killed, not just those taken in secret hunt.

The *Yolam*, by contrast (cf. pp. 113 ff.) is called the War House and the Little Sister. It is constituted around two central relics: the skull and mandible of an ancestor, and the ancestral long-bones and brush turkey foot of the firepost shrine. Formerly, two skulls were found in the *Yolam*. Though the clan of the ancestor(s) in the *Yolam* is known, this is of secondary significance and the skull serves as a representation of the ancestors of all Baktaman. Other essential sacred objects are two fires, the sacred arrows used to puncture the sacrifice at *Wonsā*, and the sacred stones for 3rd degree initiation. It also contains trophies of *female* wild pig killed in *secret* hunt, war shields, and various minor paraphernalia.

First introduction to the *Katiam* is at 2nd degree initiation, but any real understanding of its functions is not attained till after 5th degree. Some time after 6th degree men tend to take up permanent residence in the *Katiam*, but this is optional; even of the 11 men who have passed 7th degree, 2 remain resident in ordinary men's houses. Any man who has passed 7th degree initiation may establish his own *Katiam*. The *Yolam*, on the other hand, is defined as the common temple of the whole community; only one should exist. No one resides permanently in it though the cult-master may live there for periods of time. First access

248

is with 3rd degree initiation; real participation in the rites comes with 5th and particularly 6th degree.

The activities in the two temples are also consistently different. Not only is life in the *Katiam* affected by its being the normal residence of a group of men, with all the activities this implies; the organization of *Katiam* ritual is also largely decentralised and individual. Any person initiated to 7th degree is an authorized priest with authority to approach his clan ancestors; so each clan shrine is the object of independent cult. Since the bones of *all* cassowaries and wild pig should be presented to the clan ancestor whether hunted secretly or not, this involves a considerable amount of activity. When marsupials and rodents are eaten in the *Katiam*, their bones are likewise offered to the ancestor. In addition to this, the *Katiam* leader frequently organizes secret hunts and collective ritual.

The *Yolam*, on the other hand, is always the scene of communal cult — even when the cult leader alone makes small offerings through the sacred fire, he does so on behalf of all; and nothing wild must be offered that has not been taken in a secret hunt with its accompanying communal taboos. The predominant rite in the *Yolam* is thus that of whole initiation grade congregations performing collective sacrifices. Marsupials predominate in these sacrifices rather than cassowary and female pigs; and male pig is, as noted, banned. Before pacification, I expect the tenor of these offerings to have been somewhat more affected by warfare and less by taro; but an emphasis on taro fertility is definitely a predominant traditional feature. This is seen, among other things, in the association of the mystery of *white* colour specifically with the *Yolam*, whereas *red* and *black* are characteristic of *Katiam* and *Amowkam*, though both are also represented in *Yolam*. The dichotomy of drums vs. shields also defines the two former temples vs. the latter, though the *Amowkam* is uniquely characterized by its decorated façade of ancestral figures of a design similar to that of the war shields. Finally, the *Amowkam* seems to have been associated with a pattern of secret hunts reminiscent of the *Katiam*, i.e. without the emphasis on total community participation — but also without the separate clan activities of the *Katiam*.

What are the major themes that we see codified in *Katiam* and *Yolam* rites respectively? As shown, both play a part in the orchestration of the fertility mystery; but they also constitute distinctive, if partial, alternative condifications. Cast as they are in the structure of an ancestral cult, we may say that each gives a substantive codification of the relations Man-Land-Ancestors, and through their inter-

249

relations also a conceptualization of the identity and essence of each part of this triad. Man sustains the fertility of Land through his cult of Ancestors, he maintains health and vigour for the population as a whole, and for men specifically in contra-distinction to women. The cults further define the essential collectivities of men, and their connection to land as resource and territory. Let us see how the two temple systems do this slightly differently.

In the *Katiam*, Man is related to Ancestors in terms of clan; men are distinguished as connected to different clan ancestors, and they pursue their relationship to clan ancestors independently — i.e. their basic identity is codified in terms of membership in a patrilineal clan. This has implications for their relationship to Land: clan membership gives access to clan territories for hunting and gathering; it also comes closest to a ritual expression of lineal rights of succession to fallow lands and to sago and pandanus trees. The *Katiam* sacred symbols also provide a codification of the relations of man and woman: the fundamental distinctiveness of clans is expressed in clan exogamy and entails a codification of reciprocal exchange between clans, and sexuality as a bond between persons of different groups, not just different categories.

In this temple, Man relates to Ancestor through the offering of game in a relatively continuous, everyday flow of prestations, not just on special ritual occasions. In return he obtains taro fertility and plenty. This is a close metaphor to the man-woman relationship of exchange and mutual interdependence in daily subsistence; I understand the imagery as assimilating ancestral fertility and female fertility as analogous complements to man's contributions. But the *Katiam* is also like a hunting lodge in its continuous transactions with ancestors over game, and prayers for hunting luck are directed to the clan ancestors, assimilating them also to the male role in game ⇄ taro exchanges with women.

Finally, the association of 4th degree initiation with the *Katiam* gives another rendering of basically the same theme: man's individual role as a mature and virile actor vis-à-vis a female alter. The pandanus and wig imagery, the dancing, and the marathon ordeal focus on his individual capacity, blessed and authorized by the clan ancestors.

In the *Yolam*, on the other hand, the same relations are codified differently. Man is related to Ancestors as a member of a community; the skull symbolizes everyone's ancestors and man's identity is codified as member of an initiation set composed of age-mates, as part of a total congregation of all Baktaman. (This contrast to *Katiam*

250

rites is also seen in the option, uniquely open in the *Katiam*-associated 4th degree initiation, whereby others may join the novices as dancers.)

The central rites whereby Man relates to Ancestors in the *Yolam* are offerings, as in the *Katiam;* but in the *Yolam* these are always solemn sacrifices of meat sanctified through secret hunt and in no way reminiscent of male-female exchanges. The ancestor controls this hunt, not by giving hunting luck but by releasing game, which is a representation of himself; and so the commensal meal becomes a communion in which man partakes of the deity. From this arises the mystery of blessing, conceptualized in imagery such as fur and whiteness, which create taro fertility in the land.

Yolam rites also relate Man to Land as territory through their warfare potency. Through the collective strength of the community, furthered by 3rd degree initiations that emphasize solidarity above individual prowess, and by special rites mobilizing protection, like a shield, to the warriors, Baktaman lands and lives are defended and enemies are humiliated. The triad of Man-Land-Ancestor in the *Yolam* is thus constituted without the unilineal, inter-sexual, and individual aspects of the *Katiam* codifications, but with a stronger emphasis on community inclusiveness and solidarity, and a deeper level of fertility mystery.

These codifications provide answers to some basic existential questions which presumably arise in one form or another in all societies:

What are the continuities of substance and succession between the generations — generally entailing a view of man and woman?

What are the links between people and territory?

What is the basic constitution of sodalities?

In terms of anthropological conventions, the answers to such questions are usually analysed in terms of the concept of descent; and in this sense one might say that particularly the *Katiam* rites can be understood as Baktaman statements about the nature of descent. But it is also surely true that in other societies, major answers to such questions are formulated on the basis of concepts of 'property' or 'sovereignty'. It does not seem particularly fruitful to mutilate Baktaman conceptualizations by means of a preconceived anthropological notion of (the importance of) descent. Indeed if we refrain from such narrow procedures, comparison with other ethnographies is facilitated. There are some striking analogues to Baktaman codifications to be found in the 'ritual relationship' of Australian aboriginal clans and their totemic and other sites as described by Hiatt (1962, 1966).

251

Other 'ritual relationships' between groups and land are vividly expressed by Talis and Namoos in their harvest festivals (Fortes 1936), representing a codification of immigrant chiefs and autochthonous earth priests inadequately captured by means of a concept of descent, property, or sovereignty. It is by giving attention to the existential questions which they *link together,* and not by extracting what is relevant to one question only and describing this extract as 'a system', that we can grasp the structure and implications of such codifications.

In New Guinea we find a number of different codifications involving ancestors and descendants which fit a 'descent' concept most uneasily, precisely because the native codifications link the question of succession and continuity of substance with other themes: not only marriage, alliance, settlement pattern, and territory, as we have now learned to expect (Leach 1954, 1961; Strathern 1969), but also wealth and pig exchange (Bulmer 1960), personal health (Hogbin 1970), sex and pollution (Meggitt 1964), agricultural fertility (van Baal 1966). There is also clear evidence that these codifications and linkages are the subject of change, borrowing and re-casting. Thus we know from the Highlands that the Moka ceremony, and the conceptualizations it entails regarding group identity, alliance, and rank, has spread to new groups (Bulmer 1960; Strathern 1971); and that new cult forms have spread from neighbour to neighbour (cf. Bulmer 1965:148 ff., for an example).

The relevance of this to our present problem of understanding the *Katiam* and *Yolam* — and *Amowkam* — ritual syndromes is that it underscores the importance of (i) understanding each as a set of answers to *clusters* of existential questions, (ii) recognizing them as potentially alternative codifications, and (iii) acknowledging the possibility that each may have a history of its own, rather like a sect movement spreading from group to group.

I have argued elsewhere (Barth 1971) that a variety of different kinds of evidence in fact suggests a culture history in the Faiwolmin area in which each of these temple syndromes may have spread at a different time, and that ritual practices have thereby modified local communities and cultures in different ways. Baktaman equivalences are difficult to establish, and are increasingly deceptive as the distance and difference from particular Baktaman forms become greater; but there can be no doubt that temples like those of the Baktaman are found among neighbouring groups.

Thus temples called *Yolam* and containing the types of sacra which this implies for Baktaman are found in a great number of Failwol-speaking communities along the mountain slope westward from the Baktaman.

The group collectively known as Awonklamin, to the north-east, also have the *Yolam;* but their closest representatives, Kasamin village (only 2–3 hours from Baktaman village across a suspension bridge over the Murray River) have one only 6-foot square, and recognize that they 'do not know as much about' the *Yolam* as their western neighbours. Among the Kwermin, east of Baktaman, the *Yolam* is absent, and only the *Katiam* is found; it is located in the 'empty' ritual centre of a population living in dispersed hamlets. The Baktaman *Amowkam,* before its destruction, was the easternmost example of its kind; now their western neighbours the Seltaman define the eastern limits of distribution of such temples, with façades decorated with ancestral figures, as all temples are further west, and as even family houses are further north-west in Telefomin. The *Katiam* type, on the other hand, seems to be absent among western groups of the Faiwolmin.

We thus see suggestions of an age-area distribution of these temples, with *Katiam* dominant in the eastern periphery and persisting only from the central area eastwards, *Yolam* found everywhere except in the extreme eastern periphery, and *Amowkam* most recently spreading from the west (cf. Barth 1971 for details of this argument).

These distributions correlate with indicative features of social organization. The distribution of the *Yolam* is coterminous with the occurrence of nucleated villages, as we would expect from its communal emphasis. The *Katiam,* with its clan sacra, correlates with clan organization — exogamous clans in most of its range, agamous clans on the western fringe of *Katiam* distribution. Beyond these boundaries, both west, north, and east, one finds cognatic systems. (The southern boundary, as will be remembered, represents a drastic ecologic dividing line between mountain and a swampy lowland, occupied by river people of entirely distinct language and culture.)

There are also suggestions that the Baktaman population may have coalesced as a nucleated village only a few generations ago. Thus the Yeni clan has traditions that their ancestors were once settled in the northern part of present Baktaman territory, where they today have their exclusive clan lands; while Yabik clan claims the area to the southeast and has traditions of residence there. On the other hand, the largest Baktaman clan, Minkarin, has no separate territory and no tradition of separate residence, and prefers to have its gardens in the central area around the Bak stream. Thus, the collectively important *Yolam* is probably a more recent accession than the *Katiam* and may be historically connected with the establishment of nucleated, multiclan settlements. These hints of past culture history give a plausible background for understanding the present assemblage which constitutes Baktaman ritual. Probably, different and variant codifications of the themes that concern them most — the mystery of agricultural fertility; the fellowships of solidarity, congregation, and blood; the identity of man and his relationship to land — have reached them at various times, mainly from the west. They have come to them as cult or sect movements, linked to temples like the forms now identified as *Katiam*, *Yolam*, and *Amowkam*. Though in a sense alternative, such codifications need not be conceptualized as opposed — they are different insights into the constitution of reality which give life meaning and depth. The Baktaman have borrowed, thought, and reshaped these ideas; they have copied neighbours and recast the rites in a unified series of initiations, but have done so according to their own design and understanding, in a sequence and with a distribution of taboos and secrets fully shared by no other community. In this way the views of Man, Land, and Ancestors entailed in *Katiam*, *Yolam*, and *Amowkam* have retained distinctive emphasis, and yet been fused into a single body of knowledge and understandings. Thus, the skull in the *Yolam is* a member of the Yeni clan and this affects Kimebnok's relationship to him, by virtue of his own Minmurup clan status, even though *Yolam* has nothing to do with clan cult. While providing different keys to life, these temples yet seem as fully integrated in premises and values as what we find in many other cultures — e.g. in our own tradition of knowledge as between institutions like universities, theological seminaries, and teachers' training colleges. But to analyse the character and extent of such integration, we need to refocus on the actual processes of communication and transmission.

CHAPTER 29

Transmission and integration

The total corpus of Baktaman knowledge is stored in 183 Baktaman
minds, aided only by a modest assemblage of cryptic concrete symbols (the meanings of which depend on the associations built up
around them in the consciousness of a few seniors) and by limited,
suspicious communication with the members of a few surrounding
communities. I have argued that such a corpus will only persist to
the extent that its parts are frequently re-created as messages and
thereby transmitted. The immediate determinant of the occurrence of such messages may be described as social praxis. The mutual
feedback between thought and action, culture and society, may thus
best be approached through social organization.

General features of Baktaman social organization with major
implications for the flow of messages may be summarized as follows:

The community has been highly isolated and not confronted with
members of contrastive ethnic groups. This absence of any systematic
alternative to their own way of life has absolved them from the need
to question features of their customs and premises, and entails a
very incomplete and unfocused self-image.

The scale of the group is such that control of information can only
be achieved by careful secrecy, never by anonymity, and the full
social identity of all alters is always known.

Statuses are characteristically defined by imperative injunctions
and taboos. A person thus has little opportunity to signal latency of
any of his part-statuses. He participates as a 'whole person' in most
interaction and is restricted in his capacity for role switching and
redefinition of social situations, other than what follows from the
secrecy surrounding sacred places and activities.

Scenes and occasions for interaction are thus not highly differentiated, apart from the categorical distinctions created by secrecy and

taboo. There is a corresponding lack of compartmentalization of the activities of persons into different 'capacities', and limited elaboration of situational codes. The major disjunctions in the flow of information within the population derive from a) male/female segregation, whereby the sexes largely act on different arenas for audiences of their own sex, b) the segmentation of the male population into a small number of residential collectives and c) partly congruent with this, the formal barriers of secrecy separating the various levels of sacred knowledge.

Within this gross framework, the flow of messages is further channelled by the detailed structuring of interaction. Note that we are not here concerned with distinguishing communication from action, but we look at all information given and given off in interaction, i.e. the message aspect of all observed behaviour. We may usefully distinguish some parts or phases in this:

(i) triggering — what starts the message. This may be a social encounter (when Baktaman, as noted, tend to give information particularly on the location of events in the minutest detail), an exogenous event (the appearance of a wild boar in the neighbourhood, the observation of worms in a taro tuber), or an endogenous state (sickness, anxiety about enemy attack). It should be noted that without concepts to record and quantify time the Baktaman are highly dependent on such exogenous events to trigger their messages, i.e. knowledge entailed in messages which will be frequently triggered by random events has a greater chance of transmission than that which is not so linked. Linkage to ecologic cycles longer than that of taro maturation does not seem to serve this function among Baktaman.

(ii) conceptualization of response — the codification of the event in terms of the action, task, or whatever else it should elicit. The major variables here are the codification of whom it will interest and concern, the degree of urgency and necessity of response, and whether the response is an individual or a collective task.

(iii) the construction of the response — involving the shaping of the message through retrieval and activation of knowledge, decision-making and planning, with the major variables being the form of procedure, the extent of collective mobilization in participation, and the size and composition of the audience to this procedure.

256

(iv) the actual 'message' output — the knowledge it contains, whom it involves as participants, and to whom it is broadcast. Finally,

(v) audience status — whether they are or will ever be placed in a situation or status where such knowledge is relevant and positively sanctioned.

When Kimebnok stages an initiation, when a man circumspectly takes precautions against sorcery, when a specific illness is discussed in a men's house, we see knowledge codified in messages which show systematic differences with respect to these organizational features. It is my argument that this must entail systematic differences in the extent to which the different kinds of knowledge so codified will be received by audiences and thereby transmitted and retained. Bakta-man culture seen as a distribution of the total mass of Baktaman knowl-edge over various sectors and topics should reflect these differences: where transmission is effected, the stock may be large; where there is inadequate transmission the stock will shrink. Complexity is thus not merely a result of high creativity, as might be concluded from chapter 27: sheer maintenance is even more precarious. I am not able to demonstrate this for every aspect of Baktaman culture: e.g. their stock of topographical, taxonomic, and various technical knowledge is too varied and large to be encompassed in my field material. But a brief overview of the material on rite, myth, cosmology, sorcery, and concepts of disease and of society will provide sufficient data for a discussion.

Some of the most critical messages containing such knowledge are organized as initiations. The special features of this pattern of social organization were noted in chapter 11. In terms of the points formu-lated above, Baktaman initiations are (i) triggered by a state of readiness in the audience, as understood by seniors, public opinion and, increasingly with higher grades, the novices themselves. (ii) They are the collective task of knowledgeable seniors, and recognized by them as a necessity. (iii) They entail the systematization of much knowledge, and clarify issues for seniors as well as novices. (iv) They require audience participation in (many aspects of) the activities and thus become a highly significant experience for the novices. (v) They lead to a status change in the novices which authorizes them subsequently to make use of what they have learned in men's houses and temples.

We have seen how predominantly this organization is concerned with the performance of rites, largely expressive of cosmological knowledge and to some extent health, and how little of the knowledge is verbally codified, or treats of social relations. This correlates strongly with the large stock of ritual and cosmological knowledge in the tradition, and the relative poverty of myth and simplicity of concepts for society and morality. There is thus a strong suggestion that initiations serve as an effective mode of transmission. At the same time, there is other evidence that the dramatization of secrecy and taboo which generates their value and mystery also creates a reluctance among novices to receive the messages and use the knowledge they contain.

Initiations are also of necessity infrequent occasions; and it is only by the repetition of the knowledge they contain in numerous other temple performances that men become adepts in handling the sacred symbols. Such repeated messages are triggered, as we have seen, in different ways: the basic *Katiam* message of offering to ancestors results from every successful case of hunting; the *Yolam* rites are a response to concerns about taro growth, health and welfare, or warfare and security — concerns and anxieties which apparently arise with sufficient frequency to ensure adequate transmission under normal circumstances.

In other respects, there is a poor development of specialized roles which elaborate and transmit a tradition. In addition to the cult leaders in *Yolam* and *Katiam*, and the clan seniors in the *Katiam*, there are only the men's house leaders and the shaman curers. Cult leaders tend to attract assistants, who assimilate and are even instructed in certain specialist skills and knowledge; and every shaman will refer to a particular ascendant kinsman who taught him the (limited) secret knowledge he uses. Otherwise, transmission depends not on instruction but on information given off, and on the verbalizations that are triggered by rivalry to the positions, or audience demands for greater activity.

The general features of social organization which we have noted — small-scale, extensive information about alters, interaction as whole persons — would seem to be such as to facilitate such activities and thus allow for effective transmission. But in the fields of ritual, myth, and cosmology we have seen case material both of rivalry and of audience demands, which indicate how poorly and hesitantly such criticisms and evaluations are in fact articulated. The barriers to such verbalization are found in a) the explicit taboos and rules of secrecy surrounding sacred symbols, b) a more diffuse wariness and reluctance to speak about, and thus carelessly activate, occult forces, and c) a fear of sorcery reprisals from rivals and persons criticized. The transmission of knowledge as a side effect of verbal discussions is therefore quite limited on such topics.

Such avoidance of verbal discussion is not characteristic of the topic of disease, however, nor of most aspects of sorcery short of specific accusations. Here we might expect easy transmission to take place as a side effect of normal communication. However, looking at the finer structuring of communication about disease in terms of the above criteria (i)–(v), we see that while (i) discussions are frequently triggered, (iv) fora are readily available, and (v) others will be in a position to use the knowledge, there are less optimal conditions under the other two points: (ii) the response is codified as a personal and contingent task, and (iii) it may legitimately take any number of alternative forms for which there is no framework of comparison. Add to this the fact that discussion and action are as frequently interrupted and terminated by exogenous events (recovery or death) as triggered by them, and we may understand the main features of this sector of knowledge: relatively extensive and well transmitted, but unsystematized and randomly distributed in the population.

A fairly similar situation obtains for sorcery, except that communication is somewhat more reluctant and takes place relatively more in small fora than in wide public fora. But this circumspection only serves to enhance the value of the information to the audience; and sorcery beliefs consequently form a strong and well transmitted tradition despite the private secrecy that surrounds its positive performance.

Finally, conceptualization of social relations and their construction are poorly elaborated and transmitted: (i) events which might trigger messages naturally occur but (ii) are easily deflected by being defined as sorcery issues, or concerned with ritual and therefore secret obligations; finally (iii) they rarely involve collective rights or (iv) collective action. Add to this how poorly Baktaman conceptualizations of their relations to ancestors in cult equip them with the vehicles to analyse social relations, and we may understand how poorly elaborated and transmitted this field of knowledge is. Strikingly, the closest I heard to articulations of general moral principles and obligations as a framework for understanding a social situation was in Kimebnok's private musings over the attacks on him by Taneŋ (pp. 118 ff.) — perspectives that I never heard articulated to the audiences really concerned. Whatever wisdom in such matters Kimebnok and others accumulate through life is so rarely and incompletely expressed as not to become incorporated in any collective tradition; whereas the linkage with sorcery is constantly reiterated and so provides a shared premiss for knowledge.

Clearly, the didactically most powerful organization among the Baktaman is that which I have called initiations; and together with the other cult performances it transmits a complex and rich tradition. Yet in their initiations and temple organizations the Baktaman have constructed a communicative apparatus which they themselves approach with such reluctance and trepidation as to endanger the very knowledge it contains. New participants hold back and are poor learners, adepts often respond to difficulties by withdrawal. When the value of the knowledge is further affirmed and created by postponement of its transmission, this generates a tendency to over-retention and the concentration of much essential knowledge on very few hands. Such a situation entails a distinct risk of loss of established knowledge. I have cited the case of Ngaromnok's father, who hid the Warop clan sacra and died without telling where they are, with the result that the Warop no longer practise clan cult (p. 109). A more dramatic and comprehensive loss is that of the community of Augobmin, neighbours of the Baktaman across the range of mountains to the southeast. According to their own account, confirmed by Baktaman seniors who used to have trading partnerships with them, they had a system of, probably four, initiations until c. 15–20 years ago, when accidents of warfare and death removed the handful of senior and knowledgeable man. They have since had to abandon their temples and practise only a truncated 1st degree initiation; their stock of cosmological knowledge is reportedly minimal.

Both empirical data and simple reasoning thus indicate that the stock of Baktaman knowledge, and its size and distribution over topics, will reflect a long-term balance between borrowing and creativity vs. loss, mediated by a constant process of transmission through the various modes in which items of knowledge are articulated in messages during interaction. But it seems impossible to operationalize such concepts as 'stock of knowledge' or 'topic' and 'sector', and thus the proposition remains impressionistic despite its simple statement of cultural dynamics and association with relevant ethnographic data. I fall back on the common-sense contention that 7 degrees of initiation seems a lot and the elaboration of sacred symbols in the rites seems undeniably rich and complex, while a corpus of 8 myths and legends seems very little and the universe of discourse for problems of suffering or of responsibility seems constraining. I thus feel that my basic argument has been demonstrated, though I do not feel I can usefully carry this demonstration any further.

This discussion of transmission has made use of a vocabulary whereby knowledge is represented as a stock of items and may be described in sectors. Yet the parts of knowledge that combine in a tradition doubtless show features of integration — so would it not follow that each major part of this body of tradition implies its other parts, and thereby persists as a whole in transmission? Especially with the kind of tightly knit social organization summarized in the opening of this chapter, where relatively whole persons with comprehensive information about each other interact for many purposes, one might expect such integration to be particularly marked.

On the other hand, one may argue that man, by virtue of being in the world, has a welter of existential problems forced upon him, and it seems much to expect that he has anywhere developed systematic and mutually consistent answers to all of them; and perhaps particularly inappropriate to expect a small, isolated community of shifting cultivators to have achieved this intellectual feat. Beyond doubt, a relatively stereotyped repertoire of ideas and reasoning procedures will produce a certain uniformity in answers; but this is far from the kind of logico-deductive integration that seems to be implied in frequent structuralist assumptions and descriptions. I see no evidence in Baktaman tradition of the tight mutual determination implied in such a concept of integration, or of the simplicity in the process of transmission of culture that this would imply.

To discuss the issue I need to clarify my concepts and intentions. Clearly, a degree of integration is a constituting property of any system;[1] and cultural phenomena may be described as 'integrated' in a number of senses. As technical acts they are integrated with a multitude of non-cultural events in complex ecosystems; through the reciprocities of social transactions they are integrated in systems of circulation of prestations, etc. The aspect of integration that concerns us here is that of cultural codification: the extent of cognitive and emotional coherence between the symbolic categories of Baktaman con-

[1] A sensible general position is formulated by Geertz (1966:66): 'Systems need not be exhaustively interconnected to be systems. They may be densely interconnected or poorly, but which they are — how tightly integrated they are — is an empirical matter. To assert connections among modes of experiencing, as among any variables, it is necessary to find them (and find ways of finding them), not simply assume them . . . the problem of cultural analysis is as much a matter of determining independencies as interconnections, gulfs as well as bridges.'

ception. We may look at this initially as a structure: the symbols whereby Baktaman knowledge is organized, their relations to each other and to that which they symbolize. But here a difficulty already arises, in that different Baktaman subscribe to differently constituted schemata of knowledge, though largely employing the same concrete symbols, depending on their sex and initiation grade. A higher degree of consistency and integration also characterizes the symbols associated with one type of temple than the combined sum of all temple idioms. Thus a discussion of the degree of coherence and connection between the symbolic categories of an aggregate 'Baktaman culture' seen as a structure would disguise the characteristic structure of the 'Chinese boxes' of initiation knowledge and the syndromes organized around the separate temples. These structural features are inherent, not in the form and meaning of the various symbols but in the patterns of communication whereby some symbols are juxtaposed and confronted and others are not.

To investigate the nature and extent of integration in Baktaman culture we should thus show the distribution of cognitive schemata over persons and occasions; the degree of coherence and systematization of each in terms of the uses to which the symbols are put in messages; and finally the levels of shared and separate comprehension generated by such communication. Some awareness and understanding of such features have been built up in the preceding description; but I am unable to construct a representation of these various dimensions of the organization and integration of tradition in a unified model. Instead, I shall perform the following three steps in my discussion. First, I shall demonstrate the character and extent of integration in some core areas of knowledge as they are constituted in the shared understandings of senior men with advanced ritual knowledge. Second, I shall discuss the processes of communication in the Baktaman population at large, and the patterns of disjunction and integration that they generate and sustain. Third, I shall seek to identify the processes of interaction and creativity that generate a cumulatively changing tradition with a thrust towards increasing integration.

Major ways in which the symbols known by senior adepts are conceptually integrated are the following:

a) Metaphors are identified and developed as concrete symbols for general and abstract concepts, in terms of which a variety of events are related. This is particularly clear when the metaphorical bases for such idioms are defined or supplemented in the rites themselves. Thus, when dew is rubbed on young novices, the face shelter is

262

constructed so that rain can fall on their chests without washing away the pork fat from their faces, and when they are forbidden to wash in running streams (pp. 52, 54), a physical property of water has been abstracted and a conceptualization of the nature of health and increase has been achieved with the aid of this abstraction. Throwing diseased material on flowing water (p. 139), or the corpses of enemies and sorcerers into rivers (pp. 126, 149), are ritual acts which extend this abstraction to further fields of experience. By employing the same concrete symbol of water in these rites, the Baktaman construct a conceptual interrelation between them, roughly equivalent to the verbal construction: 'dew and falling rain embody accumulation, and thus the goodness of increase, growth, and health — which are properties similar but inversely related to the badness of sickness and hate which water can embody and remove, like dirt.' Without such words and ways of speaking, the Baktaman have only their concrete symbols to use as vehicles to express such thoughts. But by employing the concrete symbol of water in this fashion they have none the less integrated the codification of otherwise quite separate phenomena subsumed under verbal concepts such as health, growing big, sickness, etc. This integration, like the general concepts which it relates, emerges only obliquely from the non-verbal statements, as meta-communication entailed in the concrete rites. The clarity and precision with which the conceptual integration is achieved are consequently low, but none the less significantly constitutive of the Baktaman codification of a world view.

Another, somewhat different mode of integration results from the multiplicity of connotations of some of the core symbols of Baktaman ritual. The general proposition that one and the same concrete symbol can serve as a vehicle for several distinct metaphors has been strongly argued by Turner, e.g. 1967. In the preceding material we have seen this repeatedly, e.g. in the several distinct groups of meanings represented by fire and smoke (p. 238), or pandanus (pp. 188 ff.). The kind of integration which results from such subsumption of several meanings under the same concrete symbol is obviously loose; but there can be no doubt that they do become cognitively and emotionally linked by such an association. Moreover, the association seems to pose an intellectual problem to actors so that they will attempt to harmonize the disparate connotations of each symbol into a more coherent chord.

A final type of integration results from a codification of overarching or bridging symbols. Since each sacred symbol has its independent sources of meaning in its separate metaphors (pp. 207 ff.), they are not connected as are the symbols of a digital code. One way to weld them together in an integrated code is to connect them by such over-arching symbols. In Biblical imagery the rainbow serves, with the myth of Noah, in this way to connect the concepts of sin and punishment with God's compassion and mercy — just as it serves in natural science imagery to connect concepts of light as waves and a physical model of observers in three-dimensional space. For the Baktaman, the frequently mentioned marsupial *ubir* similarly integrates the conceptual fields symbolized by fire and by pandanus — to my understanding not in a particularly illuminating fashion, but yet so that what is otherwise separate becomes connected.

We thus find that these symbols, and the concepts that they embody, are no mere assemblage of separate solutions to existential problems; they are cognitively interconnected in several distinctive ways and thus show features of integration. But the nature of this integration is both loose and partial: they are not linked to each other in logically necessary patterns, and it would be false to attempt to construct a set of premises from which they can be deductively derived. Note the examples by which the modes of integration are illustrated: the invocation of *ubir* during fire-making, the different meanings of fire, the different ritual uses of water. Each such item increases the field or strength of integration, but cannot be deduced from any other; and each such item, and many others, may be separately added or lost in any concrete group's historical tradition. The *force* of these symbols in moulding Baktaman experiences arises less from their logical articulation than from their cryptic, vital character as the secrets of a mystery cult.

The Baktaman tradition of knowledge as a whole is more than the concrete symbols and concepts employed by senior men. The other and simpler sets known and used by junior men and by women have also been described; in principle each of these is integrated in the same ways as that of the senior men. The more important question is how these different variants relate to each other. Here, it is in the flow of communication that we can see the significant structure, rather in the formal differences and similarities between the sets of symbols. If all Baktaman shared the same symbols, there would be a simple isomorphy between the logical structure of the codes and the patterns of flow and content of messages. Shared understandings would then be confirmed through every event of communication, thus maintaining this isomorphy. But the striking fact of Baktaman life is the *absence* of such common premisses and shared knowledge be-

264

tween persons in intimate interaction. The tradition of knowledge is structured like Chinese boxes precisely in that persons have different knowledge and different keys to interpret meaning. More than half the population know only the public codifications, and must base their understandings on them, and on private experience. Sacred symbols will have sometimes discrepant, sometimes opposite meanings for alters in communication — e.g. brush turkey as a symbol of subterranean pollution or taro purity. And the very stuff of transactions in some relations — e.g. gardening activities for man and wife — must have very different meanings for the parties in transaction.

The main lines of distinction are between the levels of knowledge represented by initiation grades, and the syndromes associated with temple types. The latter are practised by the same persons but differentiated as alternative rules relating to separate scenes. The differences between the symbols and meanings of these syndromes are thus resolved in part by never being confronted with each other. The differences between the levels of knowledge of initiation grades, on the other hand, are not segregated on separate scenes but assert themselves as different premises for persons in interaction and should thus militate against mutual understanding. How then do persons achieve social confirmation of their concepts, values, and interpretations? In the case of women we may assume them mainly to obtain such confirmation in the everyday fora prominently composed of their own sex; but men of different levels of initiation live together and interact continuously.

Part of the answer lies in the position of senior men, who in a sense hold *all* the keys and can interact with different alters, and confirm their understandings, in terms of the level of knowledge they know alter to possess. Seniors conceptualize these patterns as rules of secrecy, and constrain their behaviour very consistently in terms of such rules. But because they separate and maintain the levels of knowledge with deceit and other tricks (e.g. by jumbling the species of marsupials with respect to their sacred values for lower initiates), there is no master key in terms of which all the different levels are harmonized. So the fact remains that in the normal flow of life persons with different premises will interact, confuse each other, and thus in part increase rather than resolve the puzzles of life for each other. The force of the sacred symbols in constructing a Baktaman reality arises from secrecy rather than logical coherence of form. But secrecy entails a pattern of distribution where most actors are excluded from knowledge. This exclusion affects the very processes whereby such reality is socially constructed; and so emerge the characteristic features of Baktaman tradition: at once poorly shared, poorly systematized, and puzzled and groping in thought and imagery, while yet creative, complex, moving, and rich (cf. p. 222).

I argued above that the particular ways in which Baktaman symbols are interrelated reflect a specific course and moment of history. The steps whereby this degree of integration has emerged cannot be reconstructed, beyond the tentative sequence suggested for the appearance of the temple syndromes. But the general social processes that produce this thrust towards integration can be identified. We may seek them in concrete features of social organization, rather than in a construct of Man with an innate drive to build symbolic systems. The analyses of the preceding chapters have linked observed activities which were directed at such system-building and integration to the following features of organization:

We have seen how the collective nature of many taboos, and their sanctions, entail a collective concern about the form and content of individual ritual acts. Reactions, e.g. to one man's handling of the meat of wild female pig (p. 201) systematize emotions and classifications and the extent of their sharing.

The instituted roles of cult leaders, with a pattern of open succession among the fully initiated, triggers rivalries whereby aspects of ritual performance are criticized and intellectual energy is directed at the discovery and elimination of inconsistencies (cf. pp. 112 ff.).

The organization of stable initiation sets, and their role together with the cult leader as active initiators, create occasions when complex ritual messages are collectively constructed. Besides increasing agreement, this must also increase clarity and systematization.

The combined effect of such organizational features must be both to promote certain limited kinds of intellectual creativity, and to direct it to areas where the sacred symbols are unclear or inconsistent. It is especially in these areas that incorrect or ambiguous ritual messages will occur and trigger sanctions and criticism, and these are the areas where the harmonization of connotations and associations is so problematical that creativity is stimulated by the need to achieve collective agreement (cf. the discussion of creativity, pp. 239 ff.).

Finally, the fact that public emblems of rank, and valued privileges (feathers, drums, pig slaughtering, first harvest, various delicacies) have ritual significance entails that the social tug-of-war whereby interest groups seek to redistribute such goods is constrained by, and in turn affects, ritual codifications. We saw how junior sets tried to shift the release from certain food taboos from 6th to 4th degree, but failed, while the (c) set succeeded in obtaining access to the drums for themselves. Such activity also affects an interrelating of symbols and thus furthers integration. As between the sexes, however, a similar struggle seems to persist interminably and uncreatively as an undercurrent, whereby women by intransigence and carelessness devalue the sacred world from with they are excluded, undermining its practices and breaking its taboos.

The effect of these cross-currents of secrecy and instruction, confusion and creativity, is to fashion a tradition of knowledge whereby people can live, one that provides some answers for them but leaves much in the dark. My own image for the achievements of Baktaman understanding and codification is provided by the concrete symbol of their own dance evenings. Occasionally, a score or two of adults and youths will come together at night, aided by torches and a partly overcast moon. They dress in their finery, including cassowary-feathers for the seniors, dance to their sacred drums, and sing their songs of love and violence, thereby shaping the whole scene in complex cultural imagery and positively intoxicating themselves with the force and vitality of their own expression. But if you move a hundred metres along one of their paths you find yourself outside this circle of cultural imagery; and through the trees you glimpse a panorama of immense, untouched forest-covered landscape, dwarfing man's tiny village clearing and muting his tiny noise. The command which the Baktaman achieve over their situation is, as for all of us, at best a subjective command only, asserted in those limited sectors where their awareness asserts itself. And in creating this awareness, the symbols fashioned in their rites are both their main beacons and their tools.

Contact history

The first Baktaman experience of Europeans was, as far as can be ascertained, a brief encounter with Karius and Champion in their first attempt to ascend the southern mountain ranges on their original crossing of the island in 1927. The Baktaman remember giving a pig to the strangers and receiving nothing in return. (K./C. claim to have left axes, cf. Champion 1932, p. 49.)

No further contact was made until the first Patrol Officer from Olsobip in 1964 entered the Murray valley. Pacification was announced, but had in fact been realized already, as the government threat of retaliation against raiders had spread by word of mouth from western neighbours. Between then and my arrival in February 1968, three more patrols seem to have passed through the area, each spending one day in the main Baktaman settlement.

While no Baktaman had been out of the Murray/Luap valleys till that time, they had, however, received a considerable amount of indirect information from outside. Before pacification, the Baktaman had irregular contact with members of six neighbouring communities. After pacification, both the range and frequency of these contacts must have increased. During my residence, visitors would arrive as frequently as about once a week — mostly from the Seltaman to the East, and Kasanmin to the North (cf. Maps p. 19), but including visitors from places as distant as Oksapmin and Olsobip. Baktaman also made their first visit to Olsobip at that time. Steel axes, bush knives, and industrial salt were largely available in sufficient quantities, though my gifts greatly increased the consumption of salt, and also provided a steady supply of matches. Curiosity about the outside world, however, remained low; and serious questioning of traditional cultural premisses had not started on any identifiable points.

APPENDIX II:

Demography

Some important demographic questions arise in connection with this fieldwork, particularly: a) What were the precontact dynamics of such small, isolated populations? b) How are these demographic features inter-related with features of social organization? c) What is the nature of changes resulting from pacification and contact?

Very roughly, we seem to see a largely self-contained 2-generation population, of relatively stable size with a high incidence of mortality from warfare in pre-contact times, changing into a tragically declining pacified population after first contact. But to establish these and other features of the demography with any degree of firmness is difficult since the available kinds of data are necessarily so limited.

(i) The initial government census upon contact was highly unreliable. My own field census spans a period of only 8 months' time.

(ii) Without a calendar the Baktaman can give no information on absolute age and time elapsed, except for pacification (variously interpretable as first contact or establishment of Olsobip patrol post, respectively 4 or 6 years before my fieldwork). Only relative age can, with some difficulty, be established, as can visible maturity, probably corresponding to age 15–18.

(iii) Other data available are: complete kinship network; initiation set memberships; complete (living and dead) sibling groups of all living adults; causes of death in these sibling groups, dichotomized as before/after pacification; and marital history of women — probably incomplete and unreliable. From such data, what description can be established?

Total population varied, from 183 at my first census to 185 owing to deaths, births and the return of two long-absent males, to 181 at the end of the fieldwork. The degree of isolation of this population is indicated by the fact that all but 14% of the adult residents were also born in the community.

Sex and age distribution:

	Male	Female	Total
Adult	55	46	101
Child	40	42	82
Total	95	88	183

The age distribution of males is further indicated by the size of consecutive initiation sets. Arbitrarily setting the interval between the formation of new sets at 10 years — a rough guess at a reasonable average — gives the distribution:

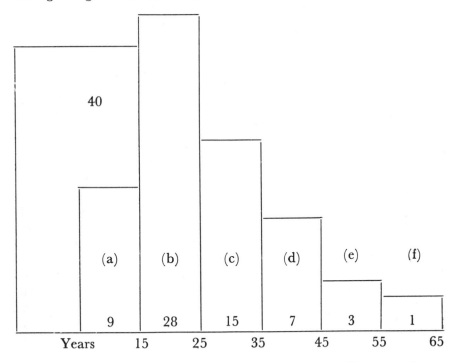

Generations: The 82 living children have the following live ascendants:

No. of parents alive:	2	1	0
No. of children	43	28	11

No. of grandparents alive:	4	3	2	1	0
No. of children	0	0	1	5	76

i.e. half the children have lost one or both parents, and only 6 of the 82 have grandparents alive. We are thus dealing with essentially a two-generation population and, since there is no evidence of a very late marriage age, a population with very short life expectancy at all ages.

Size of completed sibling groups: From every adult I collected a complete record of siblings. Since informants spontaneously gave sex of siblings who died in infancy before receiving a name, and the kinship terminology is one that specifies elder/younger, and cross-checking uncovered very few discrepancies, I regard these data as reliable. However, though I also tried to assure myself that the list included only full or uterine siblings, I am not sure that the oldest sibling sets may not include some agnatic siblings of different mothers.

Total No. of siblings:	1	2	3	4	5	6	7	8
average 3.8	3	10	11	12	6	5	0	1

Causes of pre-contact death in these sibling groups:

War	Accident	Sickness	Childbirth	Infant mortality	Total
18	2	27	1	6	54

War includes only death from gross wounds, usually immediate. Sickness subsumes sorcery-caused sickness as well as 'natural' sickness. Infant mortality comes out with an improbably low c. 10%; violent death (both sexes and all ages) with a staggering, but probably true, one in three.

Post-contact immediate effects on population are suggested by a few independent indicators:
(i) Native evaluation: the increased incidence of disease far outstrips the previous loss by warfare. Increased disease is explained by the loss of ancestral blessing caused by the change from stone to steel axes.
(ii) Population balance during fieldwork:

272

Deaths	4 adults, 2 children	..	6
Stillbirth	1		
Live births	3		3

net change — 3

(iii) Effects of a (meningitis/influenza?) epidemic in the area just prior to fieldwork: 6 deaths among Baktaman but a gross 25% of the adult population among the neighbouring Seltaman according to the patrol officer's census.

Since this increased incidence of disease probably affects all ages, as did traditional warfare, the present decline has probably not yet wrought any *structural* change in the population.

A general construction on such data suggests low fertility, relatively low infant mortality, steadily high mortality through life and low life expectancy. This picture is further supported by other data: the 8 women apparently past menopause have a total of 24 live issue, i.e. an average 3/woman. The 44 living women who are or have been married are in

first marriage	24
widowed (incl. one divorce)	6
remarried	10
twice widowed	1
thrice married	2
thrice widowed	1

Such a high rate of depletion of cohorts, also through adulthood, is highly consistent both with the structure of family and kinship among the Baktaman, with their characteristically limited ramifications. Together with the pattern of stepwise initiations of sets over extended periods it also produces the preconditions for a successful mystery cult, viz: a small elite of fully initiated seniors despite praxis of active and frequent initiations.

273

18

CENSUS:

Key:

Clan membership of adults is indicated as follows:

▲ male adult

● female adult

■ child of resident female

□ other resident child

—— marriage bond

--- other household bond

⌐ house

⌒ village grounds, kept clear of grass

Clan

A = Minkarin

B = Yabik

C = Arepmurup

D = Wanfayir

E = Yeni

F = Murukmur

G = Minmurup

H = Kobren

I = Yotmorup

K = Warop

L = Togumin

The initiation set composition (b—f) is indicated for each men's house.

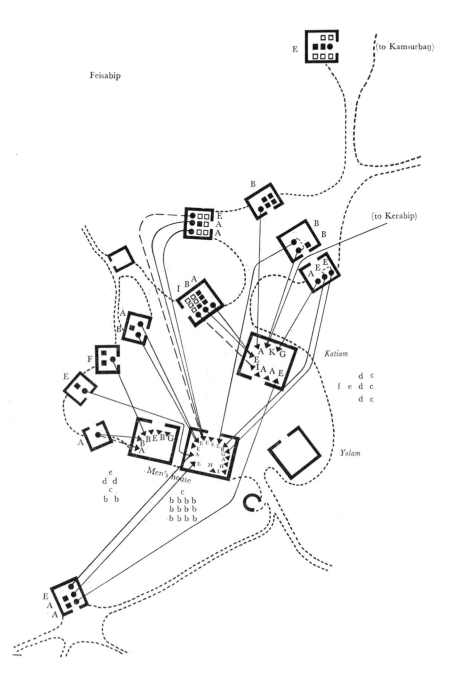

Feisabip

E (to Kamsurbaŋ)

B

(to Kerabip)

B
B

E
E
A
A

B
B

E
E

I B A

A K G
E
I A A E

Katiam

d c
f e d c
d c

A
B

F

E

A

B E B G
B
A

Men's house

E E E E
E
A
E H H

E
E
B
G
A
H I

Yolam

e
d d
c
b b

c
b b b b
b b b b
b b b b

C

E
A
A

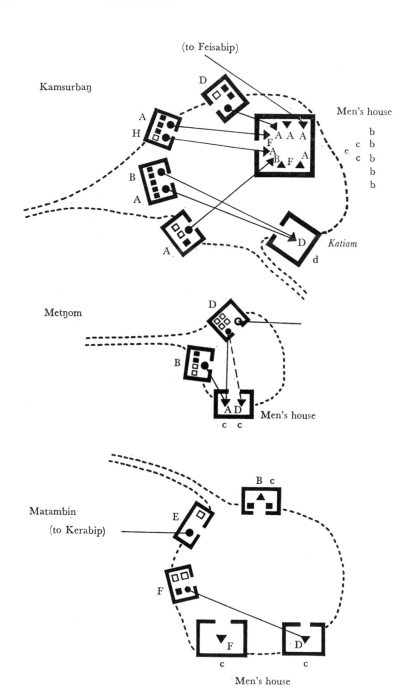

(to Feisabip)

Kamsurbaŋ

D

Men's house

A
H

A A A
F
A
B F A

b
b
c b
e c
b
b

B

A

A

D   *Katiam*
d

Metŋom

D

B

A D   Men's house
c c

Matambin

B c

(to Kerabip)

E

F

F   D
c   c

Men's house

276

Kerabip

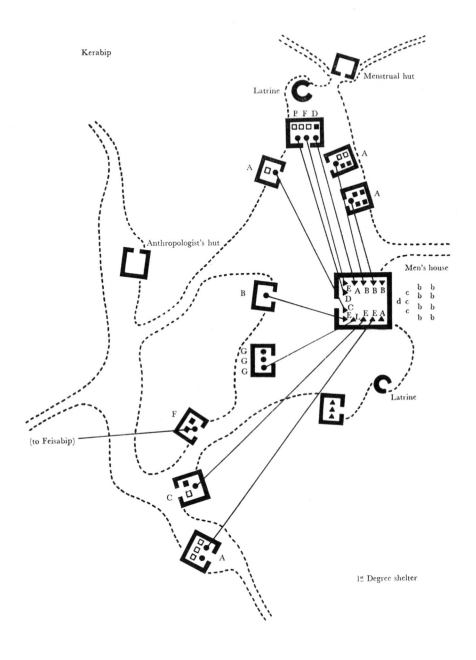

Menstrual hut

Latrine

P F D

A

A

A

Anthropologist's hut

Men's house

B

E A B B B
D
C
E L E E A

b   b
c c   b   b
c c d b   b
c c   b   b
      b   b

G G G G

Latrine

F

(to Feisabip)

C

A

1st Degree shelter

APPENDIX III:

Myths

Myth 1, see pp. 83. f.

Myth 2

'When the ancestor Brutinanim died, his son just left him on the ground and departed. After 8 moons he returned, and found that the wild pig had eaten the corpse. Only a few things remained: the ancestor's hair which had turned white, and a few of his teeth. The son took the hair and put it into a hollow tree — and it turned into ŋāp [the leaf-eating insect whose nest is used as a tray for the skull in the Yolam]. He put one tooth in a hollow tree — and it became eiraram. He put the other teeth in another tree, and they turned into yerōp (large white tree grubs). When he looked more closely, he found a scrap of the ancestor's skin which the pig had messed down into the ground. He picked it up and shook it to clear off the dirt — and it flew away as a flying fox.'

This myth was told in justification of the special sacred role of the *eiraram* marsupial mouse in ritual. It is also supposed to explain why bats, grubs and ŋāp larvae must not be brought into the Yolam.

Myth 3

'The first ancestors were an elder sister and a younger brother. The elder sister built a cult house, put wild pigs' skulls and mandibles there, but the taro did not prosper. She put cassowary pelvises there, but the taro still did not prosper. She would not let her brother into the cult house, but sent him off to hunt and garden. When he objected, she killed him with magic and then exposed his body in a tree. After a while she returned, but the body had not decomposed at all. Then she waited a *long* time, and then went and fetched the bones to put in the cult house: skull, mandible, right armbones and finger bones A *durēm* bird [wren warbler= *Malurus alboscapolatus*, a tiny black-and-white bird] came to eat insects from the roof thatching; she shot it, cooked the breast and gave half to the bones — and then the taro came up terrifically strong.

278

Her younger (live) brother did not like *her* to do the rituals, *him* to be left out. So he took nettle leaves and spread them all over the floor of the *Yolam*. When his sister came and lay down to sleep, she burned herself all over. She went to his house, lay down, and was comfortable. "What a good house you have", she said, "will you change with me?" And so the *men* took over the cult houses.'

This is a variant of the *Afek* myth first reported from Telefomin (Quinlivan 1954), with an apparently wide distribution among Ok-speaking people. It was known only to a few senior Baktaman, and identified as a story from Telefomin when told me by Namraeŋ. The account it provides of the relationship of male and female to cult practice is basically familiar from large parts of New Guinea and Melanesia; among the Baktaman it seems to provide a justification for a premiss never questioned, and thus does not constitute an important explanation in the Baktaman system of thought. Its telling was the result of my active prodding (cf. ch. 3, p. 48) and the information that a woman had originally established the cult house was received incredulously and reluctantly by the (c) initiation set audience.

Myth 4

'There were four brothers; the senior one was married and had two wives. His three brothers worked the gardens, while he went out in the forest and hunted, bringing home marsupials, wild pig, and cassowary. One day he met a tree spirit (*nāwn*) in the forest, fell in love with her, and became her sweetheart. She helped him track and hold the game; he shared everything equally with her, giving her half and taking half home to his family.

One day when the others were in the gardens, the youngest, half-grown brother went into the forest to find out what happened to the other half of all the pigs and cassowaries that his brother brought home. In a very secure hiding place he found a hut shelter with a lighted fire. He hid very well at a safe distance, and waited to see what would happen. After a while, his big brother came carrying two wild pigs. He singed them, cut them and cleaned them, and started cooking the belly piece. Then the spirit woman came: she sat down by the fire, her eyes ablaze with anger. He gave her the pork belly, but she refused it, and then accused him of knowing that his little brother was there, making her ashamed to eat. The man searched and finally found the boy where her sharp eyes had immediately seen him. So the two brothers went home with the two pigs; but the big brother was very angry, saying, why have you put me in this grave danger? When they came home, the big brother told the whole story — and everybody was angry with the little brother, knowing that the big brother now was in danger of losing his life.

The man stayed in the house a long time; then finally he went off into the forest again to hunt. He came upon a wild pig with yellow bristles, and killed it. As he started to singe it, a big rainstorm came; he took the pig and sought refuge under a *boab* tree [a tree with a wide skirt of aerial roots]. As he stood there, the roots

279

started growing down, enveloping him — he first thought it was just rain trickling down, did not notice until it was too late, and he was held tight by the roots.

His three brothers and two wives waited, and became anxious; next morning the two wives went off to look for him. They followed his tracks, came to the place he had killed the pig, to the fire he had lit, to the *boab* tree where they saw the dead pig — then saw him and started crying. The man said: "Go and fetch my brothers". The brothers came, and wanted to cut down the tree, but the man said no, then the spirit would make the tree fall down on them all. He instructed them to build a shelter on top of the ridge, carry the pig up there, and cook it. They did this, crying all the time; then in the evening when all was ready they ate the pig and stopped crying. All night they could hear the man sing the *ibēn* song; but his voice became weaker and weaker; finally he died, and the spirit fetched him up into the tree with her. But the younger brothers had meanwhile learned the magic hunting song. The tree still stands, in the forests over towards Oksapmin, but it is now dead.'

The *ibēn* song may be sung when men sacrifice pig or cassowary in the *Katiam* after a secret hunt, or it may be sung before a hunt, to make the ancestors eager and hungry for meat, so that they will help the hunter. Its text:

Kīn-ō   *ē-ī*   *kīn-ō;*   *nē-kīn-sō*   *tūyūri-kū*   *ā-i* /
Eye   oh   eye;   my eye   destroyed

kīn-ō   *diādiā*   *mugō-ū*   *sāī*
eye   I have looked at/desired   breast   why

or: Eye, oh eye; my eye has destroyed me;
       why did I cast my eyes on her breast?

Myth 5

'There were two good friends of the Yeni clan — one was married and had four sons, the other was unmarried. The unmarried one said he did not want a wife, then he avoided the nasty smell from her genitals, and becoming wrinkled and weak from copulating.

When the friends became very old, the one with the sons decided to go trading. He said: "Now you see the advantages of marrying and having sons: now my sons can carry me, I can go trading even though I am old, while you must remain in one place." So he left the single old man behind. The old man looked around the men's house, took some feathers of the palm cockatoo [*Probosciger aterrimus*] and fastened them to his back and arms — and flew up to the peak of the roof. He came down again, and waited till his old companion returned — then he flew up on the roof again. The companion cried: "Do not leave me!" But he answered: "If you had let two of your sons carry me, two of them carry you, now that would have been good, and I would have stayed with you. But now it is better that I manage by myself." And so he flew away and became a palm cockatoo.'

This myth has a more secret version which I was unable to obtain.

Myth 6

'In the village of Kibibip the ancestor Minmurup went out and caught the moon. He took it home in a carrying net, and kept it in the house. At night he would use it as a light, fastening a rope around it to hold it down and carrying it as a torch. He used it for hunting, for catching cassowary and wild pig at night. Minmurup and his wife had a daughter and a baby son. One night another hamlet made a dance, they killed pigs and brought out the drums. Minmurup and his wife went there leaving the daughter to look after the baby.

After a while the baby started crying, crying; the sister brought out the moon and showed him, and that pleased him. Later, when the baby again cried, the sister again brought out the moon — but it slipped out of her hands, went up the firepost and hung there. She was a very little girl, but tried to stretch and catch it — but it went higher. She climbed up the post, but it went higher, up to the roof, it sailed away into the sky. The people at the dance saw the moon on the sky, and wondered. Minmurup left the dance and hurried home. He scolded the daughter for letting out the moon. But she explained about the baby crying.'

Myth 7

'Some Baktaman were down by Gaboa mountain working sago. They went fishing. In a large, round pool, a woman suddenly felt her line heavy, pulled it in — and there was a child on it. The others said it was a *sabkār* (ghost of a dead person), and that she should throw it back into the water; but she took it home, fed it pork, let it suck her breast, and cuddled it. In the evening she cradled it in her arms and went to sleep with it. When all were asleep, the child got up, cut off her breast, and ran away home.

When they woke up in the morning, they noticed the child had disappeared. They roused the woman, but she did not move — turned her over, and saw that her breast was cut off and she was dead. Now one of the [live] ancestors knew how to travel to the land of the *sabkār*. He told the people to slaughter a pig, cut off the fat from its flanks; then he went off. When he came to *sabkār*-land, he asked the children the way to the house of the spirit who had been to the sago-camp. They showed him — but there was no one there. He searched and searched, finally he found the cut-off breast hidden at the top of the fire-post. He took it and hurried back, put the breast back where it had been cut off and rubbed the edges with the pork fat. Then the woman woke up. She lived on, and died a natural death later.'

Myth 8

'An Abolgobip man was pursued by enemies. To escape them he ran into a taboo area and hid — whereupon he disappeared. His two SiSo's went out to look for him. They searched and searched, and finally found a house. There was smoke coming up through the roof. They went up to the house — there was a man with a stone adze. He fought them, and then let them into his house. He was their MoBr.

Inside, the house was full of game: cuscus, cassowary, wild pig. They were given plenty to eat. After a while two boys came — they were the uncle's sons. They

281

brought plenty of birds, and more marsupials, and taro; their father ordered them to cook it and give to the visitors, who were not allowed to leave the house. They ate and ate, while the two sons ate nothing, so their father would not be angry with them.

During the night the visitors had eaten so much that their stomachs turned to water, and they had to go out and defecate. The uncle stood guard at the door; he would not let them out and struck them so they fell to the ground. When they regained consciousness, they went out and then returned to the house.

The next days the sons were again sent off to fetch more game, while the visitors were kept in the house. After three nights they were allowed to return to the village, but were told to come back on the fourth day. They stayed home four nights, and returned on the fifth day — then the house and everything had disappeared, and could not be found."

References

Baal, J. van 1966: *Dema: Description and Analysis of Marind-Amin Culture.* The Hague.

Barth, F. 1971: Tribes and intertribal relations in the Fly headwaters. *Oceania*, vol. XLI No. 3.

Barth, F. 1972: Analytical dimensions in the comparison of social organizations. *American Anthropologist*, vol. 72, No. 1–2.

Bateson, G. 1972: *Steps to an Ecology of Mind.* London.

Brookfield, H. 1971: *Melanesia. A Geographical Interpretation of an Island World.* London.

Bulmer, R. N. H. 1960: Political aspects of the Moka ceremonial exchange system among the Kyaka. *Oceania*, vol. 31.

Bulmer, R. N. H. 1965: The Kyaka of the Western Highlands, *in* P. Lawrence and M. J. Meggitt, eds.: *Gods, Ghosts and Men in Melanesia.* London.

Bulmer, R. N. H. 1967: Why is the cassowary not a bird. *Man*, vol. 2, No. 1.

Champion, I. 1932: *Across New Guinea from the Fly to the Sepik.* London.

Chomsky, N. 1968: *Language and Mind.* New York.

Craig, B. 1967: The houseboards of Telefomin Sub-district, New Guinea. *Man*, vol. 2, No. 2.

Cranstone, B. A. L. 1967: Some boards from a New Guinea *haus tambaran*. *Man*, vol. 2, No. 2.

Cranstone, B. A. L. 1968: War shields of the Telefomin Sub-district, New Guinea. *Man*, vol. 3, No. 4.

Douglas, M. 1966: *Purity and Danger.* London.

Douglas, M. 1973: Self-evidence. *Proceedings of the Royal Anthropological Institute for* 1972.

Evans-Pritchard, E. E. 1956: *Nuer Religion.* Oxford.

Firth, R. 1959: Problem and assumption in an anthropological study of religion. *Journal of the Royal Anthropological Institute*, vol. 90.

Fontaine, J. S. la (ed.) 1972: *The Interpretation of Ritual.* London.

Fortes, M. 1936: Ritual festivals and social cohesion in the hinterland of the Gold Coast. *American Anthropologist*, vol. 38, No. 4.

Frake, C. O. 1961: The diagnosis of disease among the Subanum of Mindanao. *American Anthropologist*, vol. 63, No. 1.

Geertz, C. 1966: *Person, Time and Conduct in Bali.* Cultural Report Series No. 14, Yale University.

Geertz, C. 1966: Religion as a cultural system. *A.S.A. Monograph* No. 3, London.

Geertz, C. 1968: *Islam Observed.* New Haven.

Gell, A. F. 1971: Penis sheathing and ritual status in a West Sepik village. *Man*, vol. 6, No. 2.

Goody, J. 1968: *Literacy in Traditional Societies.* Cambridge.

Griaule, N. 1965: *Conversations with Ogotemmêli*. London.

Hiatt, L. R. 1962: Local organization among the Australian Aborigines. *Oceania*, vol. 32, No. 4.

Hiatt, L. R. 1966: The lost horde. *Oceania*, vol. 37, No. 2.

Hiatt, L. R. 1968: Ownership and use of land among the Australian Aborigines *in* R. B. Lee and I. deVore (eds.): *Man the Hunter*. Chicago.

Hogbin, I. 1970: *The Island of Menstruating Men*. San Francisco.

Hubert, H. and K. Mauss 1964: *Sacrifice: its Nature and Function*. Chicago (first published 1898).

Keesing, R. M. 1972: Paradigms lost: the New Ethnography and the New Linguistics. *South-western Journal of Anthropology*, vol. 28, No. 4.

Landtman, G. 1927: *The Kiwai Papuans of British New Guinea*. London.

Leach, E. R. 1954: *Political Systems of Highland Burma*. London.

Leach, E. R. 1961: *Rethinking Anthropology*. London.

Leach, E. R. 1964: Anthropological aspects of language: Animal categories and verbal abuse *in* E. H. Lenneberg (ed.): *New Directions in the Study of Language*. Mass. Inst. of Technol.

Leach, E. R. 1968: Ritual *in International Encyclopedia of the Social Sciences*.

Levi-Strauss, C. 1964: *Totemism*. London.

Meggitt, M. J. 1964: Male-female relationships in the Highlands of Australian New Guinea. *American Anthropologist*, vol. 66, part 2.

Radcliffe-Brown, A. R. 1952: *Structure and Function in Primitive Society*. London.

Rand, A. L. and E. T. Gilliard 1967: *Handbook of New Guinea Birds*. London.

Rappaport, R. Z. 1967: *Pigs for the Ancestors*. New Haven.

Richards, A. I. 1956: *Chisungu*. London.

Ruesh, J. and G. Bateson 1951: *Communication*. New York.

Serpenti, L. M. 1965: *Cultivators in the Swamps*. Amsterdam.

Smith, W. Robertson 1927: *The Religion of the Semites*. London (first published 1889).

Strathern, A. 1969: Descent and alliance in the New Guinea Highlands: some problems of comparison. *Proceedings of the Royal Anthropological Institute for 1968*.

Strathern, A. 1971: *The Rope of Moka*. Cambridge.

Strathern, A. 1972: *One Father, One Blood*. Canberra.

Strathern' A. and M. 1968: Marsupials and magic: a study of spell symbolism among the Nborwamb, *in* E. R. Leach (ed.): *Dialectics in Primitive Religion*. (Cambridge Papers in Social Anthropology No. 5) Cambridge.

Turner, T. 1973: Piaget's structuralism. *American Anthropologist*, vol. 75, No. 2.

Turner, V. 1967: *The Forest of Symbols*. New York.

Turner, V. 1969a: *The Ritual Process*. Chicago.

Turner, V. 1969b: Forms of symbolic action: Introduction, *in* R. F. Spencer (ed.): *Forms of Symbolic Action* (AES). Seattle.

Tuzin, D. F. 1972: Yam symbolism in the Sepik. *South-western Journal of Anthrolopology*, vol. 28, No. 3.

Ucko, P. J. 1970: Penis sheaths: a comparative study. *Proceedings of the Royal Anthropological Institute for 1969*.

Index

(Key references indicated by *italics*)

breast-bone, 40, 124, 125, 138, 232
Brookfield, H., 244
brother, 25, 49, 74, 108, 111, 124, 237, 278 f.
brush turkey, 58, 115, 117, 129, 165, *235 f.*, 244
Bulmer, R., 167, 213 f., 252
burial, 125
burning, 131, 141, 187, *193*, 200; in garden, 32, 90, 234; of fur, 186; of sacrifices, 80, 86, 110, 113, 115, 116, 150, *187*, 192; of *Yolam* roof, 88, 116; sacred fires, 88, 96
burrowing, 83 f., 168, 232, 241 f.
Buryēp, 118 f., 241

calendar, 21 f.
cannibalism, 116, 126, 132, 135, 149, 151, *152 ff.*, 192
cassowary, 38, 78, 100, 110, 124, 132, *160 f.*, 165, 188, *192 f.*, 233, 234; claws, 138, Pl. 3; feathers, 54, 67, 158, 160 f.; femurs, 188; head-dress, 87, 158, 233, Pl. 11; hunting of, 40; pelvises, 60, 110, 248, 278, Pl. 17; quills, 66, 87, 158
casuarinas, 32
cave, 20, 57, 118, 125, 126, 168, 232
census, 270 ff.
Champion, I., 269
chisels, of rodent mandibles, 40
Chomsky, N., 213 fn.
clan, 25, 48, 77, 87, *110*, 120, 125, 145 f., 248 f., 253; ancestors, 61, 80 f., 109 f., 140, 193, 248 ff., Pl. 17; mythical origins of, 83 f., 93; complete list, 274
cloud forest, 29, 39, 79, 180
code of communication, *157 ff.*, 172 ff., 189, 207 ff.
collective decisions, *30 ff.*, 52 f., 63, 84, 91
commensality, 24, 26, 92, *196 ff.*
community, 33, 36, 63, 99 f., 243, 250, 255, 270 f.
conception, theory of, *77*, 202
conflict, 108, 133, 203, 245 f.
consciousness, see *finik*
contact, with Australian administration, 22, 43, 269
contrast, as basis of meaning, 160, *208 f.*
contrivance, as indication of meaning, *173*
conversation, 16, 26, 44

cooking, daily meals, 44; compared to decomposition, 126
cool zone, 29
cordylene, see *kasok*
corporate groups, behaviour, 25, 122, 197 f.
cousins, 111
crops, see agriculture, banana, taro, sweet potato
cuckoo-dove, 53, 158
cult leader, see leadership; Kimebnok; Buryēp; Taktieŋ; Kaɣimkayak; Kwonkāyam
curing, *139 ff.* 168, 193; sacrifice, 100, *139 f.*, 192
cuscus (see *nuk*), 39, 40, 182

dances, dancing, 23, 54, 66, 74 ff., 83, 87, 88, 89, 90, 93, 97, 100 f., 124, 127, 141, 145, 151, 250, 281
death, 124, 145, 234, 273
death pollution, 42, 91, 99, 124, 125, 194
debts, see reciprocity
decision-making, *30 ff.*, 52 f., 63, 84, 91, 112, 120, 122
defence, 30, 43, 147, 251
demography, 137, 145, *270 ff.*
descent, 251 f.
dew, ritual uses of, 51, 52, 54, 58, 159, *199 ff.*
disease (see sickness), 32, 138
distribution, of meat of pig, 36; of sacrifice, 89, 90, 193 f.
divination, 142
dog, 37, 83 f., 93, 124, 139, 152, 165, 168; in 3rd degree initiation, 63, 65
domestic units, 24
domestication, 34 ff.
Douglas, M., 212 ff.
dream, 153, 201
drinking taboo, 54, 60, 88, 91, 244
drum, 67, 72, 73 ff., 78, 90, 97, 98, 100 f., 119, 151, 233, 242
dubkōn tree, leaves, 54, 69 f.

eagle, 54, 66, 74, 86, 158
earth (see also ground), 93, 111
earth oven, 57, 59, 64, 71, 72, 75, 80, 98, 115, 232
earthquake, 60, 100

ecology, *28 ff.*, 253
eirarem, *69 f.*, 79 f., 81, 82, 115, 181, 182, 183, 185, *186 f.*, 192, 194, 278
emblems, of status, 52, 53 f., *158*, 187, 230, 233, 266 f., Pl. 4, 9, 10, 11
environment, *28 ff.*, 43
eggs, 40, 165, 235 f.
Evans-Pritchard, E. E., 191, 193
exchange, *see* reciprocity
execution, 51 f., 143
exogamy, 111, 250, 253

Faiwol language, 16 f., 21, 106, 111, 159
fallow periods, areas, 22, 32
fat, *see* pork fat
father, 51, 53, 108, 111, 124, 147, 148, 198, 237
fear, at 1st degree initiation, 51, 56; at 2nd degree initiation, 60; at 3rd degree initiation, 64; at initiations, 101; of ambush, 34, 128 f.; of sorcery, 109, 134 ff.; of war, 153; effects on learning, 219
feast, 36, 44, 64, 65, 71, 75, 89, 92, 93, 97, 98, 115, 117, 151, 152, 158
feathers, 40, *53 f.*, 74, 86, 120, *158*, 160, 280
Feisabip, 23, 30, 48, 60, 61, 85 ff., 96, 107, 109, 111, 248, 275, Pl. 1
female role, identity, 23 f., 33 ff., 48, 74, 77, 95, 99, 132, 147, *202 ff.*, 228, 234 f.
fence, fencing, 30, 32 f., 39, 234
fern, 125, 126
fieldwork, 6, 48 f., 84, 134, 180 f., 226, 270
finik (spirit), 67, 101, *124 ff.*, 131, 138, 140, 151, 184, 232
fire, 125, 131, 133, 158, *187*, 192, 197, 223, 232, 234; in temples, 60, 64, 65, 66, 68, 69 f., 71, 72, 76, 78, 80, 85, 86, 90, 93, 110, 113, 114, 117, 120, Pl. 16, 17; taboo 52, 55; against wild pig, 39, 234
fire making, *32 f.*, 187, 232
fire post, 69, 85, 86, 89, 99, 114, 115, 150, 237, 248, 281, Pl. 16, 17, 18
Firth, R., 226
fish, 39, 66, 76, 85, 91, 113, 116, 164, 166, 169; fishing, 41; fish poison, 41, 138

flying fox, 39, 73, 91, 165, 278
flying squirrel (*see* nuk), 39, 182
forest, 20, 28 f., 38, 51 f., 79 f., 81, 120, 132, 168
Fortes, M., 252
foster relations, 147 ff.
friend, friendship (*tayon*), 59, 88, 108, 133, 146
frogs, 39, 41, 166
funerary rites, *124 ff.*
fur, 40, 70, 78, 86, *89 f.*, 93, 99, 173, 184, *199 ff.*, 223

game, 24, *38 ff.*, 53, 69, 79 f., 89, 99, 108, 110, 116, 131, 194, 235, 250
garden, gardening, 20, 22, 24, *30 ff.*, 38, 43 f., 81, 85, 90, 115, 120, 121 f., 125, 169, 201, 232 ff., 236 f., 278, Pl. 6, 7, 13, 15; taboo, 52, 76, 80, 125, 167
garden houses, 26, 44
gate, 67, 97, 138, 243
gathering, 41 f., 250
Geertz, C., 237 f., 261 fn.
generations, 25, 251, 270, 271 f.
gestures (see also rubbing, whipping): beating, 89, 192; blowing, 73, 87, 139; breaking, 70, 85, 89; passing under, 57, 65, 66, *67 f.*, 70, 75, 89, 233; rotating, 67, 128, 140; tying, 85, 92, 96, 131
ghost, *see sabkār*
gift, 24, 53, 57, 90, 91, 129, 149, 191, 198, 235
ginger, 73, 87, 138
Goody, J., 229 fn.
grass, 34, 86, 88, 230
grass skirt, 125, 131, 230, Pl. 5
Griaule, N., 228
grief, 124 f., 158; at death of pig, 35
ground, 20, 83 f., 86 f., 92 f., 96, 99, 117, 125, 158, 167, 181, 182, 278

hair, 72, 76, 78, 86, 88, 121, 131, 132, *199 ff.*, 241, 278
hair-tying ceremony, 72 ff.
handclapping, 75, 90
hardwoods, 32, 69, 99, 138 f., 233, 234, 242, 243, Pl. 16
harvest, 31, 34, 91, 234; in connection with rites, 64, 75, 97, 116
Hiatt, L. R., 251

pork fat, 51, 53, 54, 55, 57, 67, 74, 75, 76, 88, 117, 150, 159, *199ff*, 281
possession, by spirit, 140
prayer, 17, 64, 69 f., 80, 88, 89, 90, 97, 101, 110, 115, 138, 140, 150, 152, 192, *193*, 200
pregnancy, 138, 166
privacy, 26
procreation, *see* conception
public opinion, 31, 52, 242, 244
public scenes, 26, 33, 192
purity/pollution, 20, 40, 67, 68, 73, 93, 158, *167*, 235; death pollution, 42, 91, 99, 124, 125, 194; pollution of streams 42

quills, as ornaments, 40, 63 f., 87, 92, 114, 150
Quinlivan, 279

Radcliffe-Brown, 166, 169, 184
rain, 28, 52, 54
rank, insignia of, 52, 53 f., 158, 233, 266, Pl. 4, 9, 10, 11
Rappaport, R. Z., 194
rats, 39, 168, 181, 182
rattan, 32, 84, 232, Pl. 10, 11
reciprocity, 38, 88, 110, 129, 134, 196, 235, 250
red colour, 54, 60, 61, 65, 66, 74, 77, 113, 116, 119, 126, 127, 139, 146, 159, *172ff*., 188, 232, 233; circles, 113, 140, 243; ochre, 51, 74, 96, 113, 129, 139, 140, 193, 233, 243; on skull, 64, 87, 89, 96; seeds, for hunting, 40
residence, *see* domestic units; house types; men's house; women's house
rhetoric, 5, 17, 119
Richards, A., 209
right/left, 68, 75, 125, 129
rivalry, 113, *117ff*., 204, 244
Robertson-Smith, 193
roof, 86, 88, 93, 116, 278
rubbing, as ritual operation, 51, 52, 54 f., 67, 69 f., 74, 89, 150, 151, *158ff*., 200, 237

sabkār (ghost), 55, *127f*., 137, 281 f.
sacra, 61 f., 64, 68, 78, 92, 109, 232, Pl. 17, 18

sacramental meal, 57, 132, 193; in *Katiam*, 80 f., 110, 112; in *Yolam*, 71, 113, *115f*., 152; in *Amowkam*, 97
sacrifice, 68, 71, 79, 88, 96, 98, 113, 126, 138, 139, 150, *191ff*.
sago, sago swamps, 41 f., 44, 85, 93, 97, 100 f., 128, 142, 180, 250
salt (black), 57
sām (water lizard), 100, 138, 140, *141*, 168
sarop (spirit), *128f*., 137
secrecy, 26, 50, 55, 112, 117, 138, 159, 164, 169, 185 f., 192, *217ff*., 264
secret vocabulary, 17, 51, 57, 70, 79, 83, 85, 101 f., 120, 181, 183
Seltaman, 18, 38, 43, 85, 91, 95, 96, 111, 118, 119, 120, 121, *122*, 133, 145, 146, 147, 148 f., 151, 203 f., 230, 240, 253, 269, 273
seniority, 22, 25, 50, 53, 56, 108, 265 f.
Serpenti, L. M., 202
sex roles (*see* male; female), 23 f., 77, *202ff*., 228, 232 ff., 250, 271; in agriculture, *32ff*., 234, 250; in daily routine, 43 f.; in pig tending, 34 ff.; in ritual, 47 , 74, 250; in war, 146 f.
sexual activity, 24, 26, 43 f., 48, 76 f., 111, 133, 147, 150, 152, 163, 202, 203 ff., 250, 280
shaman, *139ff*.
sharing, 38, 88, 91, 97, 110, 112, 115, 119, 126, 127, 142, *164f*., 192, *197f*., 223, 279
shield, 67, 69, 87, 89, 95, 98, 114, 124, 150, 153, 247, Pl. 18
shrine, 20, 139; for pigs, 25, 237; over dog, 37; in gardens, 99; in *Katiam*, 61, 109, 248, Pl. 17; in *Yolam*, 89, *115*, 117, 150, 236, 248, Pl. 16, 18
siblings, 25, 272
sickness, 120, 131 ff., 133, *137ff*., 142, 233, 244 f., 272 f.
sister, 25, 53, 95, 124, 148, 278 f.
skull: of ancestor, 64, 69, 87, 88, 89, 92 f., 101 f., 113, 114, 118, 120, 131, 150, 187, 233, 242, 248, 250, 278, Pl. 18; of dead person, 125; of dog, 139; of wild pig, 60 f., 110, 114, 248, 278, Pl. 17
sky, 20, 236

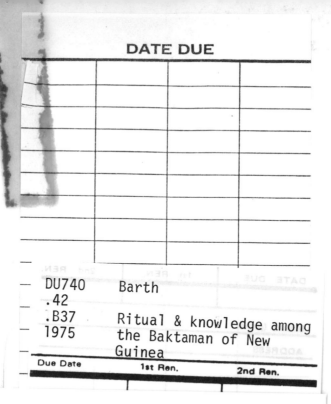